The Lights in Patmos[1]

The Origin of Spiritual Warfare

---

[1] Coverart by Ken Strickland - lifeforcepub@hotmail.com

Dedicated

To Selena Donaldson,

    Although she has not yet mastered the good fight, I pray we endeavor to fight as well as she fought.

Michael Donaldson

Shepard's Ink Publishing
Live to read, read to Live.

Copyright 2006   Michael L. Donaldson

    No part of this publication may be reproduced or transmitted in any form; or by any means electronic, or mechanical, including; photocopy, recording, or any information storage and retrieval system, without permission in writing from publisher. All scriptures and quotations used in this book used by permission. Requests for permission to make copies of any part of this work should be mailed to Permissions Department, Shepard's Ink Publishing, and P.O. Box 78211 Nashville, Tennessee, 37207.

ISBN: 978-0-9799230-0-5

Table of Contents

PART I – SOULAR ECLIPSE

Chapter 1 - A Light in the Darkness..10

Chapter 2 - The Heart of 18

Chapter 3 - Stones of Fire...27
        - The sons of God...30
        - Lucifer's Brilliance..31

Chapter 4 - The Lights in Our World..42
        - The Two Sources of Light.....................................42
            - The Bright and Morning Star.....................42
            - The Star of Morning....................................43
        - The Lights in the World...43
            - False Lights...43
            - Lost Lights 43
            - The True Light 44

PART II - TWINKLE, TWINKLE, FALLEN STAR

Chapter 5 - The Bright and Morning Star...46
        - The Godhead - The Trinity Explained....................46
        - The Trinity Confirmed...47
        - The Trinity Maneuver - Attack and Counter Attack......48

Chapter 6 - Sun and Moon Worship..50

Chapter 7 - The First Pharaoh of Egypt 58
        - The Satanic Construct..58

Chapter 8 - *"Egypt"*: The Worship of Self..62
       - The Great Pyramid of Giza....................................66
        - The Sphinx...67
        - The Theory of Soulical Man..................................67
        - A Longing for Egypt..70

Table of Contents

PART III - BEAUTY AND HIS BEASTS

Chapter 9 – Lucifer, the Bearer of Light 72

Chapter 10 - The Dragon Theory...88
    - The Mystery of the Serpent in the Garden.................90
    - The Dragon's Teeth..………………………………....103

Chapter 11 - The Ugly Beast...104
    - The Game of Death………………………………….....105
    - Satan's Kingdom Rising....................................106
        - The First Beast...110
        - The Second Beast...109
        - The Dragon's Ultimate Creation.................110
        - The Number of the Beast..........................112
        - The Name of the Beast.............................114
        - The Mother of Harlots.............................116
        - The Mark of the Beast.............................117
        - The Mark on the Right Hand....................119
        - Satan's Arc………………………………….....124
        - Devilution Phase I...................................126
        - Devilution Phase II..................................128
        - The Mule Paradox..................................131
        - Professing Themselves to be Wise...............132
        - The Scarlet Beast.....................................134
        - What About Pornography?......................137

PART IV - THE DEVIL MADE ME DO IT

Chapter 12 – Living Under Spiritual Influences..........................140
        - Spiritual Indwelling……………………….....140
        - Demon Possession...................................141
        - Spiritual Arbitration 144
        - The Spirit of the *holy gods*.......................144
            The Lying Spirit....................................145
        - Evil Spirits from God…….......................145

Table of Contents

    - UnGodly Spiritual Influences………...............…..……146
        - The Familiar Spirit……………………………………147
        - The Spirit of Whoredoms…………………147
        - The Spirit of an Unclean Devil……………147
        - The Spirit of Infirmity……………………147
        - The Spirit of Divination…………………147
        - The Dumb Spirit………………………...148
    - How Spirits gain Entrance…………………………147

Chapter 13 - Playing 'possum……………………......………152
        - Deliverance……………………………………153
        - Salvation………………………………………153
        - 'Possum………………………………………153

PART V - HOW DOES THE DEVIL DO THAT?

Chapter 14 - Satan's Tools and Applications……………………158
        - Satan's Use of Position……………………158
        - Satan's Use of Seed…………………….......159
        - Satan's Use of Time………………………161
        - Satan's Use of Utilitarianism………………161
        - Satan's Use of Bondage…………………...162
        - Satan's Use of Servitude……….....………162
        - Satan's Use of Brashness…………………163
        - Satan's Use of Guilt…………………….… 163
        - Satan's Use of Accusation…………………163
        - Satan's Use of Anger………………………164
        - Satan's Use of Personal Attacks…..………164
        - The Three Types of Permission……………..164

PART VI - LIVING IN THE SHADE

Chapter 15 - The Spheres of Demonic Influence…………………170
        - The Sphere of Sickness……………………170
        - The Sphere of Captivity……………………...171

Table of Contents

- The Sphere of Sensory Manipulation.....................171
- Deprivation..172
- Excitement..172
- The Sphere of Disease.....................................173
- The Covert Sphere..173
- The Sphere Disability......................................174
- The Sphere of Divination.................................175

Chapter 16 - Object & Animal Possession, and Natural Disasters.......176
- The Achan Theory (Object Possession).................177
- Animal Possesson...178
- The Nephilim, Rehaim, and Anakim...................180
- Natural Disasters..181

PART VII - THE GARDEN OF SECRETS

Chapter 17 - The Dusty Secret.............................184

Chapter 18 - The Edible Secret.............................192
- The Apple Theory..197
- The Lillith Theory...197

Chapter 19 - The Secret Fruit...............................200
- The Knowledge of Good and Evil.......................202
- The First Tier of the Original Sin........................205
- The Second Tier of the Original Sin....................206
- What Was the Fruit? 208
- Husbandry/Gardening......................................210
- What was the Fall?..212
- The Cause of the Fall.......................................213
- The Tree of the Accursed Fruit..........................214

Chapter 20 - Trees with Secrets............................216
- The Tree of Life..224
- The Tree of the Knowledge of Good and Evil..........224
- Cedars of Lebanon..224

Table of Contents

- The Tree for the Healing of the Nations……………..225
- The Accursed Tree………………………………………225
- The Wooden Cross………………………………………227
- The Forbidden Tree………………………………………228

PART VIII - SPIRITUAL WARFARE: SATAN'S REVENGE

Chapter 21- The Origin of Spiritual Warfare……………………232
- The Question………………………………………………233
- The Freudian Slip…………………………………………233
- Food for Thought…………………………………………234
- Windows to the Soul……………………………………235
- Seeing Without Eyes……………………………………239
- A Hedge too Small………………………………………241
- Share and Share Alike…………………………………244
- An Angel on His Belly……………………………………245
- Burning Ears………………………………………………248
- Expulsion from the Garden……………………………250
- A Quick Guide to the Fall From Grace………………251
- The Inescapable Conclusion……………………………252

Chapter 22 - Dousing the Fire ……………………………………258
- 39 Steps to Dousing Satan's Fire……………………259
- The Midst of the Seas…………………………………269

Chapter 23 - Smoking or Non-smoking…………………………280

Appendices

Appendix A - Fool's Gold……………………………………………284
- When the Tithe is Fool's Gold…………………………289
- Acceptable Christianity is Fool's Gold………………291
- The Prosperity Doctrine…………………………………298
- All That Glitters……………………………………………303

Appendix B - What You Should Know After Reading this Book…………312
Appendix C - Glossary of Terms……………………………………316
Appendix D - Symbolic Language from the Old and New Testaments……317

Acknowledgements

Thank you to the United States Marine Corps and Bushido Dojo for teaching me how to fight. I would like to thank God's Holy Spirit for teaching me when, and why to fight.

Chapter One
A Light in the Darkness

"**And this is the condemnation, that light is come into the world, and men loved darkness rather than light, because their deeds were evil** - John 3:19"

Michael Donaldson was not much of a hunter, or an explorer; and he is certainly afraid of the dark. "Why did I join one of the world's elite military organizations," I thought as he marched through the dark bushes. "Staff Sgt.," I whispered, "The squad is ready." "Move out," the Staff Sgt. ordered. I was squad leader of the first squad in the weapons company. This particular day I also planned the ambush exercise. I masterfully conceived and implemented the below illustrated plan.

11 | The Lights in Patmos

As we snuck through the dense foliage, it was apparent that the plan would be successful. The dense foliage ensured camouflage and the overlaying directions the bullets traveled trapped the enemy in two fields of interlocking fire. The idea of any ambush is to maximize fatalities and minimize escape routes, with minimal loss to your resources. In the preceding picture of the plan is so you see that no matter which way the enemy ran it was another trap. We waited quietly on the enemy, knowing that each minute of the 30 remaining minutes brought the enemy closer to the trap. The trap spelled certain destruction for the enemy because there was no way out.

The plan was simple. I found a portion of the trail where the clearing made for an inviting place for weary troops to rest. The marines lay in wait behind a fallen tree in the lower quadrant of the clearing. The log pointed straight down the path to the clearing. Along the path on the left, the entire squad waited to shoot the resting troops. We knew from intelligence that we had approximately 30 minutes before the enemy arrived. The squad dug in and waited. To add additional confusion, I decided to throw a night-illumination flare into the group. The flare added to the deceit, and gave the squad extra seconds before the enemy pointed their weapons in the right direction.

As the marines waited, I motioned to the Staff-Sgt that he saw the enemy's chem-lites. A chem-lite is a small chemical flare that glows faintly without the aid of light. The purpose of a chem-lite is that you do not lose contact with the rest of the squad while in the thick bush. Communication is important, but in the bush soldiers have to master non-verbal communication. I pointed to his eyes then pointed down the trail. This motion indicates that I saw something moving. I then put two fingers up like rabbit ears behind my head to indicate the enemy. Then I put cupped palm and using two fingers made the motions as though my hand was walking. Without saying a word, I informed my squad that the enemies patrol was near and that I could see them. We made ready. Some people put in earplugs others put in chewing gum. The heavy machine gunners made sure there links were not tangled and doom got closer.

I watched the little green glow meander through the forest getting closer. A marine knew the first light would be the point man. He was probably the safest man in the patrol. All rules of engagement say that you let the point man pass by safely to ensure that the entire patrol walks into the trap. I watched the point man get closer, waiting to spring my trap. Finally, the time was at hand. I waited until the pointman's chem-lite passed then sprung into action.

I pulled the pin on the night-illumination device and tossed it overhand from behind cover. As I looked down the trail, to find targets he saw for the first time a large tree standing in front of him. The flare bounced off the tree and landed almost on his leg. I picked it up and threw it again giving the order; "Fire, fire, fire," I ordered. My squad fired. Anything in the trap was most certainly dead.

I called cease-fire and walked out into the killing field to survey the dead. There were no dead, no injured, no bodies at all. Staff-Sgt. called a briefing and we did the post action review. "What happened?" Staff-Sgt asked. I replied, "Where is the enemy? I saw them; they were right on top of me." Staff-Sgt. Asked again, "Well, where the hell are they?" As he spoke, I saw the chem-lite again. "There!" I exclaimed trying to prove to everybody that he was not crazy. As we stood still, all the Marines started laughing and walked off. Staff Sgt. looked at I and said a few *choice* expletives. "You stupid #$@@ that is not a chem-lite that is a lightening bug." It was only then that he realized that a fool had planned the foolproof plan. The fact that I had never seen a lightening bug nor even heard of one did not seem to matter to the marines.

I explained to the Staff-Sgt. that he grew up in the Bahamas and we do not have lightening bugs. He did not care. I then asked him, "If we had been in real combat what would happen now?" Staff-Sgt replied flatly, "If we survived this #$@@ I would have killed you." Then he shouldered his weapon, mustered the troops and they walked off. They left me standing there in the dark by myself, to ponder my mistake.

I learned a costly lesson that day. Not all lights can be trusted. That bug did nothing wrong. God designed the bug to glow in a green iridescent color just like the chem-lites marines used. The problem was that I should have relied on more than just the little light to execute an ambush. Along with the light, there should have been sounds, motion, and above all bodies.

Now that you have stopped laughing, let us begin this journey by defining Spiritual Warfare.

- WAR - *is a violent, costly battle or struggle between uncompromising parties.*

- SPIRITUAL - *refers to the fact that the interactions occur in the spirit realm amongst spirit beings or powers*[2].

- SPIRITUAL WARFARE - is a *violent, costly battle or struggle between uncompromising spiritual entities.*

I use the term uncompromising because if either party is willing or able to compromise they avoid war by use of a treaties. The flesh and the spirit are irreconcilable by design. Adam's sin destroyed the flesh. The spirit is Godly by design. The flesh and the spirit cannot agree by treaty because God designed them to accomplish separate things. The flesh is not the cause of the warfare, the irreconcilable natures of the flesh and the spirit cause spiritual conflict.

The power of *choice* is the most awesome power in the universe. From this heavenly gift all life flows. Ten Commandments do not actually govern behavior they govern *choice*. Nowhere in Exodus 20 is this more explicit than in verses 3 and 4. Here God is not forbidding the existence of other gods, or even arguing the existence of other gods. God simply requires His people not to *CHOOSE,* serve, honor, or worship any other god. God in no way denies believers *choice*, He simply explains the consequences of the wrong *choice*.

The devil did not make Adam and Eve sin. The devil did not cause Judas to betray Christ. The devil did not cause man worship false gods. Satan involved himself in these episodes, but in all cases, the culprit is *choice*. When you understand what Jesus means the *Lord's Prayer*[3] then the battle is easy, and the way clear. How many nights do you think John the Baptist spent staring at the stars wondering why he did not have friends? How many days did Jesus go off to fast and to pray when there was entertainment available?

Believers, the difficulty in accepting the cup of Christ is not suffering, nor is it endurance. Believers the burden of the cup of Christ is *choice*. Remember it was not the prophecy that caused Christ to die on the

---

[2] This book only deals with the human factor in spiritual warfare it does not address war in heaven.
[3] This is not what Jesus prayed daily, this is the believers guide.

cross it was His *choice*[4]. It was not necessity that caused God to forsake His only begotten Son; it was *choice*[5]. Love is a *choice*. Sadly, sin is also a *choice*. In John 14:15 when the Master says, "**IF YOU LOVE ME OBEY MY COMMANDMENTS**[6]," He speaks of *choice*.

In the Bible's most famous prayer, we see that the burdens lie in God's hands. "**AFTER THIS MANNER THEREFORE PRAY YE: 'OUR FATHER WHICH ART IN HEAVEN, HALLOWED BE THEY NAME. THY KINGDOM COME. THY WILL BE DONE, IN EARTH AS IT IS IN HEAVEN. GIVE US THIS DAY OUR DAILY BREAD. AND FORGIVE US OUR DEBTS, AS WE FORGIVE OUR DEBTORS. AND LEAD US NOT INTO TEMPTATION, BUT DELIVER US FROM THE EVIL {ONE}. FOR THINE IS THE KINGDOM, THE POWER, AND THE GLORY FOREVER. AMEN** - Matthew 6:9-13." All we have to do is make the correct *choice*.

In the great commission, the issue again is *choice*. "**GO YE THEREFORE, AND TEACH ALL NATIONS, BAPTIZING THEM IN THE NAME OF THE FATHER, AND OF THE SON, AND OF THE HOLY GHOST: TEACHING THEM TO OBSERVE ALL THINGS WHATSOEVER I HAVE COMMANDED YOU: AND, LO, I AM WITH YOU ALWAYS, (EVEN) UNTO THE END OF THE WORLD. AMEN** - Matthew 28:19-20." Here are the *choices*:

1. Go or do not go.
2. Teach or do not teach.
3. Baptize or do not baptize.
4. Teach what He commands or do not teach what He commands.

It is in the great commission we find freedom. There is freedom in the God's commission. Like FEDEX, all God requires is delivery of His message. Believers, a Parrot can repeat words, it is time to stop spewing venom and half-truths and proclaim the truth of Jesus Christ.

In the universe, there exist things we must learn to master and things that command. In this life, we will never truly understand the three parts of the One that commands: The Father, Son, and God's Holy Spirit. However, God granted us full access to the things we must learn to master. In order to stand upright before the One that commands, we must fully

---

[4] Matthew 26:39.
[5] John 3:16.
[6] All scriptures are King James Version (KJV) unless otherwise stated.

understand the two things we must learn to master: The soul and the flesh. The dichotomous nature of the human-creation requires an equally dichotomous design in the Word of God. One such dichotomy is *choice*. The dichotomy between flesh and the soul looks like this:

Choice governs the flesh   *Submission governs the soul/spirit*

A common teaching exerts that man is a tri-part creature. However, there is no evidence in the scripture of this concept. The Bible clearly states God breathed into man and at that point, man became a living soul[7]. Matthew 10:28 confirms the dual nature of the man creature. Jesus forebodes that man should not fear the power that destroys the body, but should fear HE that destroys the body and the soul. What we teach as the third part is not the soulical man it is the imagination. God does not distinguish between the use of the term soul and spirit. He put His spirit into the man creature and called the new construct a living soul.

This book is about the two things we must master the soul, and the flesh. Later in the poem *Fire in Patmos*, we see a description of the full extent of what walking in this life consists. In life, we see: fear, solitude, trust, betrayal, misunderstanding, mercy, forgiveness, splendor, faith, idolatry; above all, we see *choice*.

According to the scriptures, men used the Isle of Patmos for punishment. I always thought of the Isle of Patmos as punishment. However, as I grew and I learned of the God that called and saved me I realized something. What I always thought of as exile and bastard-hood, was actually bewilderment in the long, lonely walk called *choice*.

<u>The Lights in Patmos</u> explores and uncovers the root of Spiritual Warfare--The concept *choice*. This book starts by explaining the nature of spiritual warfare and the nature of worship. The book then moves into the area of confused and inappropriate worship. From there the book covers spirits and spiritual influence, the nature of the beast and the ways in which humans submit to spiritual influences. As the book moves, it studies terms necessary to understand the premier events in spiritual warfare.

I attempted to draw the Spiritual Warfare line chronologically, but the Bible does not support this approach. For this reason, the information

---

[7] Genesis 2:7.

appears in a manner easy for the reader to appreciate. The book jumps around quite a bit through scripture, but this is unavoidable. The author then assembles all of this information into a picture of spiritual warfare and the actual underlying causes and effects.

It is difficult to lay down the pattern in which spiritual Warfare developed but the line is clear. The flow heart goes from Lucifer's heart out amongst the stones of fire. God throws Lucifer and friends out of heaven. The heart condition of Lucifer goes with them. Upon earth, Satan finds an impressionable human female and encourages her to explore the desires of her own heart.

The human female shares her desire with the man with whom she shares her heart. Adam partakes of his flesh, and the two give Satan the one thing God denied him-power. Prior to Adam and Eve giving Satan their power, he was the prince of the power of nothings.

Now Satan had a kingdom, he now controlled the one thing in the earth realm that God gave *choice* the human heart. Now that Satan controlled God's holy place, God left it to the creatures in control, Satan Adam and Eve. There are three things left in the earth realm He protected from Satan's control;

1. God protected the earth itself.
2. God protected the Tree of Life.
3. By protecting the Tree of Life God protected choice.

Spiritual Warfare is a violent, costly battle or struggle between uncompromising spiritual entities because neither God nor Satan will relinquish their seats of power. In all civil wars, the fighting is violent and tumultuous because the emotions contained between the people rage. Issues of trust and anger cloud the real issue. The issue is not the Satan hates God; the issue is that God will not accept Satan.

The *choice* before humans is not whether to be loved by God or not that is automatic. The *choice* is whether humans want to be loved by Satan or not. The two kings will never share a kingdom or a subject. God wants you to love Him and serve him. Satan wants you to hate God and serve yourself.

Someone has to lose every conflict, God will allow you to loose, but He cannot afford to change, or many others will suffer because of the change. Satan has no rules; he just wants to take what he can from God. The secret to Spiritual Warfare is that the only people Satan ever defeats are not stolen or taken, they *choose* to go and live in the shade provided by their father. With all the light in the world and the Light of the world it is saddening that many *choose* darkness.

Amen

Chapter Two
The Heart of One

"Therefore, shall a man leave his father and his mother, and shall cleave unto his wife: and they shall be one flesh'- Genesis 2:24."

The Lord saw that man was alone. Of all the things in Creation, God said the man's solitude was not good. There was no helpmeet for the man, according to Genesis 1:23, no creature that was like Adam. Genesis 2:21-25 sets the bond between husband and wife; that they must cling to each other. God's wisdom shows itself in this concept. God's foolishness confounded Adam and Eve, just as it confounds even the wisest of men. The statement about the couple cleaving to each other meant ALL things outside their relationship there were to ignore. Had Adam and Eve cleaved to each other there would have been no room for Satan to approach Eve.

A common misconception is that the man did not have another human being, which caused the loneliness this is not accurate; Adam did not have another Spirit filled being. Remember the beasts of the field God also formed from the earth. The beasts were like the man except the beasts had mates, flesh was never the issue. Genesis 7:22, dispels the myth that the difference was that God breathed into Adam and not the animals. All living things have the breath of God in them. There is no life without God because God is Life. To have Life means that God has put His breath in you. It is the law of God that gives eternal life.

What then makes the human creature different from the beasts of the field and a little lower than the angels? Once we determine this, we can ascertain what it meant to Satan to be 'a beast of the field? Genesis 1:26-29 and Genesis 2:21-25 give us the information we need to determine the difference between the man, the beast of the fields, and the serpent.

DIFFERENCE 1 - (Genesis 1:26-29)
"And God said, 'LET US MAKE MAN IN OUR IMAGE, AFTER OUR LIKENESS: AND LET THEM HAVE DOMINION OVER THE FISH OF THE SEA, AND OVER THE FOWL OF THE AIR, AND OVER THE

The Lights in Patmos

CATTLE, AND OVER ALL THE EARTH, AND OVER EVERY CREEPING THING THAT CREEPETH UPON THE EARTH. So God created man in His [own] image, in the image of God created He Him; male and female created He them. And God blessed them, and God said unto them, **'BE FRUITFUL, AND MULTIPLY, AND REPLENISH THE EARTH, AND SUBDUE IT: AND HAVE DOMINION OVER THE FISH OF THE SEA, AND OVER THE FOWL OF THE AIR, AND OVER EVERY LIVING THING THAT MOVETH UPON THE EARTH'.** And God said, **'BEHOLD, I HAVE GIVEN YOU EVERY HERB BEARING SEED, WHICH [IS] UPON THE FACE OF ALL THE EARTH, AND EVERY TREE, IN THE WHICH [IS] THE FRUIT OF A TREE YIELDING SEED; TO YOU IT SHALL BE FOR MEAT'.**"

1. We see that the human is the only thing God made in His own image, and after His own likeness.

2. God also gave the man dominion over the beasts of the field and over every creping thing.

3. Another difference between humans and beasts of the field is that God specifically blessed the human and instructed them to be fruitful and multiply. God instructed the man to set in motion a system so that the fruit of the man would subdue the earth.

4. In Genesis 1:29/30, God 'gave' to the man animals and fruit for his meat. *Given,* means that the man had dominion over the items.

5. The only things in the garden in Eden that Adam and Eve did not have dominion over were the tree of life and tree of the knowledge of good and evil. Evidence of this principle comes from Genesis 1:29, "**...AND EVERY TREE, IN WHICH IS THE FRUIT OF TREE YIELDING SEED.**"

This stanza proves that the tree of life and tree of the knowledge of good and evil ARE NOT trees in the natural sense. The tree of life and tree of the knowledge of good and evil do not contain *tree-yielding seeds*. The tree of life and tree of the knowledge of good and evil are therefore incapable of producing edible fruit. The tree of life and tree of the knowledge of good and evil are therefore incapable of reproducing themselves. According to scripture, God did not give the tree of life and tree of the knowledge of good and evil to Adam and Eve as meat.

DIFFERENCE 2 - (Genesis 2:20-25)

1. All the beasts of the field had helpmeets, except the *serpent* and man.

2. Nothing God formed from the earth existed before God formed them. God formed two of every creeping thing and every fowl and every beast. However, God made only one man, and only one *serpent*.

3. God formed every living thing's mate from the same earth and same components as the male of the species. Adam's mate God did not make equal to him, or simultaneously with him. God did not design Adam's mate for the sole purpose of propagating the species. God created Eve to help the man exercise dominion over the earth, be fruitful, and multiply.

4. God created the man and the woman to have a special lifelong bond that He does not make important to the other life forms. To facilitate the relationship, God did not make the man and woman from the same earth He made them from the same body. This design in the human creates a peculiar relationship. Unlike the animals which science indicates mate for life, the human male inexplicably draws to his wife. A Godly marriage contains the missing pieces needed to complete a man. This inexplicable attraction between men and women is because God dissembled the man to create the woman. The pieces she needed were more than a rib; she also took with her the breath of God. There is no way to take apart a complete unit and not modify its integrity. As a junior farmer, I learned a re*mark*able fact about digging holes. Having dug numerous holes in my yard I found out that the dirt you remove from the hole never properly fits back into the hole of origin. Similarly, the hole in Adam's side God closed; but obviously, it never reintegrated itself. Had the hole completely reintegrated, the man would not have needed a helpmeet. God also

would not have had to place flesh in the empty hole to compensate for the missing rib. Animals do not cleave to their mother and father animals wean their young. Many of the males in the animal kingdom eat their young as convenient morsels. Animals do not cleave to one another, it is not necessary for the continuation of the species. The reason man is to cleave has nothing to do with reproduction, it all centers on fidelity. Although cleaving is integral to marriage, this relationship must never supersede the will of God.

5. The use of the word flesh in Genesis mirrors use of the word in Ephesians 5:29. This thing marriage is a mystery; Paul spoke concerning Christ and the Church. The next difference between the beasts, the man, and the *serpent* is that the man had a relationship with God. The relationship between man and the Lord continues through the institution of marriage. The couple is not to become one in the numerical sense, there are to become one in the same sense that the disciples became one in Acts. The oneness is a singleness of heart, one in God. There should be one set of rules, one set of standards, and one set of goals, in a Christian household. The law of God must reign in a Godly marriage. The law of life allows marriage to function perfectly despite two imperfect people. The law of God gives a smooth even measure for life. There is no uncertainty in God, God's love, or His law.

What does this say of the man and the woman? Genesis 3:17 better explains that there can be no oneness of the man and woman if they are not one with God. Paul told us that the man and woman become one flesh. The flesh taken from Adam in the garden completed the woman. Eve drew to her husband because she was a part of Adam. The problem is that Adam was not one with Eve in his heart. Had the two been one in spirit, Eve would not have chosen to side with Satan against her husband. Likewise, Adam never should have followed his wife down the road to destruction; he would have stood fast on his relationship with God and rebuked her.

ADAM'S ROLE

God sets Adam's role and his importance to the family. Of the man, God said in Genesis 2:15-17, "**The Lord God took the man, and put him into the garden of Eden to dress it and to keep it. The Lord God commanded the man, saying, 'OF EVERY TREE OF THE GARDEN YOU MAY FREELY EAT; 17 BUT OF THE TREE OF THE KNOWLEDGE OF GOOD AND EVIL, YOU SHALL NOT EAT OF IT; FOR IN THE DAY THAT YOU EAT OF IT YOU WILL SURELY DIE'. Out of the ground, the Lord God formed every animal of the field, and every bird of the sky, and brought them to the man to see what he would call them. Whatever the man called every living creature that was its name**." In God's law, man bears responsibility for the fruit of the family. Both the blessings and the curses in this life come through the blood of the father.

EVE'S ROLE

God sets Eve's role and her importance to the family. The first thing that God dealt with was the fact that man was alone. There is no mention of the man needing help tending the garden, or bearing the burden of leadership. The man's role in the family is to rule it, rear it, and guide it. Adam was unable to fulfill this task himself. Of the woman, God said in Genesis 2:15-18, "**The Lord God said, 'IT IS NOT GOOD THAT THE MAN SHOULD BE ALONE; I WILL MAKE HIM A HELPER SUITABLE FOR HIM.' The Lord God caused a deep sleep to fall on the man, and he slept; and he took one of his ribs, and closed up the flesh in its place. He made the rib, which the Lord God had taken from the man, into a woman, and brought her to the man. The man said, "This is now bone of my bones, and flesh of my flesh. She will be called Woman, because she was taken out of Man**." To that end, God gave him a helpmeet that was suitable for him. The woman's task had nothing to do with the garden directly it was to deal with the man.

Externalization of the woman in the marriage through gender swapping and feminism exists because of the sin introduced in the garden. The curse changes the tranquility between the man and woman from sweetness to sweet and sour. No longer, do men and women complement each other as they do in kool-aid; now they are mutually combative products. The curse put the woman under man's dominion (Genesis 2:16), and fosters the desire not be under man's control.

The result of the curse is conflict between men and women. It therefore takes much longer to get the kool-aid back to its sweet flavor. The only redeeming feature in the flavoring of these drinks is that the Water has not changed. The Living Water of God's Holy Spirit keeps the conflict at a tolerable level. Christian marriages fail because after we achieve flavor one of the two additives adds or takes itself away. This alteration affects the overall flavor of not only the kool-aid but also in the fruit emanating from the family.

This is why the relationship of a husband, wife, and the word of God is important. Without the law of God, there is no life. Without knowledge of the law of God, how can one learn of His love? The love of God allows the human to flourish. God created Adam and Eve in His likeness. Adam and Eve never became one in spirit; their likenesses to God only lasted one generation. Cain and Abel were the physical proof of what transpired in the heart of Adam and his wife.

Abel like Adam tried to please God even though he was not sure how to accomplish the feat. Cain like Eve saw something else she desired and was willing to trade whatever necessary to have the cherished item. Eve was a much better wife then Adam was a husband. Eve although she was wrong took her prize to her husband to share. Although distorted, sharing is the right method between husband and wife. It was not sharing that was ungodly it was what Adam and Eve shared that cost them the Garden. Adam on the other hand, immediately blamed his wife for the problem and tried to lay the entire blame on the woman. Adam never even admitted that he was wrong.

God corrected Adam and told him that he was wrong for listening to his wife before God. The problem in their marriage was that the woman was out of control because the man never bothered to subdue the woman-flesh of his flesh. Adam should have defended his wife. If they were not going to be one with God, they should have at least been one in death. There was no unity between Adam and Eve, not in spirit or in flesh. This disunity resulted not only in a failed marriage, horrible children, hard labor, and expulsion from Eden it caused a rift between man and God. There can never be unity between man and wife and God if the man and the woman have no unity between their own hearts.

The scripture admonishes us to dwell with a woman according to knowledge and not hinder our prayers. Had Adam used his knowledge of husbandry with the woman, they would not have had their prayers hindered. Hindered prayers not only because God does not answer, it more often than not means that they never reach Him. Unified prayer requires unity. A married couple's prayer does not reach God as two separate prayers; they are one. Therefore, Mr. and Mrs. Jones' prayers come in as one prayer in heaven. When the prayers come in from separate entries God does not recognize the separate people, in His book He has an entry for the Jones'. If you wonder why your separate time in prayer is unfruitful it is not because your prayers are incorrect it is because you are suppose to pray jointly.

For too long we blamed Satan for our troubles and woes. The truth of the matter is that the problem is men. God gave women unto men as helpmeets (That which is needed to complete man); therefore, women are neither subordinates nor equals. God gave women to men, and that single fact (Genesis 2:16) has been held out over women through the ages. The actual subordination did not follow until Genesis 3:16 and it was part of the curse. The true relationship God meant between men and women summed up in one word--*tranquil*. What this would seem to imply is exactly the same type of relationship existed between Adam and his wife (Genesis 3:20) as it is supposed to exist today.

Although not exactly equals, Adam and Eve were partners. The difference between them was authority and responsibility. You cannot be equal with another person unless you share with all things. The relationship between man and his wife God never meant to be equal in the common sense of the word. The word equal has a more subtle practical use. For example, many recipes call for equal parts of different spices or vegetables. We know that Broccoli is not the same as a Tomato, if for no other reason one is a vegetable and the other a fruit. Therefore, equal must mean the *same importance* each adding unique qualities to the dish. The reason for the equal portions is to ensure that one does not overpower the other in the flavoring of the dish.

The sexual struggle between men and women is also a part of the curse in Genesis 3:16. The return to tranquility necessitates equal parts of opposing entities. The mystery of marriage Paul tells us is to see how God takes two and makes them one. The only way to do this successfully is if God puts together mutually complementary pieces. The equality is not in the amounts but in the relationship to the finished product.

We are all familiar with the revolutionary product kool-aid, and we have all mixed at least one glass. There are three components to a great glass of kool-aid, water, sugar and of course kool-aid. The finished product tastes great. However, in complete honestly no component is equal in quantity to the other. The kool-aid is necessary for the flavor, and the color, and the sugar creates the sweetness. Without the water, there would be nothing but powder. Without the sugar, the flavored, colored water tastes terrible. Without kool-aid and you simply have sugar water. To say that we add these in equal parts would be wrong. The greatest single additive is water, then sugar, and least of all the kool-aid. In this exact manner the relationship between man and woman in no way implies equality in any other manner than; *tranquility of the finished product*. The sugar in kool-aid not only sweetens the kool-aid it also tempers the bitter flavor of the kool-aid powder.

    Men have many rough edges that we need to deal with and tempered away. To Adam's kool-aid God added His sugar; but the sweetness still needs water. Through the effect of God's sugar, the world was to become a heaven of loving, caring creatures dwelling in God's garden. The woman's sweetness was to take effect flowing through the man's authority. Notice that the words in (Genesis 2:23) do not relate to an external but to an internal change. It is through an internal change; a change brought about and the cellular level, that women's beauty and power flow.

    In the relationship between humans, the principle is the same. There is no manner of equality of input; Adam had more responsibility than Eve. Eve had only two responsibilities, to be a helpmeet and to help Adam be fruitful and multiply. Feminist rhetoric socialized us to view women's role as menial and unimportant. This could not be farther from the truth. If we would but read the passages in Genesis, we would see that the parts are mutually important.

    The ability to have a relationship with God differentiates humans from every other living thing. This relationship with God Lucifer sought to destroy. The fallen angels stand unforgiven; there was no forgiveness in God for them. Undoubtedly, Lucifer planned the same unforgiveness for Adam and human kind. Lucifer intended for man to see the unforgiving side of God. Lucifer's plan was a simple plan--*Let Adam and Eve see the wrath of God and they will side with me.* God's love, however, prevailed, and saved the day.

    The oneness that was to be between Adam, Eve, and God never flourished. The reason the relationship never flourished is that Adam never tended to the relationship between he and God. Like most Christians, we leave all the work to God. God is the power; He does the miracles, forgiving, and the saving. What God does not do is cover you contribution to Him. If you have a spouse, you understand one-sided relationships. There is no greater example of one-sidedness than Christian love towards God. Adam did not need a helpmeet to cease being alone. What Adam needed Eve for was to teach him how to tend to a garden. Adam needed Eve to learn how to husband. The lessons that Adam learned from Eve he was to apply to God. Consequently, the reason Adam's solitude was not good was that Adam had no way to learn how to develop his relationship with God. Adam needed a loving relationship to base his spiritual maturity upon.

When Adam blamed Eve, he actually said more than you realize. Adam blamed the two people he had no relationship with for the problem. Adam, did not just blame Eve, he said to God, "The woman You gave me…" Adam did not cultivate either relationship, so he felt no remorse breaking faith with or blaming either person. Without unity of heart, there is no marriage. Spiritual Warfare works against marriage by attacking non-unified hearts. Satan walked into a marriage where the two people were selfish and uncommitted to each other. The man allowed God's gift destroy his domain. The woman was to help Adam learn to love God. The image of God includes unity, a loving heart: a heart of one. To be in the image of God means to have a heart like God and to love like God.

Amen

Stones of Fire

"There is little doubt that a natural mined diamond of top quality is one of the most magnificent gems. It is much coveted for its exquisite beauty, but the truth is that diamonds are just compressed crystallized Carbon. The laboratories at...were created with one mission in mind: Design classic jewelry with scientifically perfect gemstones at a cost that lets everyone experience a stone with more fire and brilliance than a mined diamond[8]."

---

[8] <u>Going Places: The Magazine for Today's Traveler</u>, January/February 2006, (P.37).

Chapter Three
Stones of Fire

"BUT IF THINE EYE BE EVIL, THY WHOLE BODY SHALL BE FULL OF DARKNESS. IF THEREFORE THE LIGHT THAT IS IN THEE BE DARKNESS, HOW GREAT IS THAT DARKNESS - Matthew 6:23."

In Ezekiel chapter 28, the Lord our God speaks to the angel formerly known as Lucifer. Several verses are of importance to this book because they shed light on some intriguing points. In Ezekiel 28:13, the Lord speaks of the *'stones of fire'*, which is a reference to the angels. Some contend that Ezekiel 28:13 refers to jewels, some the sparkling effect of the jewels, some to stars. Whichever definition you *choose*, they all indicate brightness and illumination. The verses that are of particular attention to us in the book of Ezekiel are 28:13, 14, 16, and 18.

"YOU WERE IN EDEN THE GARDEN OF GOD; EVERY PRECIOUS STONE ADORNED YOU: RUBY, TOPAZ, EMERALD, CHRYSOLITE, ONYX, JASPER, SAPPHIRE, TURQUOISE, AND BERYL. GOLD WORK OF TAMBOURINES AND OF PIPES WAS IN YOU. IN THE DAY THAT YOU WERE CREATED, THEY WERE PREPARED. YOU WERE THE ANOINTED CHERUB WHO COVERS: AND I SET YOU, SO THAT YOU WERE ON THE HOLY MOUNTAIN OF GOD; YOU HAVE WALKED UP AND DOWN IN THE MIDST OF THE STONES OF FIRE. YOU WERE PERFECT IN YOUR WAYS FROM THE DAY THAT YOU WERE CREATED, UNTIL UNRIGHTEOUSNESS WAS FOUND IN YOU. BY THE ABUNDANCE OF YOUR TRAFFIC, THEY FILLED THE MIDST OF YOU WITH VIOLENCE, AND YOU HAVE SINNED: THEREFORE, I HAVE CAST YOU AS PROFANE OUT OF THE MOUNTAIN OF GOD; AND I HAVE DESTROYED YOU, COVERING CHERUB, FROM THE MIDST OF THE STONES OF FIRE. YOUR HEART WAS LIFTED UP BECAUSE OF YOUR BEAUTY; YOU HAVE CORRUPTED YOUR WISDOM BY

REASON OF YOUR BRIGHTNESS, I HAVE CAST YOU TO THE GROUND; I HAVE LAID YOU BEFORE KINGS, THAT THEY MAY SEE YOU. BY THE MULTITUDE OF YOUR INIQUITIES, IN THE UNRIGHTEOUSNESS OF YOUR TRAFFIC, YOU HAVE PROFANED YOUR SANCTUARIES; THEREFORE HAVE I BROUGHT FORTH A FIRE FROM THE MIDST OF YOU. IT HAS DEVOURED YOU, AND I HAVE TURNED YOU TO ASHES ON THE EARTH IN THE SIGHT OF ALL THOSE WHO SEE YOU."

We need to explore the following points for this chapter:
1. Lucifer was in Eden.
2. Lucifer was the anointed cherub.
3. Lucifer walked up and down in the midst of the stones of fire.
4. Lucifer was perfect in his ways from the day that God created him, until God found unrighteousness in him.
5. God cast Lucifer out of the mountain of God.
6. God destroyed Lucifer, from the midst of the stones of fire.
7. Lucifer corrupted his wisdom because of his vanity.
8. God brought forth a fire from the midst of Lucifer.
9. God turned Lucifer to ashes on the earth.

The name Lucifer means 'Bearer of light' or 'cup bearer', in other words to carry, reflect, or be filled with Light. The concept of being the bearer of light is sublime. Lucifer was the son of the morning[9], the daystar (sun[10]); therefore, the brightest of all God's angels. The book of Job calls angels *sons of God*. Therefore, this reference to Lucifer being the *son* of the morning is not the same as the Son of God. *The Morning* is a metaphor for Light, in other words a metaphor for God. Lucifer as reflector of *Morning's Light* is therefore a son in proximity only.

---

[9] Isaiah 14:12.
[10] Likened unto the sun, God is not a literal planetary body. Nor is God the literal Morning. Lucifer is son of the Morning because the God of the Morning consecrated him. In other words, Lucifer the star of the Morning only shone because of Morning and the glory Morning possessed.

THE *SONS* OF GOD (Psalms 82:1, 89.7)

The following three scriptures show the use of metaphorical phrases, terms, and words. The title *sons of God*, refers to the *US* spoken of in Genesis. The sons of God are also the stones of fire-they are angels. The brashness of Satan appears after God cast the angels into the earth realm and he still appears when the council forms.

1. "**And it came to pass, when men began to multiply in the earth, and daughters were born unto them, that the *sons of God* saw the daughters of men that they were fair; and they took them wives of all which they *chose*.**" In Genesis 6:1-2, we see that despite the New Testament applications there is a distinct difference between the sons of men and the sons of God. The Old Testament reference were not Christian in nature they were spiritual. The references to the sons of God in the Old Testament indicated angels. This also shows that mating between humans and son of God does not bring about more sons of God. The children of unholy relationships are bastards in both worlds. God told Moses that He was I AM, in the beginning the phrase Let there be light had the same effect. When God said, "Let there be light," He was simply stating I AM.

2. "**Now there was a day when the *sons of God* came to present themselves before the Lord, and Satan came also among them**." Job 1:6 is an informative verse of scripture. This stanza not only indicates time, it indicates relationship. Here we see the term sons of God applied to angels in good standing. What we can prove through the book of Peter is that the time in which this took place occurred after the fall of Lucifer. 2 Peter 6:4 informs us that God did not spare the angels that sinned. What this means is that the Sons of God that engaged in carnality God cast asunder with Lucifer. What we have now is a meeting, an assembly, of God's righteous remnant.

After this, the New Testament references to the sons of God no longer imply spirituality they imply righteousness. The new sons of God are sons in the likeness of the son of whom the Bible says was without sin. When the Bible refers to us as sons of God, it refers to the state of our hearts, not a birthright.

3. **"When the morning stars sang together, and all the *sons of God* shouted for joy."** Job: 38 is a beautiful description of the scene in Heaven. Here we see the righteous of God performing duties set aside for the pure of heart. Lucifer can never again sing songs of praise to the Lord of Hosts. The sons of God shouted for joy, these are the remnant not swept away by Satan's tail. The twinkle we sing about in the stars is the intermittent, praiseful emanations of the stones of fire, the sons of God, the righteous angels.

LUCIFER'S BRILLIANCE

Why did Lucifer shine so brightly? Is the question we should ask? The answer is two-fold:
1. God stated that He created Lucifer to be beautiful and have the ability to sparkle and dazzle[11].
2. Lucifer was the anointed/covering Cherub. As the anointed/covering Cherub, he spent his time closest to the throne.

The real explanation for Lucifer bearing light requires us to understand the dynamics of light. Most things in the universe do not create light; they reflect the sun's light. Ocean creatures in the abyss are among the few creatures that create light. Deep-sea creatures create light because there are no natural light sources in the depths where they live. This world like the depths of the ocean is an ocean of darkness devoid of light. Since we are like God, we are to make light here in the darkness[12].

Ask any young woman, when you *choose* a diamond or gemstone you look at it under a bright, white light. The purpose of doing this is that the stone looks more brilliant and valuable under the white light. We call the brilliance in jewelry a *sparkle*. Spiritually, we would call the same sparkle *glory* or *fire*. What therefore gives the stone the sparkle is that it reflects white light. The light does not increase the value of the stone but it seems to dazzle more brilliantly in the brighter light. The fact is that the

---

[11] Ezekiel 28:13.
[12] Matthew 5:16

more light the stone reflects the more valuable we declare it to be. The brightest Light in the universe is the Lord our God and the Bible describes His glory several times as fire.

There is subtle beauty in the fact that we call God's glory *'fire'* instead of light. What makes God's glory beautiful is that light is a luminescent by product of a living thing[13]. Unlike the common light sources the sun, moon, and stars, God creates His own light[14]. Despite science's explanation that the sun and stars are light producers, God designed the sun and the stars to generate light[15]. God on the other hand, is light; God gives Himself.

How wonderful that there was light in our universe long before the sun, moon, and stars existed. Look to Genesis and see that the only source of light in the universe until verse 13 is the Lord our God. Consequently, the stones of fire are not creatures that produce light; they are reflectors of God's glory. Lucifer--the bearer of light carried and/or reflected God's glory more brilliantly because he was both closest to God, and layered in precious stones. Another reason Lucifer shone so brightly is that Lucifer was always close to God. Like the planet Mercury, which is almost a fireball itself, the closer you are to the glory of God the more you reflect His fire. We see now that the references to the stones of fire are a reference to beings that reflect the glory of God. As I lovingly write to you concerning the reflection of light, I have to pause to wonder. Were the precious stones that adorned Lucifer for Lucifer, or were they to protect Lucifer from fire in the heart of God?

Believers, there is a reason gemstones are precious to humans. Gemstones are precious because we still hold dear the things from our old lives. When the Children of Israel left Egypt, they immediately tried to continue in the Egyptian worship and lifestyle. Many of the things forbidden in Leviticus are not in themselves bad. What makes the things bad is that they are signs of the old life in Egypt they are signs of bondage. Since God's people are free, they should no longer worship or wear the signs and symbols of bondage. A side effect of Egyptian bondage was the love of 'precious' metals and stones. The Egyptians, just like many other heathen empires, cherished Gold, and gemstones as treasures. The cause

---

[13] John 1:4.
[14] Genesis 1:3.
[15] Genesis 1:14-18.

of this love was not the intrinsic value of the items[16] but an ungodly desire for 'fire'.

The desire for *'fire'* is not a normal desire like desire for food and love. The *fire* men seek is God's glory. The rulers of this age deceived humans into believing they can find God's *fire* in the gemstones and riches that formerly adorned the Prince of Darkness. Satan is the prince of darkness. Satan no longer creates, emits, nor reflects light. The lust for the light in Patmos (fools' gold) therefore came about because we tried to create the glory Satan once held. Because humans are sinful, we constantly seek fire outside God's Holy Spirit.

Humans saw what they did not have and what they desired. Eve saw that the tree was good for food and pleasing to her eyes. I like the way the New Living Testament explains this point, "**The woman was convinced. The {tree} looked so fresh and delicious, and it would make her so wise! So she ate some of the fruit. She also gave some to her husband, who was with her. Then he ate it, too** - Genesis 3:6[17]." What Eve saw was that someone had something that she did not have and it was something she wanted. What made the *tree* look good was that Eve wanted the *tree*[18]. Because Eve desired, she began to see the tree through lustful eyes. As such, Eve fell. The Tree of Life also stood in the Garden of God. This means that Eve could have just as easily *chosen* Life, yet she did not. To this day despite the fact that abundant life is available, we desire riches instead.

The father of the pit craves his former glory. Since our ancestors are fruit of Satan's tree, we have this same sinful desire in our hearts. Lucifer's problem was that he envied God's ability to create fire. As long as Lucifer only carried the flame, he was just another angel. The sin of covetousness caused Lucifer's fall. Why would the head of the fallen angels have a desire for diamonds, gold and the baubles of this world? The answer is simply yet sinister. Satan is restricted to frequent this

---

[16] The Egyptians found this truth out against the Haikso's army. The Haiksos used weapons of iron and destroyed the Egyptian armies that used Gold for weapons. Thereby proving the complete uselessness of gold, Iron and silver have more innate value if only as weapons.

[17] The Holy Bible, New Living Translation, 1996. Tyndale Charitable Trust. Wheaton, Illinois.

[18] Kingdom Principle - This is the difference between lust and normal want; lust makes anything look good.

world; he therefore, can never again bask in God's fire. Lucifer can never again bear the Light of the almighty God or shine as he once shone. Satan masters the next best thing. Satan adorns himself with the only things in this world that reflect His light, dead crystalline rocks. If you held an angel under a florescent bulb, they would not reflect any earthly type of light. However, if we put that valueless rock under any type of bulb we can watch that dead thing sparkle in the dead light of this world.

After God cast/cut Lucifer down, the Bible never again calls the devil Lucifer. There is a laudable reason for this change in Lucifer's name. Lucifer's name meant bearer of light. The instant God withdrew fire from amidst Lucifer his name changed. The Lord told His former aide de campe, that the day He created Lucifer He adorned him with *fire*. In Ezekiel 28:14 God reminds Lucifer that he walked amongst the beings of glory in the mountain of God. Just as skyscrapers reflect sunlight the angels in the Mount of God the angels reflected God's immense glory. Notice another facet of the stones of fire that make them different from humans is that they can reflect God's Light. Angels can see God and His fullness; yet live. Humans on the other hand, cannot see God's glory and fullness and live. The Lord also goes on to tell Lucifer that because of his sin he was cast from the midst the stones of fire, from amongst His jewels (shining ones). However, if you read carefully the verse still indicates that Lucifer shone when or at least as God cast him out. Credence to this passage lies in Isaiah 14:12, where Isaiah refers to Satan's former luminescence as, "…**son of the morning**."

In Ezekiel 28, the verses describe the stones as having, (emanating) *fire*. Herein the Lord explains to us why Lucifer no longer bears glory/light. Once Lucifer was the definitive measure of glory and righteousness, therefore he shone brightly, more so than anything else in the universe; except God. However, God removed His glory/light/fire from Lucifer in verse 18, "…**THEREFORE I HAVE BROUGHT FIRE FROM THE MIDST OF YOU**." God withdrew His fire and brilliance from within Lucifer and God turned Satan into dust upon the earth. The tree of dust, that bears the fruit of the flesh--called death. To this end, the devil no longer has a name. The characteristic he displays at the time or the person he uses or possesses is the title we use to refer to him. This explains why Satan has so many titles and so many forms. Satan's true form no longer emits light[19]. Lucifer can however, still masquerade as an angel.

The reason the masquerade consistently works for Satan is that Christians no longer walk with, or recognize God the Father. Like the firefly mentioned in the ambush, the emanating light of the fallen angel looks like salvation to a world in darkness. The church is no longer a light in this dark world; this causes humanity to draw to other forms of luminescence.

Expulsion from Eden not only caused death, it barred humanity from the constant presence of God. God is a creature of habit. God is the Creator of habit because He is perfect. Since His ways are perfect, He uses these ways repeatedly. We call this Godly repetition *Nature*. By emulating God's habits, God perfects His people. It is not that God wished to destroy humanity--it is because believers transformed from creatures that give God glory to creatures that revel in the flesh.

Because humans no longer meet God in the Garden in Eden, the Almighty created a holy place to meet with His children. An example of God's consistency is the concept of special meeting places. The tabernacle construct is the best example of the special meeting place. God lays out the tabernacle construct in the book of Exodus starting in chapter 25, and ending in chapter 31. The Tabernacle Construct is a simple concept.
1. The Outer Court.
2. The Inner Court.
3. The Holy of Holies.

1. **THE OUTER COURT** - is open to everybody. At this level, everyone has exposure the righteous lifestyle.

2. **THE INNER COURT** - is more restrictive. At this level, only limited access to God exists.

3. **THE HOLY OF HOLIES** - has always been a place set aside for those allowed to commune with God. Even when Moses was at the burning bush, we see that the place CLOSEST to God is the Holy of Holies. That is why Moses could not wear shoes when told to come

---
[19] 2 Corinthians 11:13-15.

closer. Moses was required to leave the trappings of this life as far from the Holy one as possible.

The tabernacle construct exists in the Bible in three scenarios. In all three versions, you see the same functions for each level.

Fig 2a - THE UNIVERSAL TABERNACLE CONSTRUCT

1. **The Universe - The Outer Court** - The universe contains all life. Human flesh experiences everything in nature first. Just as nature is open to everyone, the outer court of the tabernacle is open to everyone.

2. **The Earth - The Inner Court** - God created certain creatures to live on the earth. God set aside a special place to walk with those that passed through the outer court. We know it was by conscience design because Genesis refers to the earth as Eden.

3. **The Holy of Holies** - Garden in Eden[20] - The Garden in Eden God set aside to meet His two favorite humans. Despite queries and speculation about Nod and people existing at the same time as Adam and Eve, they exclusiveness of the Tabernacle construct did not change.

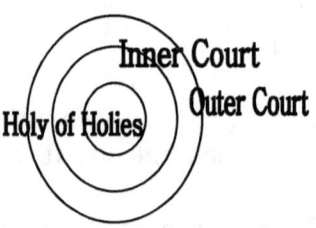

FIG 2a

---

[20] N.B. God created man before He place the garden, the need for a place to meet the man did not exist before Adam.

Fig 2b - THE TABERNACLE/TEMPLE CONSTRUCT

1. **The Outer Court** - a courtyard open to everybody.

2. **The Inner Court** - an inner courtyard restricted to priests and those with sacrifices.

3. **The Holy of Holies** - restricted only to priests.

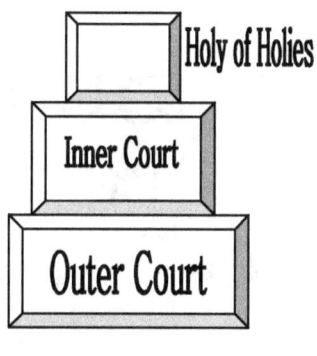

FIG 2b

Fig 2c - THE HUMAN TABERNACLE CONSTRUCT

1. **The Human Body - The Outer Court** - Everything humans experience they experience with the five sense first. Because the flesh is not discriminating, and permanently exposed to everything it is the outer court.

2. **The Imagination - The Inner court** - Incorrectly referred to as the soulical man or soul is the part of man that gives God the most trouble. Genesis 6:5 tells us, **"And God saw that the wickedness of man was great in the earth, and that every imagination of the thoughts of his heart was evil continually."** The imagination is more spiritual in nature, therefore closer to God. The imagination

is more discriminating than the outer court in that it determines what it lets in and out.

3. **The Human Heart - The Holy of Holies - "Know ye not that ye are the temple of the God, and that the Spirit of God dwelleth in you?"** 1 Corinthians 3:16 tell us that the heart is the place god set aside in the human temple to meet with His people. The consecrated heart is the holy placed God's Spirit lives in. There is no veil, guard or priest needed to invite Him in, all He requires is purity (Matthew 5:8).

FIG 2c

The tearing of the veil undid the tabernacle scenario; it affirmed the human tabernacle is God's plan for humankind. God did away for all times with the need for buildings, tents, synagogues, temples, and altars. Until Christ returns God will continue to commune with His people in their hearts.

God did not create human beings to be stones of fire. God's glory consumes human flesh before it can dazzle or sparkle[21]. This gives rise to the reason the Lord our God modifies His form when He appears to humans. The only human that ever saw God walking in a visible form was Adam, as God promised Adam died. Adam was no longer super-human as a result the man that saw God walking in the garden died.

Some argue that Moses and Abraham both saw God and lived. However, the scriptures differ with this concept in that no man has ever

---

[21] 1 Samuel 6:19.

seen all of God's glory and lived. Whether you agree or not, please do not presume to argue with God, "**And He** {God} **said, 'THOU CANST NOT SEE MY FACE: FOR THERE SHALL NO MAN SEE ME, AND LIVE'** - Exodus 33:20."

Even Christ, the tried stone, the precious cornerstone, the sure foundation was not a stone of fire. It was not in the first body that Christ ascended--but in His second[22]. Prior to the fall Adam's body was without sin. Jesus' ascension body was also without sin. In both cases, only the sinless human form is able to stand in God's presence and not suffer destruction.

David reminds us that God created man a little lower than angels. Since humans are a little lower than angels God transforms (exalts) men into new creatures, to spread light. Humans do not spread the Light of the Father; humans spread the Light of the Son. This does not mean that the two are different. It means humans reflect the Son when we live righteously. We are fruit of the Son not fruit of the Father. Jesus bought and paid for humans; we therefore, show Jesus' glory when we shine in the realm Jesus redeemed. This we do because believers live in the flesh not the spirit. How can believers look like spirits? When believers do the will of the Father people see the Son in believers; Jesus the Son of Man, Jesus the Son of God. Therefore, when we act and live like Jesus, people see Jesus in our lifestyle therefore they see the Father[23].

Sadly, the Light of this world[24] left. The Light of this world left believers in His place to shed His light in a world of darkness. We traded God's light to dazzle in the shade of another king[25]. We traded the Light of our incorruptible God for the light of our corrupt father[26], and turned God's truth into a lie. Believers, this is the single reason that the Prosperity Doctrine does not work. It is not a new doctrine or even a new move of God; it is the same old dragon still deceiving the nations[27].

---

[22] John 20:17, "**Jesus saith unto her, 'TOUCH ME NOT; FOR I AM NOT YET ASCENDED TO MY FATHER: BUT GO TO MY BRETHREN, AND SAY UNTO THEM, I ASCEND UNTO MY FATHER, AND YOUR FATHER; AND [TO] MY GOD, AND YOUR GOD'.**"
[23] John 10:30, "**I AND [MY] FATHER ARE ONE**."
[24] John 3:19, John 8:12, John 9:5.
[25] Judges 9:15.
[26] 2 Corinthians 4:4.
[27] See commentary on *Fool's Gold*.

In the Gospel of Matthew, we see the *prosperity doctrine of this age* in its purest form, spoken by the father of this age. Perhaps you will see it for what it is and return to God's Light, wealth, and peace.

"The tempter came and said to Him, 'If you are the Son of God, command that these stones become bread'. But He answered, 'IT IS WRITTEN, MAN SHALL NOT LIVE BY BREAD ALONE, BUT BY EVERY WORD THAT PROCEEDS OUT OF THE MOUTH OF GOD'. Then the devil taketh Him up into the holy city. The devil **set Him on the pinnacle of the temple, and said to Him, 'If thou be the Son of God, throw yourself down, for it is written,** *'He shall give His angels charge concerning thee: and in their hands they shall bear thee up, lest thy dash thy foot against a stone'.* **Jesus said to him, 'AGAIN, IT IS WRITTEN, YOU SHALL NOT TEMPT THE LORD, YOUR GOD'. Again, the devil took Him to an exceedingly high mountain, and showed Him all the kingdoms of the world, and their glory. He said to Him, 'I will give you all of these things, if you will fall down and worship me'. Then Jesus said to him, 'GET THE HENCE, SATAN! FOR IT IS WRITTEN, 'THOU SHALT WORSHIP THE LORD THY GOD, AND HIM ONLY SHALT YOU SERVE'. Then the devil left him, and behold, angels came and ministered unto Him** - Matthew 4:3-11."

The concept of prosperity in this age ties into the selfishness of humans. The prosperity concept of this age resembles God's type of prosperity as much as Satan's beguiling words resembled the truth in the garden. This is the subtle mastery of Satan's plan; Satan never gives up. The god of this age uses old tricks on every generation. In every selfish human generation, Satan's seeds find a place to grow in the wretched hearts of men. Like Jesus, when you too refused the garbage the devil has to offers, God and His angels will gladly minister unto you. Then you will see the effects of true wealth.

If there are to be stones in your lives, if you must *bling-bling* then let the fire in your lives flow from your heart. Let the brilliance of the love of God reflect from your heart through your life out into this dark, bleak, world in which we exist.

Diamonds are the product of years of pressure and intense metamorphosis. Righteousness is also the product of years of pressure and intense metamorphosis. There is still light in the universe, let the light you follow be the Light of the Son.

Amen

Chapter Four
The Lights in Our World

"Woe unto them that call evil good, and good evil; that put darkness for the light, and light for darkness; that put bitter for sweet, and sweet for bitter - Isaiah 5:20."

Darkness over ran the earth, God could not find a light in the earth; the Maker of the sun created a Light for this world. There are many lights in this world. Some of the lights are false, some incorrect and there is one True light. This book is about different lights and the ways lights affect our spiritual life. In the world, there are many types of lights but only two sources. God created the heavens and the earth, any other source of light is from the kingdom of God's enemy.

THE TWO SOURCES OF LIGHT IN THE WORLD
Bright and Morning Star vs *son of the morning*

How delicately different are the following two references.

"I JESUS HAVE SENT MINE ANGEL TO TESTIFY UNTO YOU THESE THINGS IN THE CHURCHES. I AM THE ROOT AND THE OFFSPRING OF DAVID, [AND] THE BRIGHT AND MORNING STAR - Revelation 22:16."	**"How art thou fallen from heaven, O Lucifer, son of the morning! How art thou cut down to the ground, which thou didst weaken the nations** - Isaiah 14:12."

You have to look closely, very closely as you would a wisp of smoke. If you stare, it disappears, if you move it disappears. There is no way to hold on to the smoke in its purest form. This is the ultimate test of the two great lights in the universe. The difference is plain to see if you let your heart hear.

1. **THE BRIGHT AND MORNING STAR** - Bright and Morning star creates light, it gives light it is the Light of the world. The son of the morning is also a light in the world, but it neither creates nor emanates light. This world is a world of darkness, anything that stands out in the dark, does so because it has traits in common with the things in it shade. A shadow for example is dark, because it has nothing in common with light. Because a shadow is the opposite of light, it appears dark, as dark as the creature it silhouettes.

2. **SON OF THE MORNING** - Isaiah 14:12. This passage shows the relationship Isaiah held with the most high. How could Isaiah know of the fall of Lucifer without a quickening from God's Holy Spirit? Here we also see what level of understanding Isaiah possessed. What mere man would understand the travesty to humanity the fall of Lucifer caused? Isaiah said that the fallen star weakened the nations. Jesus said that Satan deceived the nations confirming Lucifer is the fallen star. The son of the morning is simply a celestial being that descended from heaven. There are two sources of light in the world and they fall into to three categories or groups.

THE LIGHTS IN THE WORLD

1. **LOST LIGHTS** - "**FOR THERE WILL ARISE FALSE MESSIAHS, AND FALSE PROPHETS, AND THEY WILL SHOW GREAT SIGNS AND WONDERS, SO AS TO LEAD ASTRAY, IF POSSIBLE, EVEN THE CHOSEN ONES** - Matthew 24:24." There are entire cadres of lost lights. This the largest groups of lights. This is the largest group because the lost, mis-educated, uneducated, and deceived comprise this group. There is no intention to deceive or mislead inherent in these lights, which is why they are devastating. These lights are sincere, gentle well-intentioned people, but the pathway they illuminate leads to destruction.

2. **FALSE LIGHTS** - "**BUT IF THINE EYE BE EVIL, THY WHOLE BODY SHALL BE FULL OF DARKNESS. IF**

THEREFORE THE LIGHT THAT IS IN THEE BE DARKNESS, HOW GREAT IS THAT DARKNESS - Matthew 6:23." False lights exist for one reason only; they intend to destroy as many lives as possible. The false light is sinister because it has never existed to do well. It was born in evil, conceived in darkness and will always result in the destruction of the soul.

3. TRUE LIGHT - "**Again, therefore, Jesus spoke to them, saying, 'I AM THE LIGHT OF THE WORLD. HE WHO FOLLOWS ME WILL NOT WALK IN THE DARKNESS, BUT WILL HAVE THE LIGHT OF LIFE**' - John 8:12." Only one true Light ever walked the earth. The truth of the Son over shadowed and out shone the sun in the sky. The red giant we call *Sol* God placed in the sky at the dawn of time. God gave us the sun to mark seasons and time. The gospels record that the sun marked the beginnings of time; it twice bowed its head to the Son of God.

Unlike the Son of God, the son of the morning is restricted to be a light in this world. As we can tell from scripture, there is no true light left in this world. The Light of this world shone only once; at Golgotha then it left, and will return some other time. Jesus told us that He was the Light of the world and that when He left that Light would leave with Him. This is why the sun refused to shine at Golgotha, the Bright and Morning star is the source of Light in the universe, not the sun. It was the Bright and Morning Star that gave Himself to us in Genesis, when He moved upon the face of the dark and the deep. **"In Him was life, and the life was the light of men. And the light shineth in darkness; and the darkness comprehended it not** - John 1:4-5"

Paul asked what fellowship has light with darkness. This is never more poignant than in the wilderness experience. Discerning the light in your world requires a careful heart. No matter which light you *choose* you must judge it by where it leads. Any light that leads to, near, through darkness is not the light you wish to follow. Notice I did not say any light that causes pain and suffering. Doing the wrong thing does is not the only cause of pain and suffering. Many trials and tribulation exist for His namesake. Although loneliness, despair, and sorrow are unpleasant places, they ARE NOT DARKNESS. Darkness is the absence of Light.

Sadness is the absence of joy, without Light there will never be hope. Better to cry now and rejoice in heaven than to laugh and get fat in this life, only to perish[28]. You may wish to 'enjoy your best life now', but this is evidence that you have no intention, or hope of spending eternity with the Father.

Amen

---

[28] James 5.

Chapter Five
The Bright and Morning Star

"**I JESUS HAVE SENT MINE ANGEL TO TESTIFY UNTO YOU THESE THINGS IN THE CHURCHES. I AM THE ROOT AND THE OFFSPRING OF DAVID, [AND] THE BRIGHT AND MORNING STAR** - Revelation 22:16."

I freely admit that Revelation 22:16 is one of the many passages in the Bible that I find difficult. The Triune nature of God creates confusion; this confusion permeates throughout scriptures that ascribe more than one or two attributes to anything. The reason the Bible ascribes dual traits or application to things is that humans have a dual nature flesh and spirit. In order to minimize words and still make the Bible sharper than a two-edge sword God engineers His words this way.

One of the areas of difficulty for many Christians, one that dissuades many from the faith is the Trinity concept. Let us look together at the Trinity, so that we may further understand how it affects spiritual dynamics.

THE GODHEAD - THE TRINITY EXPLAINED

I once asked God for an easy way to explain His Holy nature. To which He responded:
- God the *Father* is the ocean.
- God's *Holy Spirit* is the salt in the ocean.
- The *Son* is a glass of salt water.

The ocean is deep and vast, its depth and marvels are without end. There would be no life on this planet without oceans. The oceans could not support the life they do without salt. In every drop of ocean, there are equal amounts of salt. A glass of salt water has the properties and salinity of the ocean. The only limitation to the cup of salt water is that it is enclosed, trapped inside the glass. Christians speak of *God in three persons* but we separate the Godhead. Each portion of the Godhead has a purpose and to explain the purposes further I use King David as an example of the Father and Son.

In the court of the king, no one but an equal or a designee may approach the king. Many people wished to speak to King David but they had to settle for a court appointee. If the appointee (the equivalent of a priest in the spirit) cannot address the issue the prince, or heir-apparent contend with the issue. If the issues are of dire importance, the king addresses it personally and makes law. It is not that the king's underlings have no wisdom; they have little to no authority. The king's court operates within the power of the king. When power is required, the king must act personally. For this reason, Jesus the prince instructs believers to beseech the Father for help and power. Remember the prince acts in the power of the king, Jesus tells us this repeatedly that He and the Father are one and that He does nothing without permission of the Father.

In Matthew 28 Jesus tells us to baptize in the name of the Father, the Son, and God's Holy Spirit. This we do because each has an area of responsibility.
- *The Father* - is responsible for the universe, balance, and keeping Satan's kingdom under control.
- *God's Holy Spirit* - operates in the earth realm under the permission of redeemed human authority.
- *The Son* - redeemed the earth realm and restored God the Father's relationship ability to help humans.

THE TRINITY CONFIRMED

Again, I openly and definitively state that the Trinity is a stumbling block for as many Christians as among the lost. Nevertheless, make no mistake the three are one. It is not for men to disagree with the God that made the heavens and the earth. 1 John gives both a record and a witness. The record is for spirits and the witness for the flesh. **"For there are three that bear record in heaven, the Father, the Word and the Holy Ghost: and these three are one. And there are three that bear witness in the earth, the Spirit, and the water and the blood: and these three agree in one** - 1 John 5:7-8"

Look closely and see that the spirit world and the flesh have different needs. In the spirit there is only need for a record, the record of I AM. Look more closely and you will see that in the earth the three agree IN ONE.

"And immediately I was in the spirit; and, behold, a throne was set in heaven, and One sat on the throne - Revelations 4:2"

There is no doubt that Jesus redeemed men, but He gives credit to the Father that sent Him. The God that so loved the world, choose to send us the begotten Son, the son He begot. They are one, in deed, one in thought and one in motivation, even though one lives in the Spirit and the other the flesh.

THE TRINITY MANEUVER

God gave man irrevocable dominion over the earth. God cast Lucifer out of the heavens and into the earth realm, but withheld power from him. Satan only has the powers of the air. God gave Adam power over the earth, the seas, and the fowls or the air. The power of the air remains unclaimed. Even Christ did not assume power over the air.

Once Satan reigned over the air, he withstood God at every juncture. The first attempt by Satan to usurp the earth occurs in the garden. Through subterfuge, Satan takes control of the earth from Adam. Since God's Holy Spirit can only operate in the earth realm through redeemed humans, the trinity maneuver became necessary.

In order to flow in the earth and not violate His own law God needed a human to retake control over the earth. There was a hindrance to God's plan--the human creature is sinful.

1. God curses the earth for man's sake, barring satanic control.
2. God seeks a human He can use to redeem the earth realm.
3. God cannot find a man righteous enough to redeem the earth.
4. God makes another human vessel specially designed for the task.
5. God uses His powers to aid this special human to complete the task.
6. Once the task is completed, God restores dominion to humans- through the redeemer of man's dominion.
7. This redeemer now having power over the flesh, the earth, the sea, the fowls of the air, the grave, and death operates freely in the earth realm via God's Holy Spirit.

In these seven steps, the Godhead maneuvered itself between man and man's adversary. You see here that the Godhead is not three persons, but one God using His integrity to repair the damage caused by Satan. If God were three separate people, this would have been exceedingly difficult, if not impossible. God did not use treachery; He used wisdom, to save humanity.

God did His part in restoring order. It falls to Christians to be lights in the world of darkness. The apathy in the faith flickers daily, no wonder Christ's return is necessary. If He were not to return, darkness would eventually take over the earth again. **"We have also a more sure word of prophecy; whereunto ye do well that ye take heed, as unto a light that shineth in a dark place, until the day dawn, and the day star arise in your hearts** - 2 Peter 1:19." Peter goes on to say that we are lights that flicker and glimmer in the darkness. Peter however adds the corollary that we must be careful in the darkness, because our light is not justified until {Christ} the Day Star rises (comes to life) in our hearts. Peters wisdom and experience shows here. Peter refers to his own trial with the crowing of the cock. Peter walked with Christ three years but was never justified, at least not until God's Holy Spirit convicts him, and he cries uncontrollably. What peter found out that day was that the flesh is not capable of serving Christ. Only a renewed (redeemed) spirit can rejoice, receive, and flow in the Spirit. Thus, the darkness in us stays in us until Light chase the darkness away. As in fable the sun chases away the moon, the rising of the Son in our hearts chases away darkness.

Amen

Chapter Six
Sun and Moon Worship

*"**But we will certainly do whatsoever thing goeth forth out of our own mouth, to burn incense unto the queen of heaven, and to pour out drink offerings unto her, as we have done, we, and our fathers, our kings, and our princes, in the cities of Judah, and in the streets of Jerusalem: for [then] had we plenty of victuals, and were well, and saw no evil** - Jeremiah 44:17."*

According to scholars, Sun and Moon worship number among the oldest forms of religion[29]. When we hear about pagan religions, we think of silly idols and ridiculous rituals. The reason we do this is that we do not know the history of Christianity. To worship a cow and not eat the cow is silly. Remember however, before the Hindus worshipped the cow, the Hebrews exalted, idolized, and worshipped the cow[30]. Pagan religions are nothing more than idol worship. Idol worshippers find peace in their form of worship. The common traits for idol and pagan religions are twofold:
    1. Idol and pagan religions both lack responsibility.
    2. Idol and pagan religions both lack the need for personal change.

WHAT CREATES IDOL WORSHIP?
To answer this let us first look to I Samuel and then to the book of Malachi. In I Samuel 8 the Children of Israel request a king to reign over them; a king of flesh and blood like every other nation. To this God responded, that the people had rejected Him[31]. The Jews said they wanted a visible king to lead them and fight their battles. The simple fact is that the Jews did not want a king to help them stay victorious and righteous; The Jews wanted a break from God's narrow path. The verse in I Samuel

---

[29] Other scriptures dealing with moon worshipped by the Assyrians as a goddess in nature are Jeremiah 7:18, 44:17, 25.
[30] Exodus 32.
[31] I Samuel 8:7.

8:20 is very similar to the verse from Exodus 32:1 let us compare them side by side.

I Samuel 8:19-20 -	Exodus 32:1 -
"**Nevertheless the people refused to obey the voice of Samuel; and they said, 'Nay; but we will have a king over us; That we also may be like all the like all the nations; and that our king may judge us, and go out before us and fight our battles'.**"	"**And when the people saw that Moses delayed to come down out of the mount, the people gathered themselves Aaron and said unto him, 'Up make us gods which shall go before us; for [as for] this Moses, the man that brought us up out of land of Egypt, we wot not what is become of him'.**"

In both cases, what is obvious is that like disobedient children the Jews wanted freedom to play. Despite the righteous leadership of Moses, the Children of Israel found value and solace in wretched, unrighteous, leadership. The children of Israel wanted a leader that was fleshly, unrighteous, and would wallow with them in the mud.

Christians love to pretend we differ from pagans. The truth; however, is that the only difference between pagan idols and Christian idols is that the Christian idol is **Self**. Is there truly a difference between pagans worshipping a snake and Christians acting like snakes? John 14:15 clearly says that if you love the Lord you will obey Him. If you read Exodus 20:3 and 4 you will notice that God calls anyone that worships (follows, obeys) anything or anyone other than Him *a hater of God*. Remember idols do not create worshippers; on the contrary worshippers create idols. This is why the commandment forbids the creation, serving, bowing before, and/or worshipping any graven images. God's genius even shines in this law. There are no cults or religions that actually worship and living things. Nature worshippers, element worshippers, animal worshippers, celestial worshippers all claim to worship the *spirit inside* the thing they worship. This is why Paul calls them fools, because their rationale is so stupid. See how close they are to the light, yet choose darkness. A man that can worship the *Totem* and carve idols representing their spirits can certainly worship the Great Chief. Any man that can worship the Dogstar (Dogans) can give credit to the creator of the star. A man once said he would rather light a candle than curse your darkness. The man had the right ideal; we must even love fools, and may God have mercy on their souls.

Christianity changed as it moved further from Christ. Down through the centuries, can we not see how farmers could fall in love with and depend upon the sun? What if I was a follower of the Way[32] and a farmer, how could I read Malachi 4:12 and not get confused? In Malachi 4:12 we find a reference to the sun. Of the 160 times the word sun appears in the Bible, it only appears capitalized *Sun*[33] twice. Of the 52 listed times for the moon it only appears capitalized *Moon* once.

Joshua 10:12 - **"Then spake Joshua to the Lord in the day when the Lord delivered up the Amorites before the children of Israel, and he said in the sight of Israel, *Sun*, stand thou still upon Gibeon; and thou, *Moon*, in the valley of Ajalon."**

Malachi 4:12 - **"But unto you that, fear my name shall the *Sun* of righteousness arise with healing in his wings; and ye shall go forth, and grow up as calves of the stall."**

The logical question - *Is the capitalized word Sun a typo in this scripture or is this reference to Christ?* If this is a reference to Christ then Sun worship is the same as worshipping the Son. Since *Sun* appears in the Bible, can we in good conscience not worship the *Sun*? If this is the case, to worship the Sun that we see and rely on, is a logical course of action.

Romans 1:20 would also seem to imply that Sun worship is an acceptable practice. Sun worshipping Christians justify Sun worshipping by saying that they simply use the great ball in the sky as a visible

---

[32] This is what people called Christianity in the Old Testament days before Christ.
[33] The *Halo* comes from Sun worship because prior to conversion King James was a Sun worshipper. The halo and wedding band exemplify the sun of righteousness.

representation of God. The problem with this seemingly harmless course of reason is that it leads future generations into Sun worship that has no affiliation with Christ. In Joshua 10:12, Joshua is not worshipping the sun; he is giving it a command. The capitalization appears because Joshua uses the sun and moon's names to address them.

People did not fall into sin because of Sun and Moon worship, the converse is true. Sun and moon worship are a result of sin. Humans have always desired something visible to worship. The desire for something visible to worship is not sinful. The desire for something visible to worship it is the result of being fleshly creatures. This desire for familiarity is only a few degrees from tribalism. We want things that look, walk, and act as we do. The flesh wants a leader it can see, and of decrepit morality. For humans it seems far more logical to believe in the visible than the invisible.

The theory of Evolution has at its core the same flawed belief in the visible rather than the invisible. How can we think that Qantas (the smallest active portion of atoms) can form what we see today yet they came from nowhere? The Lord our God asks a peculiar question of His followers, "**HOW CAN YOU LOVE A GOD THAT YOU CANNOT SEE AND NOT LOVE YOUR BROTHER THAT YOU SEE EVERYDAY?**" In this verse, God did not ponder the mystery, He comments on our hypocrisy. Worshippers those that claim to love God and not His creation--He knows are liars. Just as the sun cannot be divorced from light and heat, we cannot separate God. The scriptures tell us in the book of John that in the beginning was the word, and the word was God. Therefore, what was in the beginning before creation and during creation is still the reason for the creation. God was then, is now, and will forever be the reason for creation[34].

As it were, the creatures seeing that the Creator would never be corrupt like them, sought other forms and creatures to worship. There is a commandment forbidding creating likenesses of anything in heaven or earth or in the ocean or skies above. God leaves no room for question; THOU SHALL HAVE NO OTHER GOD BEFORE ME.

I once heard an argument that idols of crosses and churches are ok because they are manmade. This is a laudable concept, but irrelevant. The issue is not that the idols man makes are sinful; the issue is that GOD

---

[34] John 1:1-5.

DOES NOT SHARE. What folly it is to worship the sun because of its power and not worship the One that gave the sun its power. What folly it is to worship the moon because of its mysterious power and not worship the One that gave the Moon its mysterious power. When the Lord hung the moon in Genesis, He said that He gave it for light. When the Lord hung the sun, He said it was for a light by day. I would like to point out another reason sun worship is not based on any sound reasoning. There once hung a man on a cross at Golgotha. On His head, He wore thorns and above His head, men wrote 'INRI'. After a short period, that man on the cross-died. When that man died, a historical thing happened. When the Son died, the sun that the idolaters worship REFUSED to shine.

Despite man's attempt to corrupt the incorruptible God, the things God creates continue to worship Him as God. Sun worshippers and Christians have one thing in common, however; both worship the Light of the world. The lost see the light of the world as a red giant type star and believers see the Bright and Morning Star.

It is not as difficult as you think to fall away from the truth; especially, if you did not know the truth to begin with. Let us take a wonderful example of falling away. I watched a television program about the Incas. In that program, the excavators discovered a very peculiar array of stone slabs in the most sacred part of the temple (Fig I). Based on the location in the temple, researchers deemed the slabs central or at least foundational to the religion. The array consisted of six vertical stone slabs and a slab statue. The horizontal arrangement was of the same size and architecture, but it consisted of several vertical columns supporting one horizontal stone slab.

(Fig 1)

After approximately 18 months of studying the scrolls and religious texts, the researchers stumbled upon something remarkable. What the researchers stumbled upon was the fact that the slabs were not simply slabs they represented something. It turns out that the horizontal arrangement was actually a bench representing the holy day of rest for their god. What the researchers uncovered was that central to this Incan religion was the following creation story; *In six days, the Incan god created the heavens and the earth and on the seventh day, he rested.*

It is amazing, but the simple fact is that if you trace all of the world's major religions back far enough, they all have a common origin. Most current religions trace back to Egypt and from there they become easier to trace. No matter which theory you believe—(Gap, evolution, big bang, chaos, Creation etc.) like humans, all religions started the same place--*In the beginning.* Religions therefore all have commonalities.

I spent ten years in the pagan wilderness when I left Christianity. I left Christianity because Christian teaching and teachers were severely deficient. I studied and tried to convert to several pagan religions in my wandering. Here is a synopsis of that journey. If you walk backwards around the earth, you will see that religion spread with civilization and commerce. Religions also spread along the same route as commerce and civilization. As people moved about and merchants traveled, they took their belief systems along.

Regressing through time, you end up in Egypt. Going backwards through Egyptian deities, you fine Atom. Atom is the name for a sun god; from this god we get the word Atomic. You find that under the reign of the Pharaoh Akhenaton monotheistic worship of the sun emerged and became the official religion. Going past Akhenaton, tracing the kings of Egypt you find a figure that we only hear about in a negative fashion. According to researchers, the first ruler of what later became Egypt was Ham the father of Canaan. Yes, believers, the man that went on to become the first pharaoh of what was to be Egypt was one of Noah's sons. One of the eight humans God personally delivered from sin and brought safely to land. At some point in time, God was in Egypt. After years of failed fellowship with God, a pharaoh arose in Egypt that did not know the God of Abraham, Isaac, and Jacob.

Like all relationships, unused intimacy fades. The result of the waning relationship with God was that the people suffered. Many believe that the suffering was a result of God's anger, they are wrong. God does not get angry with those that fall away, He weeps. If a country did away with its police, the result would be a crime wave. The crime wave is not a result of the unemployed police officers rage. The crime wave is the result of the lack of protection. What makes the suffering in our lives subside is the protection of God. When we walk out into wilderness of our own design God is not there. Like the father of the prodigal son, he will wait anxiously for your return but He WILL not come looking for the rebellious.

When God speaks of leaving the 99, He distinctly tells us that He is looking to help the lost. Lost is not a *choice*. When a man decides to run away from home and leave the familiar places, we say he is missing. When a child does the same, we call them lost. The difference is that the man has the *choice* to leave, they child does not have that *choice*. We worry about the child because we know the dangers they will face. In the same manner, God protects us when we are lost, but He gives us up to our own stupidity when we rebel.

They children of Israel endured 400 years of slaver because they *chose to*. When their cries reached heaven, is another way of saying when they came to their senses. The story of the Israelites and the prodigal son are the same. They both discard a loving father's kindness for fleshly pleasure. Once the pleasure ends, panic sets in. Only upon panicking, does the son remember the kindness of the father wand return. You will note God does not chase those that walk away from Him…anywhere in the Bible.

I hold a Black belt in Wado-Ryu karate. I am still a student of Wado-Ryu karate. If you look at what students learn verses what the founder of the style taught there are subtle differences. Many of these differences did not come about because people tried to change the style. The fact is that for one reason or another, the further away from the source Wado-Ryu moved the more diluted the style. Some people are taller, heavier, or physically unable to do what the founder was able to accomplish; therefore, they modified the style to suit their abilities. With religion however, we have modified the truth not because we are taller, heavier, or physically unable it is to serve our lust and debasements.

People that refuse to see God as God are fools the book of Roman says. They are fools because they deny the inescapable truth. Whether we agree the sun rides across the sky from East to West, it does. Whether we agree or not, that the sun sits over 96 million miles away, it does. Most of all they are fools because any God that can make a ball of fire that keeps us warm but does not burn us is far more powerful than we can ever imagine. Any God that can make a moon that controls the tides from such a great distance, shines light on this dark wretched world, and affect the fertility cycle of the human female deserves our respect.

    It is impossible to walk anywhere on the earth God created and not see His beauty. It is ok to worship the Sun if you wish. It is ok to worship the Moon and the stars if you wish. At the end, when time ends, there will be only one Light in the universe. Anyone that does not *choose* to kneel when He rises will most certainly bow when He sits.

Amen

Chapter Seven
The First Pharaoh of Egypt

"**Now there arose up a new king over Egypt, which knew not Joseph. And he said unto his people, Behold, the people of the children of Israel [are] more and mightier than we: Come on, let us deal wisely with them; lest they multiply, and it come to pass, that, when there falleth out any war, they join also unto our enemies, and fight against us, and [so] get them up out of the land. Therefore they did set over them taskmasters to afflict them with their burdens. And they built for Pharaoh treasure cities, Pithom and Raamses** - Exodus 1:8-11."

Many people wonder why Noah cursed Ham for laughing at his drunken father. I have heard many theories discussed, none if which are laudable. Nonetheless, we look to the origins of Satan's kingdom in the earth realm. The *Satanic Construct* is what I call the Bible's cliff notes on the kingdom Satan set up here in the earth realm.

In Biblical tradition, we look at the genealogy of the Satanic Construct.

THE SATANIC CONSTRUCT

1. Satan beguiles Eve.

2. Eve shares with Adam.

3. God curses Satan.

4. God banishes Adam and Eve.

5. God curses the earth.

6. Cain slays Abel.

7. Cain flees to Nod (Scholars assert that the name Nod means w*andering or to wander*).

8. According to the records in Genesis chapter 5 approximately 7,718 years after the fall Adam and Eve, God repented making man, and was grieved in His heart.[35]

9. After the flood the earth was populated by three tribes of the children of Noah--Ham, Shem, and Japath.

10. Ham's children Cush, Seba, Mizraim, Put, and Canaan, bore children. The children of Ham; at least Cush and Canaan are verifiable enemies of God.

11. Cush goes on to sire Satan's second greatest disciple--a mighty man in the earth. Moreso than Cain, Nimrod[36] exemplified the traits and the spirit of his father Satan.

12. Nimrod built Babel, Shinar, and Nineveh. Nimrod's brother Mizraim built Cashlum and Pathrusim the lands of the Philistines.

13. Nimrod's kingdom contained Sidon, Gaza, Sodom, and Gomorrah.

14. God thwarts Nimrod's plan at Babel and scatters men. What is apparent is that the spirit chief of the Babel tribe--Satan remained in the earth.

15. The Kings from these countries wage war against Abraham.

16. Abraham flees to Egypt.

---

[35] Genesis 6:6.
[36] Genesis 10:8.

The next logical step is to address points 7 and 16 of the Satanic Construct. We look at these two points because they raise interesting questions. Where did these two cities come from? The answer is implicit in the surrounding scriptures. The *land* of Nod is not so much a place as it is a spiritual denotation. In other words, the scripture says that Cain went to Nod, just as is says Enoch built a city called Enoch. What is implicit is that Cain did not flee to a city he fled to the *Land*. In other words, Cain wandered out into the wilderness, the desolate place apart from God called Nod. The land is not Nod because it had a city called Nod. The land Nod represents the state of Cain's wandering soul.

Point 10 from the Satanic Construct is peculiar because there is no mention of the construction of Egypt. What is obvious is that Egypt was a city surrounding the lands Nimrod developed. In Genesis 12:10, there was a famine in the land, so Abram went down into Egypt. Egypt therefore was a city. Who built the city, the Bible does not spell out. Let us then look back at our genealogy in the Satanic Construct.

Mistakenly, we believe the civilization of Egypt began after the flood this is not the case. Egypt is not a place; Egypt is a state of being. Egypt in Biblical terms represents bondage in the Christian journey, not a geographical location. Egypt and all the cities like Egypt have a common origin. The origin of all the cities that came against God the scriptures does describe.

1. **"And Cush begat Nimrod: he began to be a mighty one in the earth** - Genesis 10:8."

2. **"And they said one to another, Go to, let us make brick, and burn them thoroughly. And they had brick for stone, and slime had they for morter. And they said, Go to, let us build us a city and a tower, whose top [may reach] unto heaven; and let us make us a name, lest we be scattered abroad upon the face of the whole earth. So the Lord scattered them abroad from thence upon the face of all the earth: and they left off to build the city. Therefore is the name of it called Babel; because the Lord did there confound the language of all the earth: and from thence did the Lord scatter them abroad upon the face of all the earth** - Genesis 11:3, 4, 8, 9." As we look at the scriptures, we see that Ham's

influence spread across the world through his son Nimrod. The world will feel Nimrod's influence until the return of Christ.

We see throughout time that the spirit chief who gave Nimrod his power and knowledge exists forever. We see in Revelation 18:2, that the spirit of Nimrod from Genesis 10:10 survived. Babel; the place where the languages of earth sprung, had as its source the fallen angel Lucifer. **"And he cried mightily with a strong voice, saying, Babylon the great is fallen, is fallen, and is become the habitation of devils, and the hold of every foul spirit, and a cage of every unclean and hateful bird**."

We have now pieced together a great part of the puzzle, the identity of the first Pharaoh of Egypt? Revelations again has the answer for us contained in its wisdom. **"And the great dragon was cast out, that old serpent, called the Devil, and Satan, which deceiveth the whole world: he was cast out into the earth, and his angels were cast out with him** -12:9." The angel that is wiser than Daniel, spirit chief, the evil power behind the throne was the first Pharaoh of Egypt. Lucifer the Bearer of Light gives us even more insight into the power behind the first Pharaoh of Egypt. In the chapter Lucifer the Bearer of Light, we see how the power behind the first Pharaoh of Egypt subtly under girds spiritual conflicts.

Amen

Chapter Eight
Egypt -Self-Worship

"Beware least any man spoil you through philosophy and vain deceit, after the tradition of men, after the rudiments of the world, and not after Christ - Colossians 2:18."

Descendants of Noah's son Ham went on to become the first Pharaoh of what eventually became Egypt. Egypt was the cradle of ancient civilization. As we look at the history of Egypt, we see that there was a point that Egypt honored the God of Abraham, Isaac, and Jacob.

As stated before, Egypt was not a place; Egypt was a state of heart. Egypt in biblical terms always represented a place in the Christian journey, and not a geographical location. Just as the Bible promises in Exodus, the Egyptians that you see today you will see no more forever. This was a promise of deliverance from sin and bondage, not slavery. The promise was a spiritual promise, not a promise to be free from humanity, but a freeing of souls held captive by Satan. Deliverance from bondage does not necessarily free people from the desire to sin. Lot's wife and daughters are more prime examples of this principle.

The follower of a spirit is a spiritual being. Why do we call Israel a state and not a country? It is because the entire populace believes in the God 'EL'. Therefore, Israel, the country is not a geographic location Israel is wherever the people that believe in EL reside[37]. In the same manner, Egypt is also a place where believers dwell. These are not believers in 'EL', these believers believe in 'Self'. The spirit Egyptians believe in is the false light that leads to damnation, the false light in Patmos also known as Lucifer. Genesis points out where Egypt began, and which spirit ruled Egypt. Genesis 6:3, 5, and 12 explain whose spirit inhabited the earth. We know from our studies that violence came to the human heart[38] from the father of murder.

---

[37] Psalms 22:3, "**But Thou [art] holy, [O Thou] that inhabitest the praises of Israel.**"

[38] A repository inside that fills the body with life giving blood. Whatever the heart pumps fills the body. If the heart is full of evil, evil fills the body. If the heart is pure, it fills the body with purity.

Therefore, children have characteristics of their father. Through these characteristics, we discern who is the father. The followers of Lucifer carry the spirit of Lucifer just as the followers of God are supposed to carry the Spirit of God. Because we are believers does not automatically mean that our children are believers. Although a believer's relationship with God covers their children, the children themselves, are not in a relationship with God. The relationship is like a single woman and her children living with a man. The man provides for the children not because of his relationship with the children but because of his relationship with the children's mother. The children are indirect beneficiaries of the mother's blessings. Because these are not the man's children, there is no reason to believe the children will have any of the man's characteristics.

God favored Noah just as He favored Lot. Both men lived in cities surrounded by the unrighteous; but God favored their light in the darkness. We see in both instances that the men's children did not have a relationship with God. The evidence of this lack of relationship we see in the actions of the children. No sooner did Ham survive the flood did he show the lack of a relationship with God. How could Ham see the power of God, watch Him close the door of the ark, and save Ham's life all through your father and then laugh at your dad's nakedness? Ham did this because he had no respect for God, or his father's relationship with God.

As we look through Genesis 10, we learn that Ham begat Cush, Cush then begat Nimrod. Nimrod is famous because in Genesis 11 he caused the Lord to leave heaven, come to the earth, and destroy Nimrod's plans to ascend into the heavens.

Why would a human creature wish to ascend to heaven? Why would Nimrod decide to build a tower to reach to heaven? Simple, the spirit influencing Nimrod wanted to get back to the place Lucifer once occupied. Here is a list of the four times God blocked Satan's advance in the earth realm.

1. God blocked Satan's advance by cursing the earth to keep Satan's influence out creation - Genesis 3:17.

2. God blocked Satan's advance in the garden with the Cherubs and flaming swords - Genesis 3:24.

3. God blocked Satan's advance with a flood to kill both Satan's followers and Satan's abhorrent children - Genesis 7:17.

4. God blocked Satan's advance by destroying human's ability to communicate - Genesis 11:7.

Despite Godly intervention, Satan and humans continue to strive against the Father. The Father said He would not constantly strive with His enemies[39], as always Satan did not understand the meaning. Satan did not understand that Christ was the resolution to the striving. Once God dealt Satan the final crushing blow, Christ restored the original *choice*. Jesus' death repaired the relationship between man and God. Man was again able to *choose*. God no longer intervenes to save humankind that was Christ's job.

At Babel, God took human's language, but not their ability to create. Satan simply created another language. Satan had to devise another plan. The language Satan created still exists to this day. There is only one language we consider universal--numbers. Egypt did not invent calculus to make the world a better place Egypt invented calculus it because of their philosophy of self-deification. Satan's followers desired a way to exalt themselves, a way to exalt Satan. Satan's followers invented a way to immortalize their way of life and their rebellion from God. What the world extols as genius is actually evil at work. Thousands of years later the world still marvels at what Egypt created. The world still finds self-deification an awe-inspiring religion. The only three religions not based on *self* all stem from Abraham. Although Abraham is the father of the faith, Abraham's faith came from the Father of us all. From Egypt, we get most of the world's science and many of the world's religions. Like his disciple Nimrod, Satan created a vast kingdom to worship him. Therefore, all religions fall into two categories, Abrahamic and non-Abrahamic.

Abrahamic	vs	**Non-Abrahamic**
Judaism		Hindi
Christian - Protestant & Catholic		Buddhist
Ishmaelite/Mohammedan/Islamic		Confucianism

---

[39] Genesis 6:3.

Taoists
Voodoo
Wicca
Yoruba

Despite Christ crushing the head of Satan's kingdom the limbs still exist and function. We see the power of satanic influence in the followers of God in Exodus with the Golden calf. The golden calf the children of Israel formed represented Hathor, a manifestation of Isis the Egyptian Mother. In the Egyptian ritual, Isis was the *great cow that gives birth to the Sun.* Considering the prevalence of Sun worship amongst the Egyptians, it is easy to understand how after several renditions (commonly called versions) the phrase Son of God became *sun of god.*

As we look at Egyptian architecture, we see the Satan's spirit Romans 1:20 would also seem to imply that Sun worship is an acceptable practice. in Nimrod Romans 1:20 would also seem to imply that Sun worship is an acceptable practice. . The sphinx and the pyramids exist to accomplish the same thing as the tower of Babel--They exist to be an affront to God. The premise of the tower was to ascend to heaven, overthrowing God's decision to cast Satan out of heaven. The question are these buildings an affront? Before you can understand the concept, you must understand the components.

Start the answer by looking at the following symbols.

 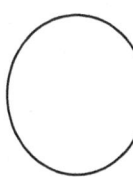 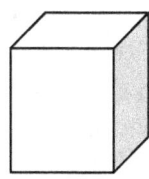

These three symbols represent the basic shapes found in architecture. The symbols each consist of 360°, which mathematically makes them complete. We know there are no perfect shapes in nature, nor any straight lines in nature. Why then would Satan use these shapes? Satan used the shapes to show that he could create perfection without the help of God. The shapes also enable Satan's architects to make buildings that last longer than they would naturally last. The Pyramids and the

Sphinx are 5,000 years old. The Pyramids and the Sphinx stand in the desert, looming out against the nothingness, to remind God of Satan.

The conjunction of the shapes and numbers creates a spiritual language that Satan uses. Satan did not pioneer numerology he simply prostituted it for his use. These four points[40] give a wealth of information to see just how intricately deceptive the light in Patmos really is.

1. *The number three represents the Trinity and hence spirituality.*
2. *The number four represents material order, earth, fire, air, and water. There are also four cardinal virtues, which are temperance, prudence, fortitude, justice.*
3. *The number seven represents wisdom and completion. It contains the three spiritual and four material values.*
4. *The number nine called the magnified square, because it represents the three spiritual virtues multiplied (enhanced) by self.*

THE GREAT PYRAMID OF GIZA

The pyramid starts on four sides (square) and rises to three sides (triangle). What The Great Pyramid allegory means is that the man-beast born on all fours is perfect. The only thing higher than the square is the triangle, which rises on four sides and ends in three. This paradigm represents the human creature evolving from a crawling pap (4 legs) to walking on a cane as a wise elder (3 legs). The pyramid allegory therefore represents the four materials and the four cardinal virtues, the best qualities of the earth.

According to Egyptians, the introduction of spirituality improves Humanity. Egyptians represent this concept with the triangle. The combination of the four material virtues and the three of spirituality results in the number seven. Seven is the number of completion. Egypt therefore represents spiritual beings with pyramids. The great pyramids of Giza stand-alone in the wilderness to show God that Satan's spirit also lasts forever through his followers. The pyramid therefore says to heaven *Long live Lucifer.*

---

[40] The Mystery of Numbers, Annemarie Schimmel, Oxford Univ. Press. 1993, New York.

THE SPHINX

Harmakhis the Sphinx is a pictorial representation of the same Pyramid allegory. Satan cannot create humans he recruits them. What Satan can do is create edifices that glorify him for eternity. Harmakhis[41] sits on four and has a human head.

Any heart not filled with God's Holy Spirit has room in it for *self*. Egypt exists in the heart of every human, saved or unsaved. Egypt still exists because selfishness still exists. Matthew 15:19 informs us that out of the human heart the issues of life arise.

The worship of *self* is the ultimate representation of satanic influence. Perversion is the truest indicator of satanic influence; this is why the Lord detested Sodom and Gomorrah. The Lord detested them because of immorality.[42] Sexual immorality constantly reminded God of the result of the war in heaven. Sodom was a reminder that the wickedness of man was great in the earth. Sodom was a reminder that man's every imagination and the thoughts of his heart are continually evil. It repented God that He made man, and man still has not changed.

THE THEORY OF SOULICAL MAN

Genesis 6:5-6 - "**And God saw that the wickedness of man was great in the earth, and that every imagination of the thoughts of his heart was only evil continually. And it repented the Lord that He had made man on the earth, and it grieved Him at His heart.**" According to scripture, it is not man's soul that is evil, God gave the soul to humanity; man's imagination is evil. We compartmentalize the human creature and pretend that his compartmental (spirit/flesh/imagination) nature makes him sinful. This is not the case. It is not the compartments but the contents of their hearts that makes men evil. Humans have the capacity to love, forgive, and exist in the holy image of God. There is no scripture to confirm the *tri-part man*; Jesus says man only has two parts. Even in the Tabernacle Construct man does not have three parts, literally they are spiritual stations used to commune

---

[41] Supposedly named by *Thothmos after the god, Harmakhis-Khopri-Ra-Tum.* http://en.wikipedia.org/wiki/Great_Sphinx_of_Giza

[42] Genesis 18:20.

with God. I cite the following scriptures to show you that there is no evil *soulical man*; man's imagination is that which is evil.

1. Genesis 11:6 - "**And the Lord said, "BEHOLD, THE PEOPLE IS ONE AND THEY HAVE ALL ONE LANGUAGE, AND THIS THEY BEGIN TO DO; AND NOW NOTHING WILL RESTRAIN THEM WHICH THEY HAVE IMAGINED TO DO**."

2. Deuteronomy 29:19 - "**And it come to pass, when he heareth the words of this curse, that he bless himself in his heart, saying, `I shall have peace, though I walk in the imagination of mine heart'--to add drunkenness to thirst**."

3. Deuteronomy 31:21 - "**AND IT SHALL COME TO PASS, WHEN MANY EVILS AND TROUBLES HAVE BEFALLEN THEM, THAT THIS SONG SHALL TESTIFY AGAINST THEM AS A WITNESS; FOR IT SHALL NOT BE FORGOTTEN OUT OF THE MOUTHS OF THEIR SEED. FOR I KNOW THEIR IMAGINATION AND THAT WHICH THEY GO ABOUT, EVEN NOW, BEFORE I HAVE BROUGHT THEM INTO THE LAND WHICH I SWORE**."

4. Psalms 2:1 - "**Why do the heathen rage and the people imagine a vain thing**?"

5. Psalms 10:2 - "**The wicked in his pride doth persecute the poor: let them be taken in the devices that they have imagined**."

6. Psalms 38:12 - "**They also that seek after my life lay snares for me: and they that seek my hurt speak mischievous things, and imagine deceits all the day long**."

7. Psalms 62:3 - "**How long will ye imagine mischief against a man? Ye shall be slain, all of you; as a bulging wall shall ye be, and as a tottering fence**."

8. Proverbs 6:16-19 - "**These six things doth the Lord hate: yea, seven are an abomination unto Him: A proud look, a lying tongue, and hands that shed innocent blood, An heart that**

deviseth wicked imaginations, feet that be swift in running to mischief, A false witness that speaketh lies, and he that soweth discord among brethren."

9. Proverbs 12:20 - "**Deceit is in the heart of them that imagine evil: but to the counselors of peace is joy.**"

10. Nahum 1:9 - "**What do ye imagine against the Lord? He will make an utter end: affliction shall not rise up the second time.**"

11. Jeremiah 23:17 - "**They say still unto them that despise me, The Lord hath said, Ye shall have peace; and they say unto every one that walketh after the imagination of his own heart, No evil shall come upon you.**"

12. Zechariah 7:10 - "**And oppress not the widow, nor the fatherless, the stranger, nor the poor; and let none of you imagine evil against his brother in your heart.**"

13. Luke 1:51 - "**He hath shewed strength with his arm; he hath scattered the proud in the imagination of their hearts.**"

14. Acts 4:25 - "**Who by the mouth of thy servant David hast said, Why did the heathen rage, and the people imagine vain things?**"

15. Romans 1:21 - "**Because that, when they knew God, they glorified him not as God, neither were thankful; but became vain in their imaginations, and their foolish heart was darkened.**"

16. 2 Corinthians 10:4-5 - "**For the weapons of our warfare are not carnal, but mighty through God to the pulling down of strong holds; Casting down imaginations, and every high thing that exalteth itself against the knowledge of God, and bringing into captivity every thought to the obedience of Christ;**"

LONGING FOR EGYPT

Rather than mimic the goodness of the Father in heaven, the human constantly *chooses* the evil in the hearts of men. The evil things men do emanate from the wicked human heart. Satan does not actually inhabit the human heart; the human heart overflows with sin. The sin that fills the human heart desires expression, like any living creature it grows and matures. Once the seed of sin grows roots it rears its ugly head through the imagination. The evil creative facet of humans worried God enough for Him to intervene. God did not overthrow Babel to punish humans; He did it to forestall the debauchery of the human imagination.

The imagination in itself is not evil it serves the human heart. The *choices* we make in our hearts the imagination simply brings to life. The fact that humans are willing to strive with God continually indicates the darkness still prevalent in the human heart. Ever since the day God expelled man from the garden man sought to return. The problem is that Satan replaced the memories of God in the garden with memories of gods from Egypt. We remember self, more clearly than we remember Eden. Not that Egypt was more beautiful, God's people, the ones that told Him we want another king, still find Egypt more attractive than Eden. We long for freedom, as any slave would. The freedom we want is to worship self, we long to return to Egypt, to swim in the Nile, to serve a pharaoh and to toil in his fields…why else do we follow the religious leaders that we *choose*?

Amen

Part IV
Beauty
and
His
Beasts

"And the fifth angel poured out his vial upon the seat of the beast; and his kingdom was full of darkness; and they gnawed their tongues for pain, and blasphemed the God of heaven because of their pains and their sores, and repented not of their deeds. And blasphemed the God of heaven because of their pains and their sores, and repented not of their deeds. And I saw three unclean spirits like frogs [come] out of the mouth of the dragon, and out of the mouth of the beast, and out of the mouth of the false prophet. For they are the spirits of devils, working miracles, [which] go forth unto the kings of the earth and of the whole world, to gather them to the battle of that great day of God Almighty - Revelations 16:10-14."

Chapter Nine
Lucifer, the Bearer of Light

"*He who fights too long against dragons becomes a dragon himself; and if you gaze too long into the abyss, the abyss will gaze into you*[43]."

This chapter is more technical that many of the other chapters. This is not to confuse but to clarify two issues.

1. God's complexity.
2. The waging of unsuccessful Spiritual Warfare.

In our synopsis we review a few Greek and Hebrew terms that we use in this chapter. I use *terms* instead of *words* because word is a singularity, whereas terms allows for several things. In legal contracts, term implies conditions or rules. We must learn to look at scriptural terms for what they are:

1. Combined or grouped words.
2. Sounds designed to convey thoughts.
3. Principles.
4. Conditions.
5. Rules.

Before we begin with our synopsis, we will look at two indexes, which illustrate the Heavenly rank of angels, and shows, why Satan detests mankind. In figure 3 and 4 we see the Heavenly order and the level of intimacy with God each order of angels enjoys. In figure 3 we see that Lucifer stood closest to God. Lucifer and Jesus are the only two spirits other than God that ever '*sit*' in heaven. Everybody else stands in heaven, showing who actually as the power.

---

[43] Friedrich Nietzsche.

Hierarchy in the beginning	Post Satan Hierarchy
The Godhead	The Godhead
Lucifer	Seraphims
Seraphims	Cherubims
Cherubims	Thrones
Thrones	Dominions
Dominions	Virtues
Virtues	Powers
Powers	Archangels
Archangels	Principalities
Principalities	Angels/Man[1]
Angels	Beasts
Man	Satan
Beasts of the field	
(Fig 3)	(Fig 3b)

In figure 3b, we see that Lucifer no longer appears close to God. Never again will Lucifer stand or sit next to God nor retain his glorified name. Satan, the devil, bastard in other words is all he will ever be. God no longer considers Lucifer His son, and does not love Him Satan is therefore a bastard[44].

Many people mistakenly believe that Satan hates mankind because God loves them. That is not the case. Satan hates mankind because men love God. It was the love of the angels Satan wanted; he already had God's love. Satan loved himself so much he thought everyone should love him not God. After all he was the most beautiful and most powerful in the kingdom.

Choice, free will is Satan's enemy. Satan hates man because they have the *choice* to worship him and the righteous do not. Exodus 20:3 speaks to this choice amongst men. When God tells us that we "**SHALL HAVE NO OHTER gODS BEFORE ME**," He was forewarning us about the great red dragon in all his forms. There are only two gods, two kings in the universe. There is the King of Kings and there is the prince of darkness. This is where it gets technical. Like Joseph came into the

---

[44] Hebrews 12:8.

bloodline and stole his brother's ascendency to the throne, man created the one creature in the universe legally able to stop Satan's ascendency. Because God had no heir, a successful revolution in heaven guaranteed Satan the throne. With God dead, or over throne Satan would no longer be prince he would be king.

Through men, god introduced an heir into the struggle. Satan does not hate men because he is jealous he hates men because they allowed God to legally pass the throne on to His only begotten Son. Now we see why the biblical tradition always plays out with two sons vying for the birthright. The two sons represent the battle between Satan and Jesus for the throne of their Father. Despite expulsion, Ishmael died a son of Abraham. Despite expulsion, Satan retains part of his birthright, which is why God gave him a kingdom.

It is necessary to explain a legal concept at this point. Many believe that the reference to the dragon whipping his tail is a reference to some Godzilla like scene in heaven it is not. The war in heaven, waged over a birthright, the birthright warfare spilled out of heaven. God had a son, like most of the princes in history, that son turned to the dark side due to pride. The son of a king, always has a legal claim to the throne, the Hebrew word for this legal claim is *tail*.

Revelations 12:4, is not a reference to Godzilla, it is a reference to a prince demanding his birthright. Like Jacob and Easu, Solomon and his brother, Ishmael and Isaac Joseph and his eleven brothers, Cain and Able, and the prodigal son - a certain God had two sons. The God had two sons because it happened that the Lord had not respect for the sacrifice and worship of his son. The son of the morning no longer glorified the Morning. When the son realized his Father's disdain, he stood before the throne and proclaimed his right to the throne. As he declared his intention, he reminded his Father of his birthright. When his Father denounced him and expelled him he *whipped his tail* and those who sought to follow their new king left. The whipping of Satan's tail is what Judges 9 describes in vivid detail.

Satan, prince of darkness is still a prince. The Greek-Hellenic stories of Zeus, Persus, Hades etc are retellings of the Christian wars in heaven. The reason men became useful was God needed another heir to His throne. He needed a creature free from satanic influence, one that would *choose* to worship Him. As He did with Rhaboam, God did not find a man worthy so He placed the position (heir-apparent) under the care of men. Through their bloodline would come a worthy Son of God. So you see Satan has only one quarrel with humans, they made his replacement.

Post Adam Hierarchy	**New Jerusalem Hierarchy**
The Godhead	The Godhead
Serapims	Seraphims
Cherubims	Cherubims
Thrones	Dominions
Dominions	Virtues
Virtues	Powers
Powers	Archangels
Archangels	Man-creature
Principalities	Fallen Principalities
Angels	Fallen Angels
Man	Satan
Beasts	
Satan	
(Fig 4)	(Fig 4b)

In order to understand the various lights in Patmos we pause to look at the nine types of angels in the Bible. To this end, we review the Nine Choirs[45] (levels) of Angels:

1. **Seraphims** (Seraphs) - *Are the highest order of angels* - Isaiah 6:2-6, Revelations 4:8.

2. **Cherubims** (Cherubs) - *Cherubim rank after the Seraphim* - Ezekiel 1.

3. **Thrones** - *are the angels of humility, peace and submission* - Colossians 1:16, Revelations 4:2.

---

[45] Choir because Choral indicates unison of expression and purpose. So these are the nine expressions of godly unison that once existed in Heaven.

4. ***Dominions*** - *Are angels of leadership;* - Ephesians 1:21, Colossians 1:16.

5. ***Virtues*** - *Known as the Spirits of Motion and control the elements.*

6. ***Powers*** - *Are warrior Angels* -Ephesians 1:21.

7. ***Archangels*** - *Are generally taken to mean "chief or leading angel"* - Jude 1:9.

8. ***Principalities*** - *Spiritual beings hostile to God and human beings* - Romans 8:38, Ephesians 1:21.

9. ***Angels***[46]- *These angels are closest to the natural world and human begins. They deliver the prayers to God and God's answers and other messages to humans* - Romans 8:38.

Strong's Complete Dictionary of Bible Words[47] defines several integral Greek and Hebrew terms used in the Bible. The listed terms describe or refer to the spiritual enemy of our faith--Satan. We also delve into certain Hebrew and Greek definition of certain type of angel. According to the book Satan, Adversary of Mankind[48] the Hebrew word used in Genesis 3:1 for *serpent* is *nachash* (*nachash*). Huie asserts that the noun form of the term would be *hanachash* (*hanachash*), which means the shinning one. Huie cites three other possible definitions of *nachash*;
1. *A diviner.*
2. *Shining brass.*
3. *To shine or glow.*

In researching the definition of serpent, I found was that the Hebrew words for *serpent* and *Seraphim* are interchangeable. "*Seraphim: burning; fiery, this word means fiery ones, in allusion, as is supposed, to their burning love. Seraphim appears represented as "standing" above the King as He sat upon His throne, ready at once to cover or minister unto Him. Their form appears to have been human, with the addition of*

---

[46] The Nine Choirs of Angels. http://www.catholic.org/saints/anglchoirs.html 5/5/05.
[47] http://www.blueletterBible.org/tmp_dir/strongs/1152631851-9061.html July 2006.
[48] Satan, Adversary of Mankind, Huie, Bryan. July 12 1997. http://users.aristotle.net/~bhuie/satan.htm.

wings. This word, in the original, is used elsewhere only of the "fiery serpents" sent by God as His instruments to inflict on the people the righteous penalty of sin[49]*."* This being the case, in the third chapter of Genesis, the word serpent may very well be Seraphim.

In Revelations 12:9 we find the word serpent used again. The Strong's number used is 3789. <u>Strong's Complete Dictionary of Bible Words</u> lists several usages of the word Seraphim;
1. *Fiery serpent.*
2. *Fiery.*
3. *Seraphim.*

The definitions Strong's gives for these terms consist of the following;
1. *Serpent, fiery serpent.*
1a. *Poisonous serpent* (fiery from burning effect of poison.)
2. *Seraph, Seraphim.*

This would mean that in Revelations 12:9 the applicable term Seraphim would make the verse read, "*And the great dragon was cast out, that old {Seraphim}, called*[50] *the Devil, and Satan, which deceiveth the whole world: he was cast out into the earth, and his angels were cast out with him*". Which would then be a clear indication of Satan's character not his appearance. Even the most ardent literalist must admit that this verse offers the most compelling evidence that the literal approach simply does not make sense when dealing with Satan. Let us dissect this verse of scripture point-by-point revealing that the common belief is inaccurate. Before beginning, understand that inaccurate does not mean incorrect. Inaccurate simply means that the translator used grammar to translate spirit and did not get close enough to the spirit to translate the truth. Many context errors appear in the Bible. Contextual errors are the inevitable result of secular people translating spiritual text.

---

[49] <u>Vine's Expository Dictionary of New Testament Words</u>. Thomas-Nelson Publishers, Nashville, (p.124).
[50] Notice scripture does not say *named* the devil. To give something a title does not morph the item its title. I cite this joke as an example, "Call me a taxi?" "Ok you are a taxi." Although this is a spoof, the point is clear. Because you called the man, a taxi does not make him one. If however that man was carrying someone on his shoulders or back calling him a taxi would convey the behavior he displayed. In the same manner calling an angel, a serpent does not make it a reptile, but the title does imply snake like qualities.

1. **"And the great dragon"** - Nowhere in the Bible does God use mythological terms, figures, glyphs, or characters. Although science does not agree on many facts, science universally agrees on one fact. Science does agree that the fabled dragon does not and never has existed. At no time in terrestrial history has there been any proof, indication, diagramming, or fossil verifying the existence of dragons. The dragon is a purely mythical creature. Could God therefore in Revelations refer to a creature that never existed? Could God be wrong? On the other hand, is it more likely that the term dragon is a metaphor for behavior, not an actual creature?

2. **"Was cast out"** - We know for certain, that at no time in any history have there been snakes in heaven. And even if there were we also know with certainty that the only things cast out of heaven were Lucifer and his core of rebellious angels[51].

3. **"That old serpent"** - Are there any snakes that live a life span of thousands of years. For this to be the same snake that was in the garden the snake would have to be millennia in age.

4. **"Called the Devil"** - Index I (p.105) gives a list of the various names the Bible calls Lucifer. These names cannot apply to two different people. Which is more likely?

    a. The snake in the garden was Lucifer and that same snake still exists.

    b. The serpent in the garden was never a snake and the fallen angel from the garden still exists.

In all Biblical demon encounters, the *demon* entity is a spirit. Does it not make sense therefore that the same spirit that existed then exists now? Would we rather believe that our adversary is a snake, a mere reptile? Perhaps this makes blaming Satan for our failure easier because a snake is flesh. This is insulting because it means that reptile is smart enough to tempt Christ, deceive nations, and manipulate kings.

---

[51] Ezekiel 31.

5. **"And Satan"** - Although the New Testament refers to Lucifer as Satan, and a serpent. None of the snakes in the New Testament are referred to as Satan. Not even the one that bit Paul near the fire.

6. **"Which deceiveth the whole world"** - This stanza precedes Revelations 20:2-3, and Revelations 20:10. I list these scriptures because there is no way to ascribe the listed actions to a snake[52]. Here we see again that the snake would have to have the ability to live another thousand years in a bottomless pit. How does an object made of matter survive in a pit with no bottom? Also, take note that verses 1-4 all deal with spiritual beings.

In Revelations 20:10 we have the *coup de gras* of references proving that the serpent was not a snake. In Matthew 13:37-42 and 49 & 50 Jesus refers to those cast into hell. God will judge the unrighteous, and the wicked, and throw them into the fire of hell. Where else in the Bible other than the Lion and the lamb reference (A spiritual reference to the reunification) does God number humans among animals? Where in the Bible are animals judged for wickedness?

7. **"He was cast out into the earth"** - Can we interpret this reference as anything but the casting out of Lucifer? Other that the snake that bit Paul, the staff that Moses and Aaron threw to the ground are there any snakes dashed to the ground? Moreover, are there any snakes cast out of heaven anywhere in the Bible?

8. **"And his angels were cast out with him"** - Obviously the angels cast out in Revelations 12:9 are the same group from Judges 9 and Ezekiel 31. NO ANIMALS IN THE ENTIRE BIBLE EVER HAD CHARGE OVER A GROUP OF ANGELS. Does it make sense that

---

[52] Revelations 20:2-3 - **"And He laid hold on the dragon, that old serpent, which is the Devil, and Satan, and bound him a thousand years, And cast him into the bottomless pit, and shut him up, and set a seal upon him, that he should deceive the nations no more, till the thousand years should be fulfilled: and after that he must be loosed a little season."**
- Revelations 20:10 - **"And the devil that deceived them was cast into the lake of fire and brimstone, where the beast and the false prophet [are], and shall be tormented day and night forever and ever."**

God employed a snake in Heaven or that the only terrestrial being in heaven was a snake?

What this plethora of information means to us is that the term used in Genesis 3:1 is not a reference to a snake but an illusion or a metaphor for Lucifer's behavior. If the entity in question were merely a snake, asp, or viper those words would have been quite effective. It appears that the Bible uses Viper, Cobra, Adder, or Asp[53], to refer to the animal and *serpent* to describe the characteristics of the creature.

The term serpent differentiates this deity from the animal. The use of serpent in this sense mimics the use of the biological term *mammal*. To speak of mammals collectively describes creatures with like characteristics. However, a mammal does not have to be a whale. There are two types of snakes; venomous and non-venomous. Although they use different killing methods, they are both lethal. Let us for a moment look at some of the hunting habits of snakes. In terms of spiritual warfare, these attributes apply to Satan and his abilities. The characteristics listed for terrestrial snakes explain in detail why the Bible explains Luciferian characteristics via metaphor.

Like snakes, Satan's followers do what comes natural to them to survive. Since exile from heaven, these traits are also natural to Satan; and he employs these tactics to find or create dust upon which to feed.

The following list of traits show Satan's similarities to snakes.

1. *"Snakes are the most streamlined and stripped down of the vertebrates. It just has the bare necessities of a mouth and a belly, a skull and spinal column."* **And the Lord God said unto the serpent, 'BECAUSE THOU HAST DONE THIS, THOU [ART] CURSED ABOVE ALL CATTLE, AND ABOVE EVERY BEAST OF THE FIELD; UPON THY BELLY SHALT THOU GO, AND DUST SHALT THOU EAT ALL THE DAYS OF THY LIFE'** - Genesis 3:14." The Lord uses this term to describe Satan's new lifestyle because God stripped Satan of so much. No longer bearing every precious stone or timbrels for praise, all Satan possessed was what he needed to survive in his new life.

2. *"As a group, snakes eat the widest range of prey. Being slow, snakes tend to eat whatever is in abundance. One reason for their*

---

[53] Genesis 49:17, Psalms 91:13, Proverbs 23:30, Isaiah 11:8, 30:6, 59:5, Acts 28.3.

success is their ability to change their diet with the seasons, eating whatever is most plentiful. Others change their diet as they grow; eating small prey when they are young and bigger prey as adults. Being "cold-blooded", they don't have to eat often and can survive in places with irregular supplies of prey." **"And the Lord said unto Satan, 'FROM WHENCE COMEST THOU?' And Satan answered the Lord, and said, 'From going to and fro in the earth, and from walking up and down in it'** - Job 2:2." The fact that Satan moves at a leisurely pace in no means indicates a lack of danger. Lava is notoriously slow moving but everybody has heard or seen the immense devastation it causes. Another reason the church of this age has spread more consistently than Christ's body is that like the snake they have the ability to change their diets. Unfortunately; for the lost, spreading the gospel is also faddish. Whatever is in 'season' on TBN and CTN is what all the churches run out and do. The snake's ability to change diet enables Satan's kingdom to grow year round--no sinner is ever out of style to Satan.

3. *"Snakes do not catch just any prey. Snakes make their calculations before catching prey. A big snake may pass over small prey that does not provide enough nutrition to offset the risk of catching it. Snakes may ignore prey too large or difficult to swallow whole."* **"Hast not thou made an hedge about him, and about his house, and about all that he hath on every side? Thou hast blessed the work of his hands, and his substance is increased in the land** - Job 1:10." This is why Satan deals with fathers and leaders because it is easier to attack a believer using a wicked leader than to penetrate the hedge of God. Although his resources are not limited, Satan can only remain hidden for so long.

My job in the Marine Corps was Mortar man. My gun crew was one of the best in the company. We could do wonderful things with our crew- served weapon but we had one severe limitation. Because Mortars are both highly mobile, and deadly they fire their rounds below a certain height. There is radar designed to detect Mortars. If the round reaches that height, it shows up on special radar. The people operating the special radar do not waste time tracking the mortar they simply carpet bomb the entire grid square. A grid square is 1,000 yards by 1,000 yards. As the enemy of the Mortar uses radar, Heaven also has radar it uses to monitor the activities of the rulers of this age. The moment Heaven detects the fiery darts of the enemy attacking His children God also devastates the grid square the darts came from.

4. *"Snakes need water especially before a moult and for making eggs. Snakes may drink from pools and streams as well as sucking dew and raindrops one by one through the tongue groove in the lip. Snakes that do not have access to freshwater, (desert and marine snakes) can get all their water from their prey. Some flatten and lifts their necks to condense the coastal fog and drink the resulting water droplets. Snakes conserve water well so their need for water is minimal. They seek humid microclimates and do not urinate."* **"Son of man, say unto the prince of Tyrus, Thus saith the Lord God; 'BECAUSE THINE HEART [IS] LIFTED UP, AND THOU HAST SAID, I [AM] A GOD, I SIT [IN] THE SEAT OF GOD, IN THE MIDST OF THE SEAS; YET THOU [ART] A MAN, AND NOT GOD, THOUGH THOU SET THINE HEART AS THE HEART OF GOD'** - Ezekiel 28:2." Demons also need water, Living water. The problem for demons is that they are dead. They no longer have access to the Living Water. Just like snakes demons absorb there 'Water' from their prey[54]. Once demons devour the lost sheep they also absorb whatever water they can. This is how demons maintain control in the world.

5. *"A snake is a fragile creature with a delicate skull, thin teeth, and many ribs that can break. A struggling prey is not only dangerous when being caught, but also when being swallowed. A desperate prey with fangs and claws can damage and even kill a snake."* **"AND I WILL PUT ENMITY BETWEEN THEE AND THE WOMAN, AND BETWEEN THY SEED AND HER SEED; IT SHALL BRUISE THY HEAD, AND THOU SHALT BRUISE HIS HEEL** - Genesis 3:15." The skull of the snake represents protection for Satan's kingdom. If the snake cannot think, it

---

[54] Luke 4:6.

cannot eat or defend itself. Many snakes with crushed head die of heat stroke, because they lose control of the necessary body functions. The skull and the spiritual crown occupy the same function for a snake. Satan's power was entirely dependent upon his crown. Jesus crushed Satan's head, since Satan's power only emanates from the hearts of ungodly humans.

6. *"For dangerous prey, a venomous snake will bite and quickly release to minimize contact with the live struggling prey. It will then track the prey in its death throes by smell and eat it only after it is immobile. If the prey is small or harmless, a snake will bite and hang on until the prey is immobilized or it may not even bother to kill it and just swallow it alive."* "**Above all, taking the shield of faith, wherewith ye shall be able to quench all the fiery darts of the wicked** - Ephesians 6:16." The only people that Satan fears are those in relationship with God. When Satan bites God's people, he must bite and release them for fear of personal damage. Lost sheep and sinner are no threat to Satan. Not only do the lost and sinners not have the full protection of God's Holy Spirit they do not resist the wiles of the devil. This is why greed, lust, and fear are so commonly used. These fiery darts act quickly in almost every life. Satan can drop a financial opportunity, sexual opportunity, or personal tragedy in most lives and quickly create havoc.

7. *"Snakes are found almost everywhere, mountains, deserts, in the sea, rivers, lakes, even in the Arctic. Snakes have developed marvelous adaptations to a wide variety of habitats."* "**WHEN AN UNCLEAN SPIRIT GOES OUT OF A MAN, HE GOES THROUGH DRY PLACES, SEEKING REST, AND FINDS NONE. THEN HE SAYS, "I WILL RETURN TO MY HOUSE FROM WHICH I CAME. AND WHEN HE COMES HE FINDS IT EMPTY, SWEPT, AND PUT IN ORDER. THEN HE GOES AND TAKES WITH HIM SEVEN OTHER SPIRITS MORE WICKED THAN HIMSELF, AND THEY ENTER AND DWELL THERE: AND THE LAST STATE OF THAT MAN IS WORSE THAN THE FIRST. SO SHALL IT ALSO BE WITH THIS WICKED**

GENERATION - Matthew 12:43-45." Demons are extremely adaptable, they are anywhere lost sheep are located.

8. *"Snakes can concave their bellies to create airspace to breathe underground. Some stick just their eyes and noses out of the sand in ambush and wiggle their tail to lure prey within strike range."* **" She was with child. She cried out in pain, laboring to give birth. Another sign was seen in heaven. Behold, a great red dragon, having seven heads and ten horns, and on his heads seven crowns. His tail drew one third of the stars of the sky, and threw them to the earth. The dragon stood before the woman who was about to give birth, so that when she gave birth he might devour her child** - Revelations 12:1-4." Satan tried everything he conceived of to block, locate, and destroy Christ. Satan finally discovered Christ's one weakness like superman Christ's weakness was His love for people. The things He loved enough to save ambushed Christ.

9. *"Snakes usually stay underground during the heat of the day and become active only at dusk or night*[55]*."* According to Judges 9:8, Satan remains in the shade because darkness is his domain. Darkness can only exist in the light as shade or a shadow. The thing Satan does not want you to see his darkness. Remember humans fear the dark. If Christians saw Satan for what he was, that would be too afraid to worship him.

Before continuing, I admonish you understand that that metaphors God uses to convey principles are not always literal. We must attempt to understand the pictures God draws. God's way of thinking is so high above ours He treats us as we treat infants when we read to them. God uses colors, sounds, and images to fill in the areas we do not understand. So that you may better understand, I cite further metaphorical examples. The exercise in listening in to the heart of God will yield innumerable blessings.

---

[55] http://www.szgdocent.org/cc/c-eat.htm 9/22/04.

1. 2 Kings 18:4 - "**He removed the high places, and brake the images, and cut down the groves, and brake in pieces the brasen serpent that Moses had made: for unto those days the children of Israel did burn incense to it: and he called it Nehushtan**[56]." Footnote 51 provides interesting insight into the serpentine motif. I find it very interesting the name given to this serpent means brass or bronze--an allusion to reflecting light or being shinny. It is also curious that the serpent episode with Moses is prophetic of Christ on the cross. We know that the Father never regards Christ in contempt. The hidden meaning must therefore refer to some attribute the two incidents share. I submit that the similarity between the two was that they both glistened. Jesus is the Light of the world. Lucifer is a wretched reflection of the Light of the world. The light in Patmos is a false light worshipped and exalted by men.

2. Proverbs 23:29-33 - "**Who hath woe? Who hath sorrow? Who hath contentions? Who hath babbling? Who hath wounds without cause? Who hath redness of eyes? They that tarry long at the wine; they that go to seek mixed wine. Look not thou upon the wine when it is red, when it giveth his color in the cup, [when] it moveth itself aright. At the last it biteth like a serpent, and stingeth like an adder. Thine eyes shall behold strange women, and thine heart shall utter perverse things.**" This passage alludes to the affect venom has on it victims'. Here we see the writer ascribing the characteristics commonly associated with liquor to snake venom. The writer describes the effect alcohol has when it blurs vision, clouds judgment and enables people to do things they would not do

---

[56] *Of copper*; a brazen thing a name of contempt given to the serpent Moses had made in the wilderness (Numbers 21:8), and which Hezekiah destroyed because the children of Israel began to regard it as an idol and "burn incense to it." The lapse of nearly one thousand years had invested the "brazen serpent" with a mysterious sanctity; and in order to deliver the people from their infatuation, and impress them with the idea of its worthlessness, Hezekiah called it, in contempt, "*Nehushtan*," a brazen thing, a mere piece of brass (2 Kings 18:4). http://www.blueletterBible.org/tmp_dir/*choice*/1152633386-4695.html. July 2006, World English Bible.

normally. Much as venom causes people to hallucinate, alcohol also has a vicious bite.

3. Isaiah 14:29 - "**Rejoice not thou, whole Palestine, because the rod of him that smote thee is broken: for out of the serpent's root shall come forth a cockatrice and his fruit [shall be] a fiery flying serpent**." This passage metaphorically prophesies about the serpents roots. The root is the source of a tree. Herein Isaiah tells Palestine to enjoy the evil seat of power that they serve. Isaiah forewarns Palestine that from their sin their master shall devise their own destruction.

4. Isaiah 27:1 - "**In that day the Lord with His sore and great and strong sword shall punish leviathan the piercing serpent, even leviathan that crooked serpent; and He shall slay the dragon that [is] in the sea**." This passage of scripture predates Ezekiel 28:2, Matthew 13:47&48, Hebrews 11:12, and Revelations 4:6, 13:1, 15:2. The Revelator saw the same thing Isaiah saw, Satan freely swimming in the *sea* and Satan looks to both writers to be the evil creature of the *sea*. The *sea* spoken of in these verses is a metaphor for humanity. This is why Satan said he sits as a god in the sea, because many people still worship him.

5. Job 26:13 - "**By His Spirit He hath garnished the heavens; His hand hath formed the crooked serpent**." A confirmation in scripture that God created Lucifer, and that His judgment resulted in the fallen angel called the serpent. Although we do not understand God's ways, they are just.

6. Psalms 140:3 - "**They have sharpened their tongues like a serpent; adders' poison [is] under their lips. Selah**." Notice the serpent used his tongue and the adder poison. This is because the adder is a snake and the serpent a spirit that speaks.

7. Jeremiah 46:22 - "**The voice thereof shall go like a serpent; for they shall march with an army, and come against her with axes, as hewers of wood**." In this scriptural-metaphor, the

slinky, winding, secretive nature of the serpent God attributes to the way in which the army will victoriously attack.

8. Micah 7:17 - "**They shall lick the dust like a serpent, they shall move out of their holes like worms of the earth: they shall be afraid of the Lord our God, and shall fear because of thee.**" Amidst the plea for help the Jews asserts the sovereign nature of the Lord. At the same time, the Jews remind readers of the timid, cowardly nature of the unrighteous. The enemy's demise to death they liken unto Satan and his followers punishment.

Despite God's effort, Christians still believe the things Satan says. This is not because Satan is convincing but because believers are not sure if God's forgiveness is true. Accusations and weakness do not bind believers, their lack of faith and lack of intimacy with God binds them. The power that Lucifer exercises over Christians is not demonic possession it is temptation. Lucifer knows that there is something in the heart of every human, which in time he can access. Through temptation, the serpent manipulates *choice*, making the wretched nature in the human heart the perfect battlefield.

Amen

Chapter Ten
The Dragon Theory

"**And there appeared another wonder in heaven; and behold a great red dragon, having seven heads and ten horns, and seven crowns upon his heads. And his tail drew the third part of the stars of heaven, and did cast them to the earth: and the dragon stood before the woman which was ready to be delivered, for to devour her child as soon as it was born** - Revelation 12:3-4."

Genesis 1:24 makes plain that animals were fashioned after their own kind. Unless there are two kinds of serpents, there must be a species of reptile not yet explored by science. Unless there are two kinds of serpents there must be a species of reptile that;
1. Looks like a snake.
2. Moves like a snake.
3. Has the power to move back and forth between heaven and earth.

This is the Dragon Theory. The dragon is a serpent that can do all of the following?
1. Fly.
2. Breathe fire.
3. Travel through space.
4. Live both in the spirit and in the flesh.
5. Exist since the creation of the world.
6. Exist in heaven.
7. Interact with nations and deceive them.

There is no known terrestrial creature that ever possessed or possesses these traits. In order to satisfy mystery, humans created a creature that could have all these traits. What is the origin of the Dragon? Strong's gives two usages and the following information for dragon;
1. Tannah (Hebrew *Tannah*-female jackal)
2. Tanniyn (*Tanniyn*-sea serpent; jackal).

> Although the root in these to terms is tan (Tan) which means to elongate, a monster (as preternaturally formed, i.e. a sea serpent or other huge marine animal; also a jackal (or other hideous land animal) dragon whale. The

name of some unknown creature inhabiting desert places and ruins. Some great sea monster, it may denote the crocodile. **Greek:** *drakon - denoted "a mythical monster, a dragon"; also a large serpent, so called because of its keen power of sight*

Through the ages the dragon image developed with the addition of scales, wings, fiery breath, a large tail, large teeth and claws, amphibiousness, crocodile skin, and a blood curdling roar. Images from scriptures and myths created the legend of a talking snake. Humans created a deceitful snake to bear the weight of human stupidity. Humans created a serpent smarter than man, but not smart enough to avoid being stepped on[57].

It appears that neither Hebrew term for dragon has anything to do with angels, fire, or flying. It appears that the dragon, like the *boogieman* is a compilation of myth and purpose. *Dragon* is name given to the evil that we find inexplicable in ourselves. Scripture contains many examples of the term dragon. While looking at the following scriptures we learn more about the creature man created to ease the guilt of his sin-filled lifestyle.

1. Psalms 91:13 - "**Thou shalt tread upon the lion and adder: the young lion and the *dragon* shalt thou trample under feet.**"

2. Isaiah 13:22 - "**And the wild beasts of the islands shall cry in their desolate houses, and *dragons* in their pleasant palaces: and her time is near to come, and her days shall not be prolonged.**"

3. Isaiah 27:1 - "**In that day the Lord with his sore and great and strong sword shall punish leviathan the piercing serpent, even leviathan that crooked serpent; and He shall slay the *dragon* that [is] in the sea.**"

4. Isaiah 35:7 - "**And the parched ground shall become a pool, and the thirsty land springs of water: in the habitation of *dragons*, where each lay, [shall be] grass with reeds and rushes.**"

---

[57] Genesis 3:15.

5. Isaiah 43:20 - "**The beast of the field shall honour me, the *dragons* and the owls: because I give waters in the wilderness, [and] rivers in the desert, to give drink to my people, my chosen.**"

6. Jeremiah 51:34 - "**Nebuchadnezzar the king of Babylon hath devoured me, he hath crushed me, he hath made me an empty vessel, he hath swallowed me up like a *dragon*, he hath filled his belly with my delicates, he hath cast me out.**"

7. Ezekiel 29:3 - "**Speak, and say, Thus saith the Lord God; 'BEHOLD, I [AM] AGAINST THEE, PHARAOH KING OF EGYPT, THE GREAT *DRAGON* THAT LIETH IN THE MIDST OF HIS RIVERS, WHICH HATH SAID, MY RIVER [IS] MINE OWN, AND I HAVE MADE [IT] FOR MYSELF'.**"

Humans find it easy to blame others for their flaws. How easy of an escape to blame the *dragon* rather than admit sin. There is always someone; especially Christians, to proudly proclaim, "*Satan made me do it.*" Sadly, those we look to for moral guidance still mimic the immature behavior of Adam, immediately point the finger in a direction, any direction that points away from self.

In all prophetic books of the Bible, metaphors are used and spirits likened unto animals and human personality types. Although Genesis is not widely understood as a prophetic book, it bears the first and one of the most important prophecies in the Bible. The first prophecy in the Bible occurs in Genesis 3, and it foretells redemption. Prophets use prophetic language whether or not they are prophesying, just as kings speak in kingly terms whenever they speak. The *serpent* in Genesis is nothing short of a prophetic metaphor.

THE MYSTERY OF THE SERPENT IN THE GARDEN

In Genesis 3:1 a common syntax error occurs, not in the text but in the application. "**Now the *serpent* was more subtle than any beast of the field that the Lord God had made. He said to the woman, "Has God really said, 'You shall not eat of any tree of the garden?"** The reference to animals God created is not to include the serpent in this story but to differentiate levels of intellect. God informs us of the same thing in

Ezekiel 28:3. "**BEHOLD, YOU ARE WISER THAN DANIEL; THERE IS NO SECRET THAT IS HIDDEN FROM YOU.**" The reference reiterates that the actual enemy is not the flesh and blood but the wisdom of the Great Red Dragon. The statement is only to show you why and how easily Satan deceives. Satan deceives because he is wiser than humans are, and because he has more spiritual knowledge than humans possess. According to Strong's Hebrew Concordance[58], the Hebrew title Satan has the following applications;
- *(Qal)* to be or act as an adversary, resist, oppose.
- *Adversary*, one who withstands.
- *Adversary* (in Genesis - personal or national).
- *Superhuman adversary*.

Many contend that Isaiah 27:1 is a literal reference to sea monsters, but it is not. The scriptures in Ezekiel 28:2 and 32:2 better explain that this is a reference to the power and conflict with Satan, not a reference to terrestrial animals. Isaiah 27:1, "**In that day the Lord with His sore and great and strong sword shall punish leviathan the piercing serpent, even leviathan that crooked serpent; and He shall slay the dragon that [is] in the sea.**" The sea in Isaiah 27:1 is the same sea mentioned in Revelations 13:1. This in turn means that the *leviathan/dragon* swam amongst the sea of believers and was a terror until God withdrew him.

If Satan possessed the ability to control and possess animals, why would 1,000 demons not be powerful enough to enter a herd of pigs without permission? The simple fact is that the humans may have *choice* but the animals do not. Luke 8:30-34, "**Jesus asked him, 'WHAT IS YOUR NAME?' He said, 'Legion,' for many demons had entered into him. They begged him that he would not command them to go into the abyss. Now there was there a herd of many pigs feeding on the mountain, and they begged Him that He would allow them to enter into those. He allowed them. The demons came out from the man, and entered into the pigs, and the herd rushed down the steep bank into the lake, and were drowned.**"

The coup de gras of this segment comes from Genesis 7:8, 14, and 15, 21-23, let us read them together before we study the contents. If the demons had to have permission to enter the pigs, then the only way they

---

[58] http://www.blueletterBible.org/tmp_dir/words/7/1153682688-3630.html. July 2006.

could enter animals was by permission. There is no record of God ever giving this permission to Satan. Neither is there any record of Satan having enough power to defeat God's will. The angels that mated with humans mated with humans because they had access to the daughters of men through the wicked human hearts.

"Clean animals, animals that are not clean, birds, and everything that creeps on the ground - Genesis 7:8".	"...they, and every animal after its kind, all the livestock after their kind, every creeping thing that creeps on the earth after its kind, and every bird after its kind, every bird of every sort. They went to Noah into the ship, by pairs of all flesh with the breath of life in them. - Genesis 7:14".
"All flesh died that moved on the earth, including birds, livestock, animals, every creeping thing that creeps on the earth, and every man. All in whose nostrils was the breath of the spirit of life, of all that was on the dry land, died. Every living thing was destroyed that was on the surface of the ground, including man, livestock, creeping things, and birds of the sky. They were destroyed from the earth. Only Noah was left, and those who were with him in the ship. - Genesis 7:21".	

1. We see that in verse eight that both clean, unclean, and the creeping things entered the ark.

2. Verse 14 reminds that every beast of the field created in the first six days had at least one other of its kind. According to Genesis 7:2-3, the clean animals went in by sevens and the unclean by twos. This means that the *serpent* should have had at least had a *'Mrs. Serpent'* to accompany him on the voyage.

3. Verse 15 confirms that despite their cleanliness the only things allowed in the ark were things that had in them the breath of life.

In other words, only those things created by God in the first six days entered the refuge.

4. Verse 21 confirms ALL FLESH UPON THE EARTH outside the ark DIED. Everything died that lived on dry land. This included the birds, snakes, and humans. Some argue that Leviathan fled into the seas and stayed there until after the flood. To this, the scripture says that everything that moved upon the land and had the breath of God died. Either way the serpent/leviathan cannot be a creature of this world, otherwise it too would have died with its mate.

5. Verse 22 and 23 make it clear that whatever the serpent was he was in the garden, *IT WAS NOT ONE OF THE CREATOR'S BEASTS. IT DID NOT HAVE HIS BREATH, AND CERTAINLY DID NOT HAVE A MATE.* This being the case the serpent in Genesis could not have been a snake or any other reptile.

The serpent referred to in Genesis is venomous. We know this by the metaphors the Bible uses to describe him. Why use the term dragon? The Bible uses dragon because fables say dragons breathe or spew fire. Nevertheless, some say angels spew no fire--to what am I referring. What the Bible refers to is the fire spoken of in Ephesians 6:16, Judges 9:15, Proverbs 30:16, and Mark 9:43. The fiery darts that Satan (the fire breathing dragon) uses against humans are:
1. Accusations.
2. Anger.
3. An unquenchable desire to destroy God's creatures.

We looked to the book of Job other traits of the Great Red Dragon. From Job 41 we take the following points[59]. I will not painstakingly line them up using hyper-scripting[60], but you should search books like Isaiah 27, 37, and Ezekiel 23, 33 and 31, and Revelations, to see how the scriptures confirm each other.

---

[59] The numbers correspond to points they are <u>not</u> the scripture verses.
[60] Much like hyper-linking on the internet. Many scriptural mysteries are answered by linking Old and New Testaments passages to find the answer.

1. **"CANST THOU DRAW OUT LEVIATHAN WITH A HOOK? OR IS HIS TONGUE WITH A CORD WHICH THOU LETTEST DOWN? CANST THOU PUT AN HOOK INTO HIS NOSE? OR BORE HIS JAW THROUGH**?" Although God is condescending Job, He points out one of the greatest truths in spiritual warfare. **Humans DO NOT POSSES the ability to capture, defeat, destroy, or control, the second wisest and most powerful creature in the universe.** We are not strong enough to pull Satan from his domain, nor can we trick him. God tells us unequivocally that only He can accomplish this feat.

2. **"WILL HE MAKE MANY SUPPLICATIONS TO YOU, OR WILL HE SPEAK SOFT WORDS TO YOU? WILL HE MAKE A COVENANT WITH YOU THAT YOU SHOULD TAKE HIM FOR A SERVANT FOREVER**?" Here God shows the subtle differences between Satan and Himself. Here God asks about petitions and covenants. In Heavenly wisdom God warns about the subtly of letting Satan whisper in the Christian ear. God also warns of Satan's devious plan. The old adage warns that those who wish to be served by magic end up magic's slave. Here God warns that all who make covenant with Satan for his service END UP SATAN'S SLAVE.

3. **"WILT THOU PLAY WITH HIM AS WITH A BIRD? OR WILL YOU BIND HIM FOR THY MAIDENS**?" This seems innocuous, a simple act of fellowship. The hint is that like a bird Satan not only flies but also seems harmless, beautiful, and controllable. Nothing is further from the truth. We sacrifice are children to demons and idols. We attempt to leash and cage demons, but like lions in the zoo, we forget that they are wild animals. **THERE IS NO WAY TO HAVE A HEALTHY RELATIONSHIP WITH A DEMON.**

4. **"SHALL THE COMPANIONS MAKE A BANQUET OF HIM? SHALL THEY PART HIM AMONG THE MERCHANTS**?" Here the pleasantudes of Satan manifest themself well. Satan's beauty is not only transient, it is discretionary. Satan; like a Venus fly trap,

morphs from beautiful to lethal at will. The problem is that people see the beauty and forget that SATAN IS NEVER HARMLESS.

5. **"CAN YOU FILL HIS SKIN WITH BARBED IRONS, OR HIS HEAD WITH FISH SPEARS? LAY YOUR HAND ON HIM. REMEMBER THE BATTLE, AND DO SO NO MORE."** Oh how wonderful an admonishment from God, a warning, you cannot kill Satan. God tells you to remember (take heed) of the actual battle. The battle is for your soul/spirit. Satan is not after your money, family, heath, job, sanity, or anything else. The attacks against these things are merely a mean to end. **Satan attacks in an effort to destroy your soul**. What can the evil one do with material things; he too is a spirit just like the Host on High. Neither team has need or use for material things.

6. **"BEHOLD, THE HOPE OF HIM IS IN VAIN. WON'T ONE BE CAST DOWN EVEN AT THE SIGHT OF HIM**?" Whoever casts their cares upon the devil is lost; they are not even smart enough to know that they should fear the sight of death. What normal person would stare into the eyes of a dragon and not fear the mighty beast? William Shakespeare warns us in King Lear, "Come not between the dragon, and his wrath."

7. **"NONE IS SO FIERCE THAT DARE STIR HIM UP. WHO THEN IS ABLE TO STAND BEFORE ME."** Here the Great Commander tells us clearly that no one is as fierce as the great red dragon. No one is fierce enough to face the dragon and remain exposed to his breath. If we are not fierce enough to face the dragon, how can we conceive of waging war against the Creator? The wrath of God brings to mind the words of Admiral Yamamoto after Pearl Harbor, "I fear we have awoken a sleeping giant."

8. **"I WILL NOT CONCEAL HIS PARTS, OR HIS POWER, OR HIS COMELY PROPORTION."** Here God's Holy Spirit promises freedom through truth tells for His children that HE will never aid Satan in deception. God will never collaborate with Satan, tempt humans, or allow Satan to pretend to be Him. God never vouches

for Satan's beauty, nor allows His people to believe in the lies of the enemy. If you fall for the temptation of Satan in the wilderness, it is because you did not listen to, or do not hear from God.

9. **"WHO CAN DISCOVER THE FACE OF HIS GARMENT? OR WHO CAN COME TO HIM WITH HIS DOUBLE BRIDLE**?" A Godly reminder; the layers of the anointing Cherub will never allow you to see his true nature. There are many layers under Lucifer's scales, and to his shade. This king NEVER allows his followers access into his innermost self. Reference to the double bridle is a warning about the raw power of this beast of the field. The bridle is a leather strap used in harnesses for horses and cattle. The bridle tethers to the beast of burden and via a mouthpiece controls the animal. The metal mouthpiece causes the animal pain, which controls the beast. The double bridle indicated the strength of the beast, and the level of resistance. The double bridle stops the tether from breaking under strain. The double bridle also allows the owner to apply more tension to the mouthpiece for stubborn animals.

10. **"WHO CAN OPEN THE DOORS OF HIS FACE? HIS TEETH ARE TERRIBLE ROUND ABOUT**." Many Christians believe that through God's Holy Spirit they are more than conquerors. What they do not understand is that Christians NEVER conquer Satan in the Bible. Many cite the passage in Revelations that says that with the strength of their witness Jesus overcame Satan. They cite this passage to imply that believers fight and defeat Satan. This is not the case. This is not what the Bible says in the passage. What the Bible indicates in this passage is that God's love and mercy vanquished adversarial competition. In Job, we see Satan compete for the soul of a man. The reason God chose Job was that He knew Job would win. Job was not just righteous; he was righteous in all his ways, there was none like Job. God and Lucifer played the age-old game of kings--*Bring out your champion.* God and Lucifer played this game many times in the Bible with varying results.

1. Adam vs. Eve--*Satan won.*
2. Cain vs. Abel--*Satan won.*
3. Abraham vs. Melchizedek--*God won.*
4. Joseph vs. Judah--*Satan won.*
5. Joseph vs. Potiphar's wife--*God won.*
6. Potiphar vs. Potiphar's--*God won.*
7. Joseph vs. Pharoah--*God won.*
8. Moses vs. Pharaoh--*God won.*
9. Sampson vs. Delilah--*Satan won.*
10. Elijah vs. Jezebel--*God won.*
11. David vs. Saul--*God won.*
12. Jeremiah vs. King Nebuchadnezzar--*God won.*
13. Daniel vs. King Nebuchadnezzar--*God won.*
14. The prophets vs. the kings--*God won.*
15. Jesus vs. Satan (in the earth)--*God won.*
16. Jesus vs. Peter--*God won.*
17. Jesus vs. everyone He faced--*God won.*
18. Saul vs. Jesus--*God won.*
19. Paul vs. Pilot--*God won.*
20. Jesus vs. Lucifer (in heaven)--*God won.*

Satan's teeth guard the entrance to his kingdom. Satan's teeth are the same arrows, and darts he tries against people to make them fall. Satan's teeth are terrible because they deceive even the wisest of men.

11. "**HIS SCALES ARE HIS PRIDE, SHUT UP TOGETHER WITH A CLOSE SEAL. ONE IS SO NEAR TO ANOTHER THAT NO AIR CAN COME BETWEEN THEM. THEY ARE JOINED ONE TO ANOTHER. THEY STICK TOGETHER, SO THAT THEY CANNOT BE SUNDERED. BY HIS NEESINGS A LIGHT DOTH SHINE, HIS EYES ARE LIKE THE EYELIDS OF THE MORNING.**" Satan that serpent, the great red dragon has scales on his hide. These scales do not protect Satan they are evidence of the callous nature in his heart. Satan has no mercy in him, no compassion, and loves no one. The air cannot get between the scales because there is no room in Satan's heart for anything but his pride. If there is no air in Satan, and the scales are air tight it makes sense that he cannot be a living animal--they need air.

12. "**OUT OF HIS MOUTH GO BURNING LAMPS. AND SPARKS OF FIRE LEAP FORTH. OUT OF HIS NOSTRILS A SMOKE GOES, AS OF A BOILING POT OVER A FIRE OF REEDS. HIS BREATH KINDLES COALS. A FLAME GOES OUT OF HIS MOUTH.**" This passage reflects the same description that Jesus gives for Gehenna. The attributes of hell exude from the king of the underworld. The King of Light and mercy exudes these traits, why should the dark lord not have these traits. These attributes also explain Satan's appellation Great Red Dragon, because these traits are traits of the fabled dragon.

13. "**IN HIS NECK REMAINETH STRENGTH. AND SORROW IS TURNED INTO JOY BEFORE HIM.**" This stanza is about the haughty nature of Lucifer. This single trait caused him eternity, and position near the throne. God also reminds us that the things, which cause sorrow, Satan delights in. Satan loves to see Christians lament and wail, why do you think the tormentors of Christians have always been so sinister. Sorrow rarely drives Christian's closer to God. The more sorrow Satan introduces into a believer's life the better chance to win that soul.

   The reference to the neck of Satan speaks to Satan's kingdom. The neck not only attaches the head but it moves with the head and allows the head to control the rest of the body. The beasts, antichrist, atheists, unrepentant sinners, and the haters of god, comprise the neck of Satan[61].

14. "**THE FLAKES OF HIS FLESH ARE JOINED TOGETHER: THEY ARE FIRM IN THEMSELVES THEY CANNOT BE MOVED.**" Sadly, Satan like the villain in Silence of the lambs wears the skins of his victims as trophies. Obviously, the red dragon has no flesh of his own. The flakes of his skin therefore are his followers. The pride of Satan's kingdom is the sinners spoken of in Romans 1. Those that have removed themselves from the sight of God adorn Satan's body like the precious jewels he once wore; they are his prize possessions.

---

[61] This explains the *B*easts ability to recover from the wound in Revelations 13.

15. **"HIS HEART IS AS FIRM AS A STONE: YEA; AS HARD AS A PIECE OF THE NETHER[62] MILESTONE."** The hardness of stone is unarguable. Like the lava, which burns hot then cools to cold black stone, the price of darkness has volcanic ash for his heart. Fire and brimstone erupts from Satan's heart to attack the saints. Satan has no other weapons that weapons he can form from his abode. People make weapons from the abundant materials. What the abundant materials are in the underworld except death, fire, misery, evil, and pride.

16. **"WHEN HE RAISES HIMSELF UP, THE MIGHTY ARE AFRAID. BY REASON OF BREAKINGS THEY PURIFY THEMSELVES."** Even the mighty men of old like Nimrod, the Nephilim, Rehaim, and the Anakim fear the father of the pit. This fallen angel has power of which we cannot conceive. Imagine the power one wields who would stand in front of God and defy the Creator of the universe.

17. **"THE SWORD OF HIM THAT LAYETH AT HIM CANNOT HOLD: THE SPEAR, THE DART, NOR THE HABERGON[63]. HE ESTEEMS IRON AS STRAW; AND BRASS AS ROTTEN WOOD. THE ARROW CANNOT MAKE HIM FLEE. SLING STONES ARE TURNED WITH HIM INTO STUBBLE. DARTS ARE COUNTED AS STUBBLE. HE LAUGHS AT THE SHAKING OF A SPEAR."** No weapon formed against us shall prosper, are Paul's words. No human weapon, or warrior that fights against Lucifer shall win; these are the words of God. Unlike Goliath, our slung stones will not fell Lucifer and we shall surely not behead him Satan. Satan laughs at the shaking spears of humans. The spears do not shake in rage or anger but in fear of the darkness of the evil one.

18. **"SHARP STONES ARE UNDER HIM: HE SPREADETH SHARP POINTED THINGS UPON THE MIRE."** Like modern minefields, Satan lines pathways with sharp objects. This has a dual effect. First, it makes the weak change paths from the straight and narrow

---

[62] Lower.
[63] Lance.

to the wide, well travelled pathway to hell. Secondly, this has the effect of making the righteous that stay the course pay the price. Like Jesus and the 39 strips, the numerous floggings of Joseph and Paul, Stephen's beheading, and Peter's inverted crucifixion--Satan's sharp pointed teeth cause even the strongest saints pain. Revelations warns that in the last days satanic forces will wear down the saints.

19. **"HE MAKES THE DEEP[64] TO BOIL LIKE A POT. HE MAKES THE SEA LIKE A POT OF OINTMENT."** Lucifer once sat in the seas of God. As keeper of the throne, Lucifer knows the secrets of the dark. His volcanic heart causes the deep to boil. Wherever the prince of hell abounds his presence manifests. In Judges 9 Satan gives insight into the fire that comes forth from him. I endeavored not to hyper-script but in this case, I must. In the chapter stones of fire, God removed the fire from Lucifer. Where then does the fire come from? The fire comes from the darkness itself. Remember Satan did not create the darkness; he is lord of the darkness. God banished the cherub to the place He designed for those that hate Him. The fire removed from the midst of Lucifer was glory. The fire comes from the bramble, the dragon, the devil is the fire spoken of in Proverbs 30:15-16. This fire is not glory; it is rage, evil, and venom spewing from the heart of a once beautiful angel.

20. **"HE MAKES A PATH SHINE AFTER HIM. ONE WOULD THINK THE DEEP TO BE HOARY."** Like the giant slug, Satan leaves a slimy, glistening, trail. The angel that once shone brighter than all the other stones of fire no longer leaves a trail of glory. As Lucifer--the bearer of light fell he changed into Satan--the angel of darkness. Now the Leviathan leaves a trail of death and ashes wherever he goes. The shinning described in this verse is not a reference to light it is a reference Satan giving his people his power. This is a reference to the antichrist and other enemies of God like Nimrod and Egypt.

---

[64] Ezekiel 28:2.

21. **"ON EARTH THERE IS NOT HIS EQUAL, WHO IS MADE WITHOUT FEAR."** This passage explains why Jesus was necessary. If Jesus is the second Adam and crushed Satan's kingdom without fear, then God meant for Adam to do the same. Now you see why destroying Adam was so important to Satan. Adam had dominion over the fallen angel. Before Adam understood his kingdom, it was gone. God sent the second Adam to be Satan's equal. Like Ishmael and Isaac, the king had two sons. One of his sons had a birthright and the other had a covenant and blessing; they still fight to this day. The two princes of God's kingdom still wage war for the Throne on God.

22. **"HE BEHOLDETH ALL THINGS HIGH."** According to God, Lucifer is wiser than the prophet Daniel. He therefore maintains and monitors all things important to God; this is how he maintains his target strategy.

23. **"HE IS KING OVER ALL THE CHILDREN OF PRIDE."** Jesus reminds in Luke 8:44 that we have the traits of our father the devil. This stanza is about the haughty nature of Lucifer. Solomon warns us that pride brings man low. Through pride, the more sorrow Satan fosters in believer's lives the better chance to win that soul.

Now that we see what the Creator has to say about Satan, we get to understand more of the power Satan wields over our *choices*. This does not mean that Satan has power over our *choice*, what he does is modify the things that are available for our *choice*. The power of Satan resounds in this verse from Judges 9; **"If in truth you are anointing me as king over you…"** it is *our choice* to serve in Satan's shade. As a reward for bad *choices*, Satan gives his strength. Satan's strength manifests in many forms from many places.

Let us look together at Index 1 and the 30 various appellations ascribed to Satan. This list is to elucidate metaphors and names in the Bible are there for our understanding. Of the listed titles, is there any evidence of Satan transforming himself into any of these 30 characters? If Satan changed into all of these things and constantly changed forms, how would Christians recognize Satan? The answer is simple. It was in the Spirit in Jesus that recognized Satan each time he appeared. Darkness when held to the light will always fade. Satan's darkness is not in color or luminescence but in deed. The content of Satan's heart allows believers to discern Satan's spirit. Satan's heart is full of lies, deceit, murder and envy--one of which you find in God.

The scriptures call Satan:
1. *Abaddon (destruction, to perish)* - Revelations 9:11.
2. *The accuser of the brethren* - Revelations 12:10.
3. *Adversary* - 1 Peter 5:8.
4. *Angel of the bottomless pit* - Revelations 9:11.
5. *Appollyon* (Greek version of *Abaddon*) - Revelations 9:11.
6. *Beelzebub* - Matthew 12:24, Mark 3:22, Luke 11:15.
7. *Belial* - 2 Corinthians 6:15.
8. *Devil* - Matthew 4:1, Luke 4:2, Revelations 20:2.
9. *Our Common Enemy* - Matthew 13:39.
10. *Evil spirit* - I Samuel 16:14.
11. *Father of lies* - John 8:44.
12. *Gates of Hell* - Matthew 16:18.
13. *Great red dragon* - Revelations 12:3.
14. *Liar* - John 8:44.
15. *Lying Spirit* - 1 Kings 22:22.
16. *Murderer*- John 8:44
17. *Power of darkness* - Colossians 1:13.
18. *The Prince of this world* - John 12:31, 14:30, 16:11.
19. *The Prince of the demons* - Matthew 12:24.
20. *The Prince of the power of the air* - Ephesians 2:2.
21. *Ruler of the darkness of this world* - Ephesians 6:12.
22. *Satan* – 1 Chronicles 21:1, Job 1:6, John 13:27, Act 5:3.
23. *The Serpent* - Genesis 3:4, 2 Chronicles 11:3.
24. *The Spirit* - Ephesians 2:2.
25. *The Tempter* - Matthew 12:43.
26. *The god of this world* - 2 Corinthians 4:4.
27. *Unclean spirit* - Matthew 12:43.
28. *The wicked one* - Matthew 13:19, 38.
29. *Kingdom of, to be destroyed* - 2 Samuel 23:6.
30. *That old Serpent* - Revelations 12:9, 20:2.

(Index 1)

Index I lists the satanic titles to show you a most important point. **OF THE LISTED TITLES, THE BIBLE NEVER CALLS**

SATAN YOUR PRINCE OR YOUR RULER. What a wonderful God we serve that He reserved these titles for Himself[65].

THE DRAGON'S TEETH (Job 41:16)

In Greek mythology, Dragon's Teeth feature prominently in the legends of the Golden Fleece. In each case, the planted dragon's teeth grew into fully armed warriors. The Great Red Dragon plants his teeth in the lives of believers. Unwittingly, saints allow his teeth to germinate and grown in their hearts and lives. Before saints realize that they are in trouble, the teeth grow into fully armed warriors. The Dragon's teeth are not as sharp as they are lethal. Their lethality stems from the fact that the dragon planted them in the hearts of men. Because they do not have to gain entry, the effect an internal error has is far more intense than if they dragon forced his way inwards.

Summarizing this chapter, believers you need to understand that you are free forever from Satan's grasp. Nevertheless, like a liquor store, Satan sits on many corners waiting to serve you. The liquor never walks out of the store and attacks you but advertisements produce the same end. Demon possession more accurately is influence, manipulation, and or utilization. There is only one type of person that demons can possess--the willing. This book is about *choice*. Since Jesus destroyed Satan's kingdom, we ARE FREE. There are many pitfalls and pangs in life, but it does not follow that we have to give in to them. We are not oversimplifying the concept or downplaying the power of Satan, he has no power. All power that Satan possesses and wields humans delivered to him[66]. All power Satan as he has because people CHOSE to relinquish it to him.

Amen

---

[65] 1 Peter 2:25.
[66] Luke 4:6.

Chapter Eleven
The Ugly Beasts

"**And I saw as it were a sea of glass mingled with fire: and them that had gotten the victory over the beast, and over his image, and over his mark, [and] over the number of his name, stand on the sea of glass, having the harps of God**" - Revelations 15:2."

In this chapter, we analyze the confusing components the *B*easts, the mark of the *B*east, the name of the *B*east, and the number of the *B*east. Compartmentalization of this study is unintentional, but we must try to understand the mysteries of the Kingdom of Heaven. The *B*easts are just such a mystery. The *B*east's seven components like tires on a car make the whole but are quite separate.

1. The *Dragon* and the *B*east.
2. The First *B*east.
3. The Second *B*east.
4. The Number of the *B*east.
5. The Name of the *B*east.
6. The Mark of the *B*east.
7. The Scarlet *B*east.

The book of Revelations, like most prophetic books, Revelations communicates in metaphors, symbols, numbers, and unclear time lines. There are certain things not open to interpretation or opinion; numbers are an example. It is for this cause the Bible uses numbers in prophecy.

All of God's mysteries are Revelations, or re-veiled information. God is not secretive, He is careful. In the history of this planet, there has been no animal as despicable as the human creature. Though God loves the human creature, He is careful to prevent self-destruction. Do you believe that those same creatures that invented weapons of mass destruction would not use Heavenly secrets to murder each other?

Other than Revelations, there is no other book in the Bible that I am aware of that affords the believer a blessing for reading and hearing. I would like to point out that the book of Revelations paints a picture that gives believers the ability to clearly identify Satan the enemy. God gave this information so that those who read with understanding are able to distinguish the *Beast* from fables. The Bible refers to the *Beast* as a beast not because of physical attributes but because of his level of unrighteousness. The Bible refers to the *Beast* as beast because he no longer stands righteous before God. Like a beast of the field, the *Beast* is a common--ungodly creature.

THE GAME OF DEATH

Satan uses a *GAME OF DEATH* to mimic God's Trinity Maneuver. Satan uses the first *Beast* to counter Adam; whom God gave irrevocable dominion over the earth. However, the first *Beast* has a more sinister use. Jesus never actually returned unfettered control of the earth to men[67]. If man has complete control, again he WILL give it away again. Therefore, Jesus redeemed dominion unto men. As the Son of man and the Son of God or as the Romans called him INRI-King of the Jews it was Jesus' charge to care for the earth. This He did by giving care of the kingdom to God's Holy Spirit. This is why the *GAME OF DEATH* requires the first beast to come from the *sea*. Despite human teaching, the power in the earth is God's Holy Spirit[68]. The *Beast* knows whom he must bypass to get what he wants. Therefore, the *Beast*'s first attack is against the power in the earth. The war in heaven never ended; it moved into the earth, and then returns to heaven. To take the earth this time, the *Dragon* does not battle two cherubs with flaming swords he battles the King. Sadly, as it was with Hannibal the King, when INRI fights this time

---

[67] John 14:16, 14:26, 16:7-8.
[68] Matthew 28:19 - that is why we baptize thusly, the Father and Son do not maintain the power here in the earth.

He fights alone, His subjects leave His care to follow a god of their own understanding.

    2. Satan uses the second *Beast* to counter Jesus[69]. Lucifer gives his *Beasts* the powers of the air and the power over death.

    3. Satan uses the scarlet *Beast* to counter God's Holy Spirit. Because of God's law, spirits can only operate in the earth realm through humans. God has the Trinity maneuver and the *Dragon* has *the game of death.*

Regardless of the numerous interpretations and assertions about the *Beast*, the scripture makes one point clear. It is not the first, second, or scarlet *Beast* we must fear it is the *Dragon*. We worry so much about the *Beast* that we forget, "**The *Dragon* gave him his power, his throne, and great authority**." Despite ranting about the Antichrist, the tribulation, signs, and wonders the power behind the evil throne is and always has been the *Dragon*.

SATAN'S KINGDOM RISING

THE FIRST BEAST - (Revelations 13:1-11)

    "**Then I stood on the sand of the sea. I saw a beast coming up out of the *sea*, having ten horns and seven heads. On his horns were ten crowns, and on his heads, blasphemous names. The beast which I saw was like a leopard, and his feet were like those of a bear, and his mouth like the mouth of a lion. The *Dragon* gave him his power, his throne, and great authority. One of his heads looked like it had been wounded fatally. His fatal wound was healed, and the whole earth marveled at the beast. They worshiped the *Dragon*, because he gave his authority to the beast, and they worshiped the beast, saying, "Who is like the beast? Who is able to make war with him?" A**

---

[69] 1 Corinthians 15:45.

mouth speaking great things and blasphemy was given to him. Authority to make war for forty-two months was given to him. He opened his mouth for blasphemy against God, to blaspheme his name, and his dwelling, those who dwell in heaven. It was given to him to make war with the holy ones, and to overcome them. Authority over every tribe, people, language, and nation was given to him. All who dwell on the earth will worship him, everyone whose name has not been written from the foundation of the world in the book of life of the Lamb who has been killed. If anyone has an ear, let him hear. If anyone is to go into captivity, he will go into captivity. If anyone is to be killed with the sword, he must be killed. Here is the endurance and the faith of the holy ones."

The First *Beast* comes from the *sea*, the same sea of souls mentioned in Revelations 17:15. The First *Beast* is not an oceanic creature but a human with numerous ties to European history. The First *Beast* has the power to heal himself because he is a spiritual creature. The wound in the neck speaks to the injury Jesus caused crushing Satan's kingdom. Although Jesus defeated the *Dragon*, the *Dragon* Humans did NOT ALLOW the *Dragon* TO DIE. God's mercy did not spare Satan, humans kept their god alive by giving him back what Jesus redeemed. Jesus redeemed human *choice* from satanic control--we gave it back. The reason the wound 'heals' is that Satan rebuilt his kingdom. The scripture describes the wound as fatal, but this does not mean that the first beast resurrected himself; it means he had a wound that if left untreated would lead to death. This in and of itself is not unique, but it shows that Satan regained a great deal of power over the flesh.

Because of the power of the first *Beast* people of the world, worship the *Dragon*. The *Beast* served to bring glory to his master, the power he waged war. It is important to see that the *Beast* is not the terror in the earth realm, because he draws his power from someone else.

The *Dragon* not only gives the *Beast* the mouth with which to blaspheme, he tells the *Beast* what to say. Under the power and control of the *Dragon*, the first *Beast* leads to the earth into rebellion against God. For 42 months, the *Dragon* and his first *Beast* wage war against the saints and win.

The *Dragon* gave the first *Beast* the authority to control humanity. Control over the earth God gave to men. Satan stole control; Christ redeemed control and returned it to men under the authority of God's Holy Spirit. Satan through years of merchandising regained support from men and eventually men in power give control to the *Dragon* another time.

The scripture tells us that the people worship the first *Beast* as a powerful agent of the *Dragon*. Although they seemingly worship the *Beast*, they actually worship the *Dragon*, because he is the power behind the *Beast*'s miracles. Much like the Holy Trinity Satan creates a trinity of his own. Despite calling on Christ or the God's Holy Spirit, we worship the Father in heaven. Despite which *Beast* we worship we worship the father of the *Beast*; the *Dragon*. In another stroke of Genius Satan simply mimics the model God set up for His people, and uses the Opiate of the masses to control the earth.

Make no mistake, the ultimate cold war results under the power of the first *Beast*. All those that do not belong to Christ WILL join the *Dragon* whether they want to or not. Those that will not worship the *Beasts* will endure torment and ultimately death. God foretells that this will be the most difficult wilderness saints ever endure, a time when God gives evil rule over the earth.

In Genesis six men's evil repented God. Again, in Genesis 18 the evil found in Sodom and Gomorrah waxed great in the sight of God. Mankind tested God's patience in these events, and God destroyed evil rather than endure evil. Under the reign of the first *Beast*, God promises that the saints would face the sword and fatigue. Ironically, this is all the first *Beast* does. Many willingly illiterate Christians believe that the first *Beast* relates to 666, but he does not. The reason Christians know so little about their second greatest enemy is that they will not read about him. Moreover, I say *him* intentionally; all the ℬeasts are male in gender or power. Both ℬeasts are not male because women are less evil; the ℬeasts are male because the male of the species carries dominion. Man is not more capable, God saw fit to use the male because the man carries the seed. Just as in humans the male determines the sex of the baby; in the spirit, the man determines with tree the seed bears; Godly or ungodly fruit.

THE SECOND ℬEAST - (Revelations 13:11-18)

"I saw another beast coming up out of the *earth*. He had two horns like a lamb, and he spoke like a *Dragon*. He exercises all the authority of the first beast in his presence. He makes the earth and those who dwell in it to worship the first beast, whose fatal wound was healed. He performs great signs, even making fire come down out of the sky to the earth in the sight of people. He deceives My own people who dwell on the earth because of the signs he was granted to do in front of the beast; saying to those who dwell on the earth, that they should make an image to the beast who had the sword wound and lived. It was given to him to give breath to it, to the image of the beast, that the image of the beast should both speak, and cause as many as wouldn't worship the image of the beast to be killed. He causes all, the small and the great, the rich and the poor, and the free and the slave, to be given marks on their right hands, or on their foreheads; and that no one would be able to buy or to sell, unless he has that mark, the name of the beast or the number of his name. Here is wisdom. He who has understanding, let him calculate the number of the beast, for it is the number of a man. His number is six hundred sixty-six."

The second ℬeast comes from the *earth*, which means it is fleshly. The way in which Satan gained power originally was through Adam. Again, we see that a human gives Satan his *choice* and in return, Satan gives power. The second ℬeast comes up out if the *earth*, a beast of the field; a clay pot (human) specially prepared to serve his father. The second *Beast* speaks like a *Dragon*, the great red *Dragon*. The second *Beast* unlike the first *Beast* has no spiritual connection to God.

People are most familiar with the Second *Beast*. The second *Beast* is the least powerful but most famous. The second *Beast* is the most human, not in action but in deed. The second *Beast* dedicates 100% of his energy, gifts, and talent to his father the *Dragon*. Christ performed wonders because He submitted whole-heartedly to the Father the second *Beast* serves his king 100%. The second *Beast* is also the most complex to explain. The second *Beast* performs great signs in the earth, solidifying the control the *Dragon* has on the earth. Jesus called us an evil and rebellious generation, and our actions confirm it with the *Beast*. Knowing that if we love as Christ loved, men may identify Christians; Christians *choose* to follow signs and wonders. God declares, just as they did with the golden calf, His people follow and worship the *Beast*.

THE DRAGON'S ULTIMATE CREATION

"**For God so loved the world that He gave His only begotten Son**." What makes the antichrist the antichrist--ever wonder? It is not that the antichrist is against Christ that makes him *anti*, it is that he is the antithesis of Christ. Look closely to see the marvel in Satan's plan--he too made a son. It took Satan thousands of years to finally enable and deceive humans into completing what God slowed down in Genesis.

1. "**And the Lord said, 'BEHOLD THE PEOPLE IS ONE AND THEY HAVE ALL ONE LANGUAGE, AND THIS THEY BEGIN TO DO AND NO NOTHING WILL BE RESTRAINED FROM THEM WHICH THEY HAVE IMAGINED TO DO. GO TO LET US GO DOWN AND THERE CONFOUND THEIR LANGUAGE THAT THEY MAY NOT UNDERSTAND ONE ANOTHER'S SPEECH'** - Genesis 11:6-7."

2. **"And God said, 'LET US MAKE MAN IN OUR IMAGE, AFTER OUR LIKENESS AND LET THEM HAVE DOMINION OVER THE FISH OF THE SEA AND OVER THE FOWLS OF THE AIR AND OVER THE CATTLE AND OVER ALL THE EARTH AND OVER EVERY CREEPING THING THAT CREEPETH UPON THE EARTH'. So God created man in His own image; In the image of God created He him male and female He them** - Genesis 1:26-27."

3. **"And the Lord God formed man of the dust of the ground, and breathed into his nostrils the breath of life; and the man became a living soul** - Genesis 2:7."

Satan painstakingly developed a relationship with men. The thing that God wanted the creatures made in His image not to do was create a living creature dedicated to Satan. Sure, there have been horrible people down through history but none has the breath of Satan. The one major thing Satan cannot do is create life, so he gave a living human his spirit.

Revelations 13 says that this image of the *B*east, (begotten son of the *B*east) had the breath of the *B*east. Unlike the followers of Satan who filled their hearts with evil, this person was born to serve his father's will. Through generations of practice, beginning with Nimrod Satan engineered his spiritual offspring. Like any good son, the only thing the antichrist wants to do is please his father Satan. To this end, the antichrist implements a system that glorifies his father's ego, evil, and hatred of God. Under this world system, the *B*easts give their father a tribute worthy of a god. God told His people that He would put His mark in their hearts that they would be known by love. Satan marks his people's heart as well that their hatred of God shows in their deeds.

THE NUMBER OF THE ℬEAST

We are all familiar with the tri-numeric 666. We ascribe it as the *'mark'* of the ℬeast, but scriptures clearly indicate that this is not correct. **"Here is wisdom. Let him that hath understanding count the number of the beast: for it is the number of a man; and his number [is] Six hundred threescore [and] six** - Revelations 13:18." Six hundred threescore [and] six therefore *is not the mark* of the ℬeast it is the *number of the* ℬeast. More than simply a number, 666 is an eternal marker and Godly buoy. Satan is the ultimate deceiver but he does have employees and workers in this world. With fallen angels, demonized humans, and false Christs how are believers to discern which is which? God makes a point of describing the enemy so there will be less confusion

One way to discern the enemy is to understand why this distinction is important. Understanding that this numeric is simply part of a puzzle and not the ultimate clue it is the beginning. Here the Master took the time to make sure that despite religious teaching and useless rhetoric we know that the ℬeast is A BEAST OF THE FIELD JUST LIKE HUMANS. This means that this there is nothing HEAVENLY about the ℬeast he is no more HEAVENLY than you or I.

The kabala is a Hebrew number system traditionally taught to men after the age of thirty. In the kabalistic, system numbers listed side by side mean to add. Therefore 666 is actually 6+6+6. This of course adds up to 18. We however have two numbers side by side which when added total 9. The number of months for a human is 9 and the numerological value for a man is 9^{70}.

This painstaking effort by the Lord compels us not to see this ℬeast as any other thing than a manipulative creature. The fact is that God reiterates the results of Satan's fallen state to believers. Although

---

[70] The number nine is comprised of the four natural elements fire, water, earth, and air, combined with the number five, which numerology attributes to human life forms. Therefore, the combinations would imply that the creature is a life form made from the same natural elements as Adam. <u>From a Fishing Trip in Patmos: The Disciple-maker's Edition</u>.

Satan forms weapons against you, they are no more powerful than a weapon formed by your next-door neighbor.

Revelations 13:18 is the antithesis of Revelations 21:17. Here we see that the punishment in Revelations 13:18 is lowering Satan to a level below humans. In Revelations 21:17, we see the reward for righteousness is the exaltation to the level of angels.

Revelations 13:18 -	Revelations 21:17 -
"Here is wisdom. Let him that hath understanding count the number of the beast: for it is the number of a man; and his number [is] Six hundred threescore [and] six."	**"And he measured they wall thereof, an hundred and forty and four cubits, according to the measure of a man, that is, of the angel."**

When you see the word beast, it is the same beast referred to in Genesis 3:1. A beast is a lower life form a form devoid of Godliness. It is not the beast's appearance that is beastly it is the *B*east's nature that is *B*eastly.

Satan uses deceit because he is severally limited in spiritual power. Satan's power like Voodoo[71] only works through the willing. Satan has no more POWER over you than a regular human being.

The first chapter of Romans, describes worshipers of the creature instead of the Creator. Self-deification keeps humans in a precarious relationship with God. A creature: a human like us, with the power to do miracles cannot help inspire worship. How wonderful to serve a powerful king that can perform miracles, yet has our same fleshly, debase, perverted, selfish desires. Throughout human history, many such corrupt leaders existed. We must wonder why it took so long to depose those leaders. It was simply because there were so many people that shared in

---

[71] *Voodoo*, or *Santeria* originated in Khemit (ancient Egypt). A magician-prince named Vodoun (Voodoon) used his evil magic to control and manipulate. Owing to the slave trade, Voodoo found its way to Haiti and Cuba where the deceptive practices taught by a dead magician still exist. This Craft is concentrated in those two countries because these were the two countries the earliest slaves were transported. Much like the children of Israel did in the wilderness the slaves brought their slave religion with them.

their wicked leader's desires. It is imperative to remember despite the powers granted[72] to the Anti-Christ he is not Lucifer. The Anti-Christ is only human.

THE NAME OF THE BEAST

The concept of the name is very important. Revelations 19:12 gives a wonderful elaboration into why the name of God does not appear anywhere. "**His eyes [were] as a flame of fire, and on his head [were] many crowns; and He had a name written, that no man knew, but He Himself.**" Who but God could explain His majesty? Who could name Him or describe Him? God did tell us His name. God said I AM is His name, and He explains why in I AM is His name Romans 1:20, "**For the invisible things of Him from the creation of the world are clearly seen, being understood by the things that are made, [even] his eternal power and Godhead; so that they are without excuse.**" All heavenly names have meaning. More than meaning, heavenly names are the essence of the creature. Because names are the essence of the creature God keeps His name to Himself, lest we use the ultimate power in the universe for evil. Just as the name, Jesus[73] means *Jehovah is salvation* the names of God's chosen often give explanation, destination, or attributes of the creature.

There is a reason the Tetragrammaton[74] (YVHV) came into existence. Men do not know the name of God. What we believe to be His name was not legal to speak. God so loved the world that He gave His only begotten Son. God did not give us His name. Nowhere in the cannon or in any other accepted text do we find the actual name of God. **I AM** is not God's name, neither are the other 78 titles[75] in the Bible. According to Kabalistic tradition, the Tetragrammaton has a numerical value of 78. There are seventy--eight titles for God in the Bible. Micah'El means *like God*, Gabri'El means *messenger of God* and Isra'El means *people of God*. The Father therefore only calls Garbri"EL when a message is needed, Micah'EL for war and Isra'EL for worship. This is

---

[72] Revelations 13:2.
[73] Jesus's actual name is Yeshua in Hebrew.
[74] Meaning four-tiered or four-part name, *Yod-Heh-Vau-Heh* which we pronounce *Yahweh*.
[75] Appellation--from the French, *to call*. These 78 titles are not names. Just like Pharaoh, prophet, or wife, are not titles. Each person has an actual name.

also the reason God changed the name of many people in the Old Testament. The person's name changed to indicate the relationship change between the person and God.

The name of the *Beast* is a more difficult concept to explain. The reason for this is that the name of the *Beast* is simply not listed. "**And the smoke of their torment ascendeth up forever and ever: and they have no rest day nor night, who worship the beast and his image, and whosoever receiveth the mark of his name** - Revelations 14:11." This lack of a name is undoubtedly a result of expulsion from Heaven. When we excommunicate a child they become a non-person, their name also voids. When we disown children, we not only negate them in our lives we negate the person formerly known by that name. Although we do not physically negate the person, their name was a part of the relationship once shared. The fact is the fallen angels forfeited their names. Fallen angels are spiritual bastards serving a bastardly overlord. The *Beast* was obviously expelled, but none of Satan's minions are named in the Bible.

There is a reason Lucifer no longer has a name, look with me to the answer found in Hebrews 12:9, "**But if ye be without chastisement, whereof all are partakers, then are ye bastards, and not sons.**" Satan no longer has a proper name because he is dead. Only the living have names, this is why Revelations 20:12 says, "**And I saw the dead, small and great, stand before God; and the books were opened: and another book was opened, which is [the book] of life: and the dead were judged out of those things which were written in the books, according to their works.**" No name, title, or appellation not entered in the Lamb's book of life is alive. This is why the shed Blood of Christ is the only way to enter, it brings life to the dead.

The *Beast*'s name links more to the *Beast*'s mark than his number[76]. The book of Revelations again sheds more light on the name concept with its description of the Horsemen of the apocalypse.
"**And I saw, and behold a white horse: and he that sat on him had a bow; and a crown was given unto him: and he went forth conquering, and to conquer. And when he had**

---

[76] Revelations 14:11.

opened the second seal, I heard the second beast say, 'Come and see'. And there went out another horse [that was] red: and [power] was given to him that sat thereon to take peace from the earth, and that they should kill one another: and there was given unto him a great sword. And when he had opened the third seal, I heard the third beast say, Come and see. And I beheld, and lo a black horse; and he that sat on him had a pair of balances in his hand. And I heard a voice in the midst of the four beasts say, 'A measure of wheat for a penny, and three measures of barley for a penny; and [see] thou hurt not the oil and the win'e. And when he had opened the fourth seal, I heard the voice of the fourth beast say, 'Come and see'. And I looked, and behold a pale horse: and his name that sat on him was Death, and Hell followed with him. And power was given unto them over the fourth part of the earth, to kill with sword, and with hunger, and with death, and with the beasts of the earth** - Revelations 6:2-8".

Each Horseman has a description, but only one has a name. The name matches the horsemen's task, or the judgment the horsemen carry not the way the horsemen look. In the same manner as the four horsemen, the *B*east has tools and indicators. However, the *B*east's name, whatever the name maybe is tied into his deeds not his appearance.

THE MOTHER OF HARLOTS

Revelations 17:5 and 19:12 help clarify the names and the marks. Revelations 17:5 **"And upon her forehead [was] a name written, mystery, Babylon the great, the mother of harlots and abominations of the earth."** Surely, those that contend that 666 is a literalism cannot possibly believe that there is going to be a woman running around the city with this scripture tattooed on her forehead.

Moreover, why would this woman have this variety of names? Would it make sense that these are not names, but indications of whom or what she represents?

1. *MYSTERY* - The Bible always refers to Spiritual issues as mysteries. The term mystery is appropriate because a mystery is something, uncanny and out of the ordinary. What better description of a spiritual item.

2. *BABYLON THE GREAT* - A reference to Satan's strong holds. This is a reference to either king or kingdom.

3. *THE MOTHER OF HARLOTS* - Jezebel, Delilah, Salome, and Mary, are the names of some of the more famous women in the Bible's loose women line up. This woman does not represent the women but the spirit that is the influence behind the lewd lifestyle.

4. *ABOMINATIONS OF THE EARTH* - Everything in the earth realm that God detests, this entity represents. An abomination is something that outrages God. Unlike sin, and many other human action that sadden God abominations anger Him.

THE MARK OF THE *B*EAST

The *mark* of the *B*east is by far the most difficult variant of the *B*east with which we deal. This is a difficult variant because we have so much tradition and so little understanding of the *B*easts. Believers, adhere to the common inaccuracy of a 666 cattle-brand or Microchip as the *mark* of the *B*east. Look to Revelations 19:20 and see that this is clearly not the case. **"And the beast was taken, and with him the false prophet that wrought miracles before him, with which he**

deceived them that had received the *mark* of the beast, and them that worshipped his image. These both were cast alive into a lake of fire burning with brimstone." The confusion undoubtedly arises from the story of Cain and Able in Genesis 4:15 wherein God *mark*s Cain. "**And the Lord said unto him, 'THEREFORE WHOSOEVER SLAYETH CAIN, VENGEANCE SHALL BE TAKEN ON HIM SEVENFOLD'. And the Lord set a *mark* upon Cain, lest any finding him should kill him**." Come, let us reason together, and read with understanding. There was only Cain, Able, Adam, and Eve near the garden. Who else would have known about Cain's deeds? The *mark* on Cain was not punishment it was an identifier. If God wanted to punish Cain, does it not make more sense to either kill him or let someone in Nod slay Cain? Moreover, why was there punishment set aside for whoever slew Cain? To understand the punishment, you must remember that Cain murdered Able out of jealousy. Jealousy existed between Cain and Able because God rejected Cain's mediocre sacrifice and accepted Abel's first fruit. Cain's sin was covetousness like his father Satan; violence blossomed in Cain only after evil blossomed. Therefore, the *mark* of Cain is not a blemish or brand, but the product of Cain's deed. Cain after all is the first murderer on this planet. Cain introduced murder to humanity. Therefore, the one that murders a murderer is more wicked that the first. Cain was the first murderer but the subsequent murders are evidence of Satan's influence.

God has an inhuman way of looking at humanity. God sees the hearts of men. God is more interested in the motive than a deed. When a man murders, God sees what was in his heart that caused the man to murder. All God needs to see is that what is in the murderer's heart is not of God. Although Cain committed the first murder, God waived judgment. After God set forth the law, anyone that murdered, God judged as a murderer.

I find it noteworthy at this point to bring to your attention that at no time does Genesis 4:11-15 specify the type of tattooing, brand, blemish, or discoloration on Cain. Preachers and theologians sold the concept of Microchips and all other forms of fables. Genesis 4:11-15 certainly does not indicate any type of technology.

THE MARK ON THE RIGHT HAND

Why is the mark of the beast placed in the right hand of those that follow the ℬeast? Psalms 109:5-6 - "**And they have rewarded me evil for good, and hatred for my love. Set thou a wicked man over him: and let Satan stand at his right hand.**" The purpose of using the right hand is that the right hand represents authority, will, might, or *choice* of the person. The wedding band rides on the left hand in conventional marriages and the right in homosexual marriages. The mark on the right hand represents the same thing Nimrod's tower, the pyramids, and the sphinx represent--rebellion against God.

In terms of power, the word seat means *post of authority*. The throne room has two seats, the throne and the lesser seat on the right. The seat on the right is only lesser because God sits on the throne.

1. Exodus 15:6 - "**Thy right hand, O Lord, is become glorious in power: thy right hand, O Lord, hath dashed in pieces the enemy.**"

2. Psalms 17:17 - "**Shew thy marvellous loving kindness, O thou that savest by thy right hand them which put their trust [in thee] from those that rise up [against them].**"

3. Ecclesiastes 10:2 - "**A wise man's heart [is] at his right hand; but a fool's heart at his left.**"

4. Matthew 26:64/Mark 14:62 - "**Jesus saith unto him, 'THOU HAST SAID: NEVERTHELESS I SAY UNTO YOU, HEREAFTER SHALL YE SEE THE SON OF MAN SITTING ON THE RIGHT HAND OF POWER, AND COMING IN THE CLOUDS OF HEAVEN'.**"

5. Matthew 27:29 - "**And when they had platted a crown of thorns, they put [it] upon His head, and a reed in His right hand: and they bowed the knee before Him, and mocked Kim, saying, 'Hail, King of the Jews'.**"

6. Mark 10:40 - "**BUT TO SIT ON MY RIGHT HAND AND ON MY LEFT HAND IS NOT MINE TO GIVE; BUT [IT SHALL BE GIVEN TO THEM] FOR WHOM IT IS PREPARED.**"

7. Mark 16:19 - "**So then after the Lord had spoken unto them, He was received up into heaven, and sat on the right hand of God.**"

8. Acts 7:55-6 - "**But he, being full of the Holy Ghost, looked up steadfastly into heaven, and saw the glory of God, and Jesus standing on the right hand of God, And said, Behold, I see the heavens opened, and the Son of man standing on the right hand of God.**"

Psalms 48:10 tells us the right hand is full of righteousness. Jesus sits at the right hand because He is full of righteousness. Satan never sat at the right hand; he sat in the seat of God. Lucifer sat in the seat because God only allowed him to keep the seat warm and do God's bidding. Like Potiphar, Lucifer was merely steward. Jesus is the prince, heir to the throne, a marker of the righteousness of God in men.

A person who receives the mark of the beast acknowledges disdain for God and in the words of Isaiah the show of their countenance shows against them, "**The shew of their countenance doth witness against them; and they declare their sin as Sodom, they hide [it] not. Woe unto their soul! For they have rewarded evil unto themselves. Say ye to the righteous, that [it shall be] well [with him]: for they shall eat the fruit of their doings** - Isaiah 3:9-10."

The penalty for *receiving the mark in their right hand or their forehead*[77] is because this allegiance with God's enemy is unholy and in God's mind the bearer of the mark hates Him. To worship another god, and bear his mark, (a right reserved for ownership) is to align with that spirit chief against God. It is better to die for righteousness sake that to stand before the throne bearing the mark of another God. GOD MAKES NO ROOM IN HEAVEN FOR THE CHILDREN OF ANY OTHER GOD.

---

[77] The receptacle for the imagination

There is only one reason the Bible gives the number of the 𝓑east. It is to indicate to us that the 𝓑east is human. *Therefore, the mark of this human must be a human characteristic.* There is a book in the New Testament that not only mentions the 𝓑east but also gives clear concise indicia of the *mark*s (characteristics) of the 𝓑east. The tri-numeric 666 links the 𝓑east to humanity. Conversely, the tri-numeric 666 also links humanity to the 𝓑east. Starting with Romans 1:21, we look together to see what *mark*s God has given to use to discern the children of the 𝓑east.

"Because, knowing God, they didn't glorify him as God, neither gave thanks, but became vain in their reasoning, and their senseless heart was darkened. Professing themselves to be wise, they became fools, and traded the glory of the incorruptible God for the likeness of an image of corruptible man, and of birds, and four-footed animals, and creeping things. Therefore, God also gave them up in the lusts of their hearts to uncleanness, that their bodies should be dishonored among themselves, who exchanged the truth of God for a lie, and worshiped and served the creature rather than the Creator, who is blessed forever. Amen. For this reason, God gave them up to vile passions. For their women changed the natural function into that which is against nature. Likewise also, the men, leaving the natural function of the woman, burned in their lust toward one another, men doing what is inappropriate with men, and receiving in themselves the due penalty of their error. Even as they refused to have God in their knowledge, God gave them up to a reprobate mind, to do those things which are not fitting; being filled with all unrighteousness, sexual immorality, wickedness, covetousness, malice; full of envy, murder, strife, deceit, evil habits, secret slanderers, backbiters, hateful to God, insolent, haughty, boastful, inventors of evil things, disobedient to parents, without understanding, covenant breakers, without natural affection, unforgiving, unmerciful; who, knowing the ordinance of God, that those

who practice such things are worthy of death, not only do the same, but also approve of those who practice them."

I enumerate the traits for you so that you may see that the component parts comprise only one *mark* of the 𝓑east. The components are therefore traits or indicators of the spirit of the 𝓑east manifest in people. I point this out to show you that the listed traits the behavior indicates the influence of the 𝓑east --not possession by the 𝓑east.

Ba) Full with all unrighteousness.
Bb) Full of sexual immorality[78].
Bc) Full of wickedness.
Bd) Full of Covetousness.
Be) Full of malice.
Bf) Full of envy.
Bg) Full of murder.
Bh) Full of strife.
Bi) Full of deceit.
Bj) Full of evil habits.
Bk) Secret slanderers.
Bl) Backbiters.
Bm) Hateful to God.
Bn) Insolent.
Bo) Haughty.
Bp) Boastful.
Bq) Inventors of evil things.
Br) Disobedient to parents.
Bs) Without understanding.
Bt) Covenant breakers.
Bu) Without natural affection.
Bv) Unforgiving.
Bw) Unmerciful.

Let us look now at the evidence of this 𝓑eastly nature found in the Book of Genesis. I will indicate via the '**B**' trait found in the above

---

[78] N.B. These people are full of these traits. They do not simply exhibit them. For example, one instance of sexual immorality does not qualify. The people Paul warns about constantly engage in sexual immorality.

list. For example, if the people are unmerciful I will place '**Bw**' beside the scripture. Genesis 18:20-26 - "**The Lord said, 'BECAUSE THE CRY OF SODOM AND GOMORRAH IS GREAT, AND BECAUSE THEIR SIN IS VERY GRIEVOUS**{Ba}, **I WILL GO DOWN NOW, AND SEE WHETHER THEIR DEEDS ARE AS BAD AS THE REPORTS WHICH HAVE COME TO ME. IF NOT, I WILL KNOW** {Bq}'. **The men turned from there, and went toward Sodom, but Abraham stood yet before the Lord. Abraham drew near, and said, 'Will You consume the righteous with the wicked** {Bt}. **What if there are fifty righteous within the city? Will You consume and not spare the place for the fifty righteous who are in it? Be it far from You to do things like that, to kill the righteous with the wicked, so that the righteous should be like the wicked. May that be far from You. Shouldn't the Judge of all the earth do right?' The Lord said, 'IF I FIND IN SODOM FIFTY RIGHTEOUS WITHIN THE CITY, THEN I WILL SPARE ALL THE PLACE FOR THEIR SAKE'**."

Let us look further at the evidence of this 𝓑eastly nature found in the Book of Genesis. Genesis 19:19:1-17 - "**The two angels came to Sodom at evening. Lot sat in the gate of Sodom. Lot saw them, and rose up to meet them. He bowed himself with his face to the earth, And he said, 'See now, my lords, please turn aside into your servant's house, stay all night, wash your feet, and you can rise up early, and go on your way'. They said, 'No, but we will stay in the street all night'. He urged them greatly, and they came in with him, and entered into his house. He made them a feast, and baked unleavened bread, and they ate. But before they lay down, the men of the city, the men of Sodom, surrounded the house, both young and old, all the people from every quarter** {Bb}. **They called to Lot, and said to him, 'Where are the men who came in to you this night? Bring them out to us, that we may that we may know them** {Bb}. **Lot went out to them to the door, and shut the door after him. He said, 'Please, my brothers, don't act so wickedly** {Bu}. **Behold now, I have two daughters which have not known man; let me, I pray you, bring them out unto you, and do ye to them as [is] good in your eyes: only unto these men do** nothing; for therefore came they under the shadow of my roof {Bn}. **And they said, Stand back. And they said [again], this one [fellow] came in to sojourn, and he will needs be a judge: now will we deal worse with thee, than with them. And they pressed sore upon the man, [even] Lot, and came near to break the door** {Bp}. **But the men put forth their hand, and brought Lot into the house to them, and shut the** door {Be}. **And they smote the men that [were] at the door of the house with blindness, both small and great: so that they wearied themselves to find the door. And the men said unto Lot, Hast thou here any besides? son in law, and thy sons, and thy daughters, and whatsoever thou hast in the city, bring [them] out of this place: For we will destroy this place, because the cry of them is waxen great before the face of the Lord; and the Lord hath sent us to destroy it** {Bm}. **Lot went out, and spoke to his sons-in-law, who were pledged to marry his daughters, and said, 'Get up! Get out of this place, for the Lord will destroy the city'. But he seemed to his sons-in-law to be joking. When the morning came, then the angels hurried Lot, saying, 'Get up! Take your wife, and your two daughters who are here, lest you be consumed in the iniquity of the city** {Ba}'.

We see in the last portion of Lot's story to show that unrighteousness can exist in those we love, but only at a lower level. What happens to pre-existing evil in our hearts is like any other fertilized seed it GROWS.

SATAN'S ARC

The purpose of all the above information is to remind you that the 𝓑east has no power over you. Here we see in Genesis 19:30-38 the actual power the 𝓑east has in our lives. Although God found Lot to be righteous, there was a lingering desire for the old ways in Lot's wife (1) and evidently in his daughter's (2).

1. Genesis 19:19:26 - "**But his wife looked back from behind him, and she became a pillar of salt** {Babcfijs}."

2. Genesis 19:19:30-38 - "**Lot went up out of Zoar, and lived in the mountain and his two daughters with him; for he was afraid to live in Zoar. He lived in a cave with his two daughters. And the firstborn said unto the younger, 'Our father [is] old, and [there is] not a man in the earth to come in unto us after the manner of all the earth** {Bbijqrsu}. **Come, let's make our father drink wine, and we will lie with him, that we may preserve our father's seed** {Bbijqrsu}'. **They made their father drink wine that night: and the firstborn went in, and lay with her father. He did not know when she lay down, or when she arose** {Bbijqrsu}. **It came to pass on the next day, that the firstborn said to the younger, 'Behold, I lay last night with my father. Let us make him drink wine again, tonight. You go in, and lie with him, that we may preserve our father's seed** {Bbijqrsu}'. **They made their father drink wine that night also. The younger went and lay with him. He didn't know when she lay down, nor when she got up** {Bbijqrsu}. **Thus both of Lot's daughters were with child by their father** {Bm}."

Just like he always does Satan tries to mimic God's tools. Noah had an arc, which carried the Godly seed away from destruction and allowed it to continue. In the same manner, Satan used Lot's daughters to carry the same perverse seed that made Sodom and Gomorrah wax great in the site of God. Lot's wife longed for the lifestyle that displeased God, He turned her into a pillar of salt. Like the composition of earth, the human body is mostly water. When God removed His water from lot's wife all that remained was dust (salt). WE NEED GOD TO LIVE. The same daughters, virgin daughters that seemed so innocent and were almost victim's of the perverse men—fooled everybody. Lot's daughters were as perverted as the men their father offered them to. As far as them only wanting to carry their father's seed they could not have referred to Lot, because there were many men in the city of Zoar that could have come to them. The father seed they referred to was a seed that would continue the bloodline from Sodom and Gomorrah, the seed they want to carry was the seed of their father Satan. Not in the literal sense but in the sense of perpetuating the lifestyle that made Sodom and Gomorrah debase.

DEVILUTION PHASE ONE

Devilution phase one exists in verses Romans 1:18-25. In phase one; unrighteousness becomes prevalent, waxes great before the Lord and God gives them up to uncleanness. Verses 24 and 25 are extremely intricate. In Romans 1:24 God gave people up to do what was in their hearts. In the Lord's Prayer, Jesus requests that the Father deliver Him from Evil. Jesus' prayer spoke of this evil.

Let us pretend the human heart is an ant farm. In Fig. 5 we see an illustration of the devilution process as it continues and begins to manifest physically. Because we are using illustrations, I will not use sexual immorality to explain the devilution.

(FIG. 5)

In Fig. 5 your child sees an Ant farm and immediately decides that he has to have it. Because you refused to buy the Ant farm for your child they became unruly, disgruntle, and completely disgusting. Their behavior becomes so bad that you simply stopped preventing their getting the ant farm.

Using whatever means the child finds necessary, they acquire the treasured Ant farm. You and your child are already out of fellowship, and you see things in your child you never thought possible. Although you are disgusted with your child, you still set rules and require the ants stay in their container because they are fire ants. Your child like any other child does not care about the consequences. The child wants what they want and will do ANYTHING to get what they want. Despite the fact that what we desire is harmful to ourselves and to our relationship with God, we will not stop until we have the Ant farm.

Romans 1:25 point out where the child is really in trouble. Raging against God's mercy is dangerous but not as deadly as being outside of His grace. In verse 25 the Creator and the Protector of the worlds removes His protection from us. Like Job and the hedge no matter how wretched our hearts are God still keeps us separated from the true nakedness spoken of by Adam. Fig. 5a illustrates the phase spoken of by Paul in verse 25.

(FIG 5a)

Notice in the figure most of the retaining walls are missing. Now the unclean things of this world have complete unfettered access to us. There no longer remains any protection from God, nor are there any self-restraints. Circumcision (self-restraint) only exists because we have a relationship with our parents. Once we destroy that relationship there are no boundaries, and no safe zones. Now we can wholly desire our new toy and give 100% attention and energy sin.

Creature worship lowers the child to another type of behavior. Our body, which once tried to serve God, now serves itself. With no rules and the fear of punishment gone there is no reason not to commit to this course or for the action to end. This irreverence develops a new condition in our lives.

DEVILUTION PHASE TWO

Romans 1:25-32 explains Devilution phase II. In Devilution phase II, the ability to reason and to see the truth no longer functions. The child *chooses* to invert their imagination and exchange it for a fruit that is pleasing to the eyes. Since decency no longer abides with the child, or does common sense, the child creates all manner of vile activities.

(FIG 5b)

Fig.5b depicts what happens when sin totally consumes our lives. Here you find your child living like the Ants in order to survive, surrounded by the dirt that the ants inhabit. Like the prodigal son found out, the longer you live like a pig the more you become a swine. Eventually, you even learn to eat and sleep like a swine to survive in their new life.

In Romans 1:27, we now get a visible accounting of what occurred in the heart of the child. Much like the example in Fig.5b we now see just how far the child is willing to go to seek pleasure. Notice, I did not say happiness: there is no happiness cut off from God. There is pleasure in sin, like there is euphoria in drug use. However, I DEFY you to find a happy drug user. Many lie and say they are happy, but I say to you check their personal lives, financial status, arrest history, and mental stability.

What we have come to accept as flakey, is actually dysfunctional behavior, and sin manifesting in the life of the lost.

An example of sin manifesting in the life of the lost appears in Romans 1:26. We teach that Romans 1:26 is the beginning of homosexuality and that is true, but only part of the problem. Yes, there is a beginning to homosexuality as there is with all sin. There is no such thing as gay at birth. By sheer definition, homosexual behavior involves sex; sex with a person of the same sex. It is impossible to be a homosexual, and not be sexually active. Devoid of secondary sexual characteristics[79], there is no natural sexual activity in the human kingdom. The human creature is not truly sexual until it has the ability to reproduce.

Sex in humans serves a variety of purposes. Some of the sexual purposes are good while others are bad. God however, only ordained a few purposes for sex, marital sex. The simple fact is God ordained sex for four purposes in humanity. The scriptures indicate that God ordained sex for the purposes of:

1. Enjoying the marital state, this includes sexual satisfaction, companionship, and nullifying adultery - Ecclesiastes 9:9.
2. Reproduction - Genesis 1:28.
3. A pleasurable incentive for reproduction - Genesis 3:16.
4. A bond developing relationship between a man and a woman - Genesis 2:24.

The design of the human stomach enables digestion. You may consume dirt if you like but it will not change the stomach's design. No matter how Beastly humans behave, their human design remains unchanged. Sex is the same. Molestation, incest, pornography, and rape of children may look sexual but it is not. There is nothing natural about a sexual desire for children, a desire to rape, a desire to molest, or a desire to harm. Even in the animal kingdom, sex is ALWAYS consensual. Sex is purely for procreation in the animal kingdom it therefore has to be consensual. In the animal kingdom, the menstrual cycle is the basis of consent for the female. If there is no egg for fertilization, there is no reason for sex.

The normal state for female animals is to desire sex when they are able to produce children. The unhealthy sex drive in mankind like all the

---

[79] A phase commonly called puberty, this is the phase in which we become fertile.

other sin came from the father of sin and evil. Fallen angels brought sexual perversion to the earth. 2 Peter 2:4 and Genesis 6:1-2 shed light on the origin of deviant sexual behavior in humans. The other part of *unnatural use* involves things like sado-masochism, bestiality, bondage, torture, and humiliation.

As devilution continues, more of Satan's traits emerge. God finally removes all remnants of Himself from the person. This is not to say that God cuts them off completely it is because they no longer wish to come home. No matter what your child becomes, you are still a parent. You are expected to stay normal regardless of how *B*east like your child becomes--and do not go out after them they must come to their senses. People shrink when they think of God cutting off people. It is because they do not understand God. When I took survival swimming, they taught that if the person you are attempting to save is too violent or resists, you pull them under the water. Once they have calmed down or passed out, you continue the rescue. If they continue to drag you under because of their behavior, then you simply let go. This is not inhumane; this is life, God is not inhumane God is Life.

Once God closes the door to your spirit, He no longer draws your spirit[80] to Him. Believers, this is when you are dead to Him[81]. Does this mean that homosexuals are going to hell? Of course they are, but they will have a lot of company. This is clearly written in the Bible in I Corinthians 6:9, **"Know ye not that the unrighteous shall not inherit the kingdom of God? <u>Be not deceived</u>."**

1. **Fornicators** shall not inherit the kingdom of God.
2. **Idolaters** shall not inherit the kingdom of God.
3. **Adulterers** shall not inherit the kingdom of God.
4. **Homosexuals** shall not inherit the kingdom of God.
5. **Abusers** of themselves with mankind shall not inherit the kingdom of God.
6. **Thieves** shall not inherit the kingdom of God.
7. **Covetous** shall not inherit the kingdom of God.
8. **Drunkards** shall not inherit the kingdom of God.
9. **Revilers** shall not inherit the kingdom of God.
10. **Extortioners** shall not inherit the kingdom of God.

---

[80] John 6:44.
[81] Luke 15:24.

11. **Enviers** shall not inherit the kingdom of God.
12. **Murderers** shall not inherit the kingdom of God.

All the people on the list of 𝓑eastly behavior are the same. The act of homosexuality does not define the person. On the contrary, the wretched, Godless, God hating heart creates homosexuality. This is what differentiates homosexuals from fornicators. **According to the Bible fornicators hate themselves and *homosexuals hate God.*** This difference causes the response from God that resulted in Sodom and Gomorrah's destruction. God does not tolerate those that hate Him, no matter what they do, or how they manifest their hatred.

According to human science, there are seven criteria for life:
1. Living things are made of cells.
2. Living things obtain and use energy.
3. Living things grow and develop.
4. Living things reproduce themselves.
5. Living things respond to their environment.
6. Living things adapt to their environment.
7. Living things maintain a chemical composition that is quite different from their surroundings.

Based on this list, we see that 𝓑eastly creatures do not qualify as living, by science or by Godly definition. Of the catalogued sexual perversions, NONE of the practitioners can reproduce their sexual perversions at birth. Black babies are black at birth and chickens are chickens at birth. What are homosexuals, rapists, or child molesters at birth--nothing there has never been a child born engaging in sexual activity? No human has ever come forth from the womb sexually active. According to studies, even the majority of hermaphrodites *choose* only one sexual orientation. However, hermaphrodites do not reproduce hermaphrodites.

THE MULE PARADOX

No naturally occurring species is born with the inability to reproduce. Mules are hybrids bred for farming. A by-product of the mutation is that all mules are male. If humans stop the cross breeding donkeys and horses, the Mule species will cease to exist. Albinism is similar. A Bengal Tiger is orange and black. If one of the litter is Albino, it is considered rare; but the albino tiger is also an anomaly.

Homosexuality, which is by no means rare, is of the same candor as the mule paradox. Homosexuals can neither reproduce nor maintain their species; a consequence of a lifestyle that is not natural. For this reason, recruitment and secretive bi-sexuality is important. Homosexuals must increase their flock the same way drug dealers do. For this reason both groups offer a product that appeals to a certain population of people inclined in that direction. In other words, if you are not inclined to use drugs there is no temptation for you. However, if you are already hypersexual, experimental, (like the people in Sodom and Gomorrah, and Romans chapter one) or an extremely curious person, homosexuals only have to get your inhibitions low enough to get you to 'experiment'.

When pre-pubescent children become sexually active, it is for one of two reasons;
1. They saw some else do it.
2. They were victims of molestation.

Pre-pubescent children have no sex drive they are only acting out. Sex drive is not arousal. Arousal chemicals make the genitals function so there can be sexual activity.

Believers, God tells us He is both jealous and wrathful, why must we anger Him. It is not that God hates sex--God hates SIN. God conditionally allows all the sex we desire. Paul says sex should occur virtually unceasingly--as long as it is with your wife. Remember, God said we would have Life, which requires one set of chemicals and the sex drive another. The *sex drive* (Commonly referred to as *horny*) is nature's way of keeping the human race alive. It is like the body producing insulin and making you feel hungry. *Arousal* on the other hand, affects the organs and pleasure centers differently.

Therefore, the same--sex marriage concept cannot reconcile itself with God's plan set forth in the book of Genesis 1:12. In this principle, the seeds God ordains reproduce seeds of like kind. This is why we call the process reproduction and not production. Sin produces homosexuals; conversely, copulation reproduces humans.

PROFESSING THEMSELVES TO BE WISE

There is a fundamentally irreconcilable flaw in the homosexual credo-I was born this way. Heterosexual children develop secondary sexual characteristics without coaching, assistance, or tools. If lesbianism and homosexuality were natural then why do the practitioners of the lifestyles mimic heterosexual behavior? Why dos there need to be a feminine male and a masculine female? Why do both sides use sex toys to mimic heterosexual intercourse? In addition, most compelling of them all WHY WOULD A LESBIAN WANT TO HAVE A CHILD? If you were born to be lesbian as normal people were born to be heterosexual, you should have no normal desires. God would not give creature the desire to reproduce if it did not have the ability. A lesbian should have no desire to do anything normal females do, which includes maternity. Why do I say this? Because maternity naturally requires input form a male. A species that was born to be the antithesis of heterosexuality (God's will) would not need contributions, in any form to reproduce.

The subtlety of the same sex marriage has nothing to do with sex. The object of Satan's war is to elevate his kingdom, or at least stalemate God's kingdom. The sin of adultery prohibits that lifestyle's acceptance by God, but what if man made a law and adultery was legal? What would happen if fornication and adultery became *marriage?* If this legalization occurred then I Corinthians 6:9 would no longer apply to homosexuals. Here we see the latest attempt by Satan to regain a foothold in the earth. Another tower of Babel draws neigh and when completed man will not be restricted by God. If we can change the laws against this sinful behavior, then where do we stop...will murder eventually become legal?

The summation therefore is clear. The clearest evidence of the *mark* of the Beast comes from Genesis the 6th, 18, & 19 chapters. In these chapters, the Bible describes a lifestyle of sexual immorality. The issue is not the sex it is what desires the sex: the heart condition. In both cases, God was not attempting to destroy sex or sexuality but the wicked wretched hearts that *choose* to worship something other than God[82].

In the Story of Lot, we find a vivid example of the traits of the Beast. In this story, we missed something vitally important in our dealing with homosexuality. Homosexuality was not and is not a curse; it

---

[82] Genesis 18:20.

is an indication of how far you are from God. Homosexuality is a physical measure of unrighteousness. Remember the scriptures say that the sin in Sodom waxed great before God. God did not specify that the sin He referred to was fornication. God did not destroy the city because of fornication or sexual immorality but because of the grievous level, and variety of sin in the city[83]. We do not see what the scriptures point out clearly in regards to sexual immorality. In order to understand we must look again to Romans and then to I Corinthians 6:18-20. Beginning at Romans 1:18, we see that Paul only deals with two actual phases of devilution[84].

THE SCARLET BEAST - (Revelations 17:1-8)

"And there came one of the seven angels which had the seven vials, and talked with me, saying unto me, 'Come hither; I will shew unto thee the judgment of the great whore that sitteth upon many waters: With whom the kings of the earth have committed fornication, and the inhabitants of the earth have been made drunk with the wine of her fornication'. So he carried me away in the spirit into the wilderness: and I saw a woman sit upon a scarlet colored beast, full of names of blasphemy, having seven heads and ten horns. And the woman was arrayed in purple and scarlet color, and decked with gold and precious stones and pearls, having a golden cup in her hand full of abominations and filthiness of her fornication: And upon her forehead [was] a name written, MYSTERY, BABYLON THE GREAT, THE MOTHER OF HARLOTS AND ABOMINATIONS OF THE EARTH. And I saw the woman drunken with the blood of the saints, and with the blood of the martyrs of Jesus: and when I saw her, I wondered with great admiration. And the angel said unto me, Wherefore didst thou marvel? I will tell thee the mystery of the woman, and of the beast that carrieth her, which hath the seven heads and ten horns. The beast that thou sawest was, and is not; and shall ascend out of the bottomless pit, and go into perdition: and they that

---

[83] Genesis 18:20.
[84] Evolving devilish characteristics.

dwell on the earth shall wonder, whose names were not written in the book of life from the foundation of the world, when they behold the beast that was, and is not, and yet is..."

In the interest of thoroughness, we discuss the third beast mentioned in Revelations. This *Beast* is less famous, but more easily explained. The Scarlet *Beast* is simply a man given a great deal of power by the rulers of the largest regimes. The references to heads and mountains narrows down the possibilities for the lineage of Scarlet *Beast*. This also explains why the beast is scarlet and why the woman (church) rides away with him. The color scarlet is synonyms with wealth, as it was in the virtuous woman. This woman gets carried away with the wealth of this *Beast* and is swept away by him away into the wilderness. This metaphor represents the church falling in love with the world and following the world out into a place separated from God.

Is God a man that He should lie? He told us the He punished those that hate Him. That rule has not changed. The manner in which God achieves a goal may vary, but the principle is everlasting. The *mark* of the *Beast* is therefore not a literal *mark* but a life style; a life style filled with immorality, and hating God. When we look to the scriptures to see which lifestyle most readily encompasses these traits we see the answer plainly.

The *mark* referred to on the forehead and the hands is not literal, but refers to the thoughts and deeds of the lifestyle. The *Beast* requires trading and business only be conducted between homosexuals. Like Lot in Sodom, if you are not of the lifestyle they exclude you and punish you as an outsider[85]. The *Beast* requires that he feed you what he wants you to eat. What the *Beast* wants you to eat is the same thing he feeds on-- death. The summation of the information is;

---

[85] Revelations 13:17.

1. The number of the *B*east 666 is also the number of a man. We explained clearly that this is to reassure us that the *B*east is a human being just like you and I.

2. The name of the *B*east will always be *Death,* not the name in the literal sense, but this is who the *B*east is. Since we deduced that spiritual names are properties it is the property death that best describes the *B*east.

3. The *mark* of the *B*east is a perverse, God hating lifestyle best exemplified by sexual perversion and homosexuality. This mark, sign, feature, indication, symbol, or indicator of the *B*east is the evidence of his effect.

Many contend they were born to be homosexual. Many babies are born crack babies, mentally retarded, or missing limbs, does this mean that it is correct or the intended way? In the same manner, there can be no species of human deficient of the tools to comply with God's command to be fruitful and multiply that occur naturally. In order to be natural you must have all the tools required to function within Godly parameters. Even the retard can perform most of the things needed to stay within the design. We call them retarded from the French, which simply means late. No matter how late the person is they can still comply with God, the *choice* not to comply with God is what makes homosexuality an alternative life style, not the sex. The *choice* to worship the creature rather than the Creator is what keeps God at odds with those that hat Him.

Despite rhetoric that people are homophobic, to stand and say that the lifestyle is wrong is what Christians are required to do. We have laws that say a person of more than three years age difference commits rape, whether the child victim gave consent or not. In this relationship, we say that the child cannot make an informed choice to have sex—yet we allow these children to join the military, drive cars, and apply for their emancipation from parents. If *choice* is the operative component, and it must be by their own definition—alternative lifestyle, then why still prosecute statutory rape? If this lifestyle was forced upon you like most people say, then what makes the homosexual different from the retarded person? Do we not monitor and care for the retarded person whose aberration was thrust upon them, and do we not tested them to make sure they do not reproduce retarded children. If this is the case then why are homosexuals treated any differently than the others people with abnormalities?

    I love all people, but I have rules that forbid my accepting every type of behavior. The homosexual lifestyle and the Christian lifestyle cannot reconcile because GOD DOES NOT TOLERATE PEOPLE THE HATE HIM. Can a Christian be a homosexual or vice versa? Absolutely just as my child could grow up to be a rapist, but it is neither acceptable nor desirable to God.

WHAT ABOUT PORNOGRAPHY

    Let us first agree that although Jesus did not articulate concerns with pornography He covered it in many ways. Lust is the easiest manner to define pornography, but there is also adultery and idolatry. 99.91% of people that undertake pornography use it to satisfy a need, this is what makes it sinful and dangerous. It is not the act of sex that is sinful, or watching sex, it is watching someone else have sex that God disdains. If you and you wife make home movies it still only involves you two, and is covered under the undefiled bed. If you are watching pornography, what possible purpose could it serve other than extra-marital sexual desire? You do not need to purchase the Kama Sutra to find new positions, just keep living. People are curious and experimental because they have been exposed to things they were not normally exposed to.

For thousands of years married couples enjoyed sex without porn. What made Playboy and Hustler so appealing was the brought to the public the dark secrets hiding in many homes. As we discussed what made the men in Sodom go after the two angles is that God hating must spread by merchandising and trafficking (recruitment) as it did in heaven. The reason homosexuals pushed porn is to recruit and bring Satan's Arc to rest in new territory. Once exposed to the spirit of whoredoms the person under their influence travels the darkness trying to regain righteousness, and it can be a long arduous journey. Many of the damaged people in the world were damaged to plant a seed. Satan tilled their soil grow his crops. To you I say deliverance I still available but you have to *choose* to accept it.

Amen

Part VII

The Devil Made Me Do It!

"And the devil, taking Him up into an high mountain, shewed unto Him all the kingdoms of the world in a moment of time. And the devil said unto Him, All this power will I give thee, and the glory of them: for that is delivered unto me; and to whomsoever I will I give it. If thou therefore wilt worship me, all shall be thine - Luke 4:5-7."

Chapter Twelve
Living Under Spiritual Influences

"**And the devil, taking Him up into an high mountain, shewed unto Him all the kingdoms of the world in a moment of time. And the devil said unto Him, All this power will I give thee, and the glory of them: for that is delivered unto me; and to whomsoever I will I give it. If thou therefore wilt worship me, all shall be thine** - Luke 4:5-7."

This chapter is not exclusively about demon possession because not only demons *possess* humans. For the purpose of this book, we use the accepted terms *possession* to mean demonic in nature, and *indwelling* to mean heavenly in nature. The concepts of spiritual possession and spiritual influence change between the Old and the New Testaments. The spirits do not change the difference between the Old and the New Testaments is CHRIST. Since Christ crushed Satan's kingdom, demons lost the power Satan spoke of in Luke 4:5.

SPIRITUAL INFLUENCE - INDWELLING

Like many spiritual aspects of the Christian faith walk, the difference between heaven and hell is a thin, almost imperceptible line. God's people do not cross the line because of satanic power; they cross the line because what they desire is on the other side (*choice*). People do not backside or apostatize because of pain, they *choose* to leave the faith because of anger, fear, laziness, and disappointment. Even those that blame God for their misfortune do not leave because of pain; they give in to desire.

To accomplish His will God uses the same type of methods we associate with Satan. It is not that Satan used these methods first; Satan learned the methods while he served in heaven. God used spiritual influences numerous times in the Old Testament. When God or the *Spirit of the Lord* moved in the Old Testament, this was a spiritual influence.

SPIRITUAL INFLUENCE - DEMON POSSESSION

What exactly is demon possession? This is an intricate question, but there is an answer. Demon possession means something in the Old Testament and a different thing in the New Testament. Thanks to Jesus, Satan does not have the same power as he wielded in the Old Testament. In the Old Testament Satan's power to influence humans was direct. In the New Testament, *possession* more accurately defined as *under the influence*. Strong's Hebrew Concordance defines demon possession thusly, 1139[86]--*daimonizomai {dahee-mon-id'-zom-ahee} - to be under the power of a demon*. Think of possession in terms of rental cars. No matter how long you rent or how many miles you drive, the car does not belong to you. Although you are in physical control of the vehicle, you do not own it. Even if the rental agency demands the car's return, and you refuse, you will never legally own the car. With demon possession, it is also this way, because of the Cross--demons can no longer legally own you.

Jesus settles the principle in Matthew chapter 12. What Jesus is clear on is the fact that the person under the demon is a willing participant. Jesus does not tell us why the spirit leaves the man. Jesus says the demon (unclean spirit) walks through the dry (waterless, devoid of Living water) places seeking rest. Many of us do not understand the dynamics of ownership and squatting, because we live in a system that uses credit to buy houses. In poorer or war torn countries, dwelling places often depend on strength, wealth, or violence. Consequently, we must ask what the demon seeks rest from? The answer again involves Jesus. Mark 5:7 says the following, "**And cried with a loud voice, and said, 'What have I to do with thee, Jesus, [thou] Son of the most high God? I adjure thee by God, that thou torment me not'**." The thing most feared by demons and that cause demons the most torment is the righteous Spirit of God flowing in the earth, ebbing from God's people. The reason demons wander about is not an assertion of power but an indication of the demon's powerlessness. *God evicts all demons.* What the demons are doing when they traverse dry places is seeking out another sin-filled temple in which to dwell[87].

---

[86] http://www.blueletterBible.org/tmp_dir/strongs/1152800410-5044.html.
[87] 1 Peter 5:8.

As always, the next portion of Jesus' explanation is an admonition against believers. When the demon cannot find a sinner nearby the demon returns to his old home. When the demon comes home, the demon finds the entire house under renovation[88]. When God's Holy Spirit comes, He cleans up all the garbage, and makes the place beautiful for Himself. The problem as Jesus astutely points out is that we are a wicked generation. We do not fill our hearts with the Lord; but with the wiles, treasures, and traits of the evil one.

The demon recognized immediately the work of the Temple Guardian[89]. The homeless demon seeing the new state of his former house, immediately goes and gets seven more wicked sprits, to dwell therein. This is a peculiar reaction for a homeless person, but not an evil spirit. If a normal person found a new, free, house they would move in and horde the discovery. Demons are not selfish they are *mission oriented*. Demons are not selfish; the demons' mission is self-centered. Demons have no problem sharing spiritual-houses; they all thrive on the same thing--death.

In the book <u>From a Fishing Trip in Patmos</u>, we discussed Hebrew number system. The Hebrew number system the number seven is the number of completion. The use of the number seven explains several things about our demonic roommates. One thing the use of the number seven explains is why the new state is worse than the last[90]. The new state becomes worse because evil completely fills the house leaving no empty room. Use of the number seven also explains that the state is worse because if you did not defend against one spirit you have even less chance against seven.

Do you really believe that Satan's forces fear Christians? Satan's forces only fear the Christ in the *Christian*. Discerning that the Temple Guardian's sweet fragrance filling the place the demon goes and gets help to wage the battle. The seven more wicked demons actually wage war against God's Holy Spirit and the war rages in your imagination. The seven new demons come to expose things more debase than before. Many say that the battle is for your mind but it is not. The Bible clears this up

---

[88] For details on the renovation read Exodus 25-31 how much time, effort, and care, God put into building the Tabernacle.
[89] 1 Peter 4:19.
[90] 2 Peter 2:20-22.

for us in two scriptures, Matthew 5:8, and Matthew 15:18 & 19. The mind (vain imaginations) is simply a creative segment for your sin. For example, if you have lust in your heart all the imagination does is create and devise various of ways to fulfill your lust. They may call the movie *1001 Erotic Nights*, but what the movie depicted first took place in somebody's wicked mind.

Here is the play-by-play activity that takes place in the battle for your heart.

1. The evil spirit living in the heart is seductive and subtle. God's Holy Spirit on the other hand, is a gentle, so He evicts the demon, without condemning the house.

2. God's Holy Spirit comes into the nasty sin filled heart, sweeps it, and restores it.

3. When the evil spirit returns; having been in Heaven, the demons immediately recognize the work of the Righteous One.

4. The evil spirit goes away, and gets seven more spirits, returning to the battlefield of your heart.

5. Unlike television, the two competing spirits do not war they court.

6. God's Holy Spirit comforts, and guides and the evil spirit tempts and pleases.

7. God's Holy Spirit recommends you *choose* righteousness; the evil spirit tempts and pleases.

8. The heart *choose*s.

9. If the person *choose*s sin, God's Holy Spirit sadly departs; leaving an open invitation to forgiveness. The evil spirit enhances the pleasurable opportunities of the sinful experience.

10. If the person *choose*s righteousness, God's Holy Spirit plants Himself in between the heart and the demons and protects the heart as long as it

wishes to stay behind His hedge. The evil spirit enhances temptation and tries to win the heart back with new pleasure for your flesh.

Often times the approaches of the two competing spirits look the same but the scriptures remind us NEVER say that God tempts us. The easiest way to understand this difference is that if you give in to God you do not sin. If, however, you give into the evil ones you sin. For example, God causes you to lose your job; you can get another job or simply sit at home feeling sorry in which case you have not sinned. On the other hand, you can steal, sell drugs, or sell your body in which case you have sinned.

Regardless of whether the original issue was lust, murder, strife, or envy, the returning spirit is now even more prevalent in your thoughts than ever before. The different ways that the evil spirits contrive to fulfill your lust now come in seven times more opportunities. Can you imagine 8008 Erotic Nights? The pleasurable experiences in life become more difficult to escape the more they please. This is why the new state becomes more difficult to escape than the last state.

SPIRITS OF ARBITRATION

It is complicated to explain God's use of spiritual influence without creating confusion. I therefore describe God's benevolent use of influence as arbitration. Definitions of arbitration are, *Intercession, mediation, negotiation, settlement.* These characteristics describe God's influence better than indwelling or possession. In the following instances, the method used by the Father is more familiar to us, as possession, but it is arbitration.

1. **THE SPIRIT OF THE *HOLY GODS*** - "**There is a man in thy kingdom, in whom [is] the spirit of the holy gods; and in the days of thy father light and understanding and wisdom, like the wisdom of the gods, was found in him; whom the king Nebuchadnezzar thy father, the king, [I say], thy father, made master of the magicians, astrologers, Chaldeans, [and] soothsayers** - Daniel 5:11." The spirit of the holy gods is what the Belshazzar's queen called God's Holy Spirit. The queen was not familiar with *The Way* enough to know God but she learned of Him through Daniel's prophecies. Through prophets

and miracles, the spirit of the holy gods--more accurately known as God's Holy Spirit influenced people in the Old Testament.

2. **THE LYING SPIRIT - "Now therefore, behold, The Lord hath put a lying spirit in the mouth of these** - 1 Kings 22:22, 1 Kings 22:23, 2 Chronicles 18:22." The word lie has at its core, the concept of untruthfulness, but we know that God does not lie. The Lying spirit is not actually God. God needed to intercede into the plans of a king. Rather than directly put His hand into the plan God asked an angel to go down and convince the king to change the plan. In order to change the king's mind indirectly, the spirit volunteered to be a *lying spirit.* The angel then proceeded to lie to the king through the king's prophets giving King Ahab information that caused him to change his plans. The lying spirit put in the mouth of the prophets, this God allowed to aid Jerusalem.

3. EVIL SPIRITS FROM GOD - **"And it came to pass on the morrow, that the evil spirit from God came upon Saul, and he prophesied in the midst of the house: and David played with his hand, as at other times: and [there was] a javelin in Saul's hand** -1 Samuel 18:10." Of those familiar with this scripture many misunderstand the concept. The term evil in this context is more like malevolent than evil. This spirit is not one of the fallen angels; it was evil in the sense that it tormented Saul. The influence of this spirit directed Saul to a place God could intervene. Because of the effect the evil spirit from God had on Saul, God had to appoint and new king; David was born.

   a. Exodus 12:23 - **"For the Lord will pass through to smite the Egyptians; and when he seeth the blood upon the lintel, and on the two side posts, the Lord will pass over the door, and will not suffer the destroyer to come in unto your houses to smite   [you]** ."

   b. Judges 9:23 - **"Then God sent an evil spirit between Abimelech and the men of Shechem; and the men of Shechem dealt treacherously with Abimelech."**

c. 1 kings 22:23 - "**Now therefore, behold, the Lord hath put a lying spirit in the mouth of all these thy prophets, and the Lord hath spoken evil concerning thee.**"

d. 1 Samuel 16:14 - "**But the Spirit of the Lord departed from Saul, and an evil spirit from the Lord troubled him.**"

In the above listed scriptures the phrase an evil spirit from the lord DOES NOT MEAN DEMON. An evil spirit from the Lord is just that. When the Lord has need of spirits to do His bidding, He simply orders them to the task. In some instances, these tasks are not pleasant and friendly. Many times the Lord deals with the loathsome human spirit, by cajoling, or tormenting a person. This word torment has not evil/demonic overtones. Torment is the act of making uncomfortable a creature you have authority over. God may not control the flesh, but He has open access to spirits. God would not openly force His will on the human creature, so He uses spiritual influence--He never gave man complete dominion over the spirit.

UNGODLY SPIRITUAL INFLUENCES

1. **THE FAMILIAR SPIRIT** - "**Then said Saul unto his servants, seek me a woman that hath a familiar spirit that I may go to her, and enquire of her. And his servants said to him, Behold, [there is] a woman that hath a familiar spirit at Endor** - 1 Samuel 28:7, 1 Chronicles 10:13." The familiar spirit is probably the most common spiritual influence we encounter. This entity like a mattress, by itself is not evil. Just as the marriage, bed is undefiled, and the bodies of dead young men line the way to the prostitute's bed. The familiar spirit, makes itself available to pleasure, this spirit unlike the others entices pleasurable pursuits rather that vile, self-destructive, and morose. The familiar spirit has an inviting disposition, much like the spirit of divination. Like Cleo, the *psychic* the familiar spirit is friendly and eager please. The familiar spirit is not eager to please you, but the dragon. No matter how friendly the familiar spirit, it serves the dragon. It is friendly to you so that they can steal your soul.

2. **THE SPIRIT OF WHOREDOMS** - "**My people ask counsel at their stocks, and their staff declareth unto them: for the spirit of whoredoms hath caused [them] to err, and they have gone a whoring from under their God** - Hosea 4:12." The spirit of whoredoms is a spirit of excess, sexual excess and immorality. Unlike lustful eyes that crave everything, the spirit of whoredoms is sexual in nature.

3. **THE SPIRIT OF AN UNCLEANLINESS** - "**And in the synagogue there was a man, which had a spirit of an unclean devil, and cried out with a loud voice,** - Luke 4:33, Luke 11:24, Mark 1:26, Mark 5:2, Mark 7:25." The unclean devil is another way of calling the spirit a demon. The word Devil seems to be of Eastern origin and pronounced *Devi*, which means spirit. The clarification here is the word unclean, which informs the reader that this spirit is not from God. Many times the name or clear intention of the spirit is not clear, but by its words or actions, one can determine whether it is clean or unclean.

4. **THE SPIRIT OF INFIRMITY** - "**And, behold, there was a woman which had a spirit of infirmity eighteen years, and was bowed together, and could in no wise lift up [herself]** - Luke 13:11." Sin and demons caused Infirmity and diseases. This woman could not heal because a demon possessed her. As long as the demon inhabited the woman not medicine would work. When Jesus healed the woman, He said she was free from her infirmity, free of the spirit. As proof that Jesus had the power to forgive sins, He *forgave* this woman and freed her from demonic bondage.

5. **THE SPIRIT OF DIVINATION** - "**And it came to pass, as we went to prayer, a certain damsel possessed with a spirit of divination met us, which brought her masters much gain by soothsaying** - Acts 16:16." The spirit of divination (I like to call it the Cleo spirit) is the spirit involved in fortune telling and tarot cards. People like Nostradamus, wizards, witches and fortunetellers tie into the spirit world via the spirit of Divination. What this spirit does is give the person tapping in access to the spiritual realm. Remember all spiritual laws God set in place. Whether or not the *sons of god* still live in heaven, they still are spirits. Just as God used the lying spirit in Kings Satan's unclean

spirits also speak to people. This relationship is how the Antichrist and the first *Beast* get their power.

6. **THE DUMB SPIRIT** – "**And one of the multitude answered and said, Master, I have brought unto thee my son, which hath a dumb spirit;** - Mark 9:17." The dumb spirit controls the speech center. Just like John the Baptists father could not speak until the Lord allowed him to speak, the dumb spirit prevents the possessed person's talking. The purpose of the dumb spirit is to create misery and despair in both the victim and the people trying to help the victim.

HOW SPIRITS GAIN ENTRANCE

According to Satan, men gave him ALL the earthly authority he possesses (Luke 4:6). This statement by the deceiver of humankind is the ultimate statement of demon possession. This statement sets all demon possession in place. The Dark Lord clearly states that all his power derives from HUMAN *CHOICE*, not from his own power. I pointed out that the Bible ***never*** calls Satan your ruler. Jesus calls Satan our father because of our actions, not because of his authority.

Choice is the unwitting focus of this book and now you see why. In Genesis what repented God was what human *chose*. You see all through the Bible bad *choices* displease God. We see in John 14:15 that God gauges *choice* to determine human love. The same ungodly *choice* gives Satan power over our lives.

In the adversarial game of chess, there are two pivotal moves: check and checkmate. When Christ was born, Satan was as they say in Chess '*in check*'. Jesus' death '*check-mated*' Satan. Jesus informs all interested parties that God gave Him ALL power (in heaven and in earth). All the power returned to God's throne via the house of David. The reinstitution of power means that ALL demon possession post--Christ is a result of human ***choice***.

This concept may shock you but it is the truth. There are many ways to leave your house untended, thus inviting demons. Demons can enter your house through the strong man, through weaker vessels, or through sinful vessels. This is why the Bible requires deacons and elders to rule their houses well.

I once had a friend tell me that God told him to pray for the doors in his house. He then went on to say that he walked the entire house praying for all the doors in the building. I asked him did he really think that God wanted him to pray for the closet and the bathroom doors? I asked him did he think it was more likely that God mean that he should pray for the people in his house. A door is a point of entry into a building. The people in our lives are the doors by which Satan and God enter. Many do not understand that is was the same principle Jesus spoke about when He said that no man goes to the Father but through Me. Jesus is the fleshly door that enabled the Spirit of the Lord into the house (Earth).

Believers, demons enter or respond to four states in our lives:

1. **The Sinful State** - drives a wedge between you and the Lord allowing space for Satan to enter.

2. **The Unsaved State** - has little to no protection from the wiles of the devil. All the wicked imaginations and lusts of the flesh and heart are fully exposed to the unsaved.

3. **The Rebellious State** - is Satan's favorite state. Here we turn away from and refuse the guidance of the Master. It is in this state the Bible says we are practitioners of witchcraft[91].

4. **The Complacent State** - In this luke-warm state, we have some protection from Satan but are displeasing to God. This state we most commonly call backsliding. In this apostate state we often ignore, overlook, or simply do not address demonic influence. It is like having a *buzz or tipsiness*. We are not drunk so we ignore the fact that we are physically and mentally impaired. In this state, we actually lay down one of our best weapons against Satan...Alertness. Alertness is on the list in Ephesians as a component of the "whole" armor of God. This means that as a spiritual weapon it is no less important than the other components.

Does this list mean that demons do not attack the righteous? Not at all, demons attacked Jesus. Demons attacked Jesus but they could not tempt Him. When the demons attacked Jesus they did not win, and they do not have to defeat us. What Satan could not do was convince Jesus to break fellowship with the Father.

---

[91] 1 Samuel 15:23.

Mark 5:12-23 ends this chapter. We discussed possession and indwelling in this chapter. Mark 5:12-23 shows that demons have no *choice* when it comes to Christ's authority. No matter what preachers teach, the scripture **must** be our standard for truth. Matthew 28:18 confirms that Christ rules in Heaven and on Earth. If Christians are Christ's people then their King provides for their spiritual safety, growth, and maturation. No one can pluck us from the hand of our King, but we can choose to leave at any time.

Anytime you see a believer backsliding, lost, sinning, or destroyed, they *choose* to be there. Nothing gets past Christ unless you allow it inside. Once demons enter your heart, Christ is not responsible for controlling the amount of damage the evil ones do. If you purchase a Pitbull despite the warnings against the breed and take it home, the dog is your responsibility. Can you then blame the pet-store when your animal (the one you purchased and brought home) destroys your home, attacks and kills your children? A sad tale nonetheless but you are responsible for the sin you allow in your life. Demons only add a variety of opportunities to fulfill the loathsome desires that fill that human heart, they do not create them.

Amen

Playing 'Possum[92]

---

[92] <u>National Audubon Society Field Guide to North American Mammals</u>, Revised 1996; Reader's Digest: North American Wildlife Revised 1982.

Chapter Thirteen
Playing 'possum

"Woe unto them that seek deep to hide their counsel from the Lord, and their works are in the dark, and they say, Who seeth us? And who knoweth us - Isaiah 29:15."

One day I saw a boy walking down the street with a stick. As he walked, an Opossum walked across in front of him minding its own business. Then for no apparent reason, the boy began to club the 'possum. After hitting the 'possum several times it fell down on the ground lifeless. The boy prodded the lifeless form several times, and then walked away. After several moments the 'possum got up, looked around, then hobbled into the safety of the bushes.

Satan and his minions master the art of 'playing possum'. Often times Satan simply plays dead. Many believers proclaim themselves delivered by prayer or because some preacher laid hands on them. They then move into this new, freer lifestyle away from all the old demons. As with all believers the moment torment stops--the prayer and the fasting stops. We misinterpret peace as a sign that God has moved in our lives. If God delivered you, it was not so you could just be happy--it was to build your faith and make you useful.

Believers, the scriptures remind us that any man that says he is without sin is a liar[93]. This is not to say that we are not trying, we simply have not succeeded. The heart of a man is wicked, and Satan knows this. He knows that all he has to do is either wait for the opportunity or create the opportunity and the man WILL FALL. Each time God blesses your prayer, and fasting, it is so you will see the benefits of a life of prayer and fasting. If prayer and fasting freed you once - then a lifetime of doing it will yield lifelong peace and freedom.

After moving into the *delivered state*, we walk along assuming that we are forever free from the torment. Let us look together at Exodus to

---
[93] 1 John 2:8.

see that this is not the case. I will attempt to show you that deliverance and salvation are separate. One is for the body and the other the soul.

1. **DELIVERANCE - "And Moses said unto the people, 'Fear ye not, standstill, and see the salvation of the Lord, which he will shew to you today: for the Egyptians whom ye have seen today, ye shall see them again no more forever'."** We see deliverance from sin, bondage, and torment, in Exodus 14:13. The children of Israel moved out of Egypt. Now they no longer lived under the whips and pain of Egypt. God freed the children of Israel from slavery and torment. Much like detoxification, God can get us away from that which causes pain and anguish in our lives. The problem lies in our desire to return to that state once freed. God closed the Red Sea so the Egyptians could not follow and the Jews could not return. The shed Blood of Christ is not so restrictive, you may return to Egypt whenever you desire.

2. **SALVATION - "And Israel saw that great work which the Lord did upon the Egyptians: and the people feared the Lord, and believed the Lord, and his servant Moses."** We see salvation of the soul here in Exodus 14:31. Here we see the minds condition of the people change. Here we see the beginning of abundant living--belief in God. It was not that the children of Israel did not believe in God; they lived removed from intimacy with God for 400 years and forgot the God that loved them. This was a slow beginning to the return to the bosom of the King of Kings.

3. **THE 'POSSUM - "THEY HAVE TURNED ASIDE QUICKLY OUT OF THE WAY WHICH I COMMANDED THEM: THEY HAVE MADE THEM A MOLTEN CALF, AND HAVE WORSHIPPED IT, AND HAVE SACRIFICED THEREUNTO, AND SAID, THESE [BE] THY GODS, O ISRAEL, WHICH HAVE BROUGHT THEE UP OUT OF THE LAND OF EGYPT**[94]**."** Here we see the 'possum coming back to life in Exodus 32:8. As we see, the problem with the people is that their hearts did not change. Although they had both salvation and deliverance, they did not have their minds and hearts renewed. Renewal is the pivotal stage that prevents believers from falling back to their old ways.

---

[94] Hebrews 10:26 and 2 Peter 2:20-22 indicate that the problem is a heart condition.

Because of God's mercy, He closed the Red Sea atop the Egyptians; and He closed the sea Himself. This served two wonderful purposes and one prophetic purpose.

RED SEA PURPOSE ONE - As the Lord promised, the sins that bound us we will never have to deal with again. When we accept Christ, His blood does exactly what the Red Sea did; cover and drown our captors. Believers, salvation is not merely a wiping clean of the slate, it is a freeing from our former owner, Satan. That is what redemption is all about; switching masters.

RED SEA PURPOSE TWO - The Red Sea forever prevents returning to the place/state/sin once enjoyed. Regardless of what you do you will NEVER AGAIN be the same. 2nd Peter reminds us that we can return to sin, but it will be worse than before; never the same.

THE PROPHETIC PURPOSE - Prophetically, the Red Sea represents the Blood of Christ and what the shed Blood of Christ did for the world. **"FOR THE LIFE OF THE FLESH IS IN THE BLOOD: AND I HAVE GIVEN IT TO YOU UPON THE ALTAR TO MAKE ATONEMENT FOR YOUR SOULS THAT MAKETH ATONEMENT BY REASON OF LIFE."** Leviticus 17:11 for all time explains why the Red sea and finally the shed blood of Christ was necessary and why it had the effect they both had on life.

What Satan does, is wait for the heart condition to revel itself. He does this by playing 'possum. Satan knows that in ALL cases he simply has to wait and not tempt or torment you a while. He knows that if he plays 'possum long enough we no longer consider sin a problem. The moment we stop praying and fasting for deliverance--Satan pounces. This in no way means that God failed--on the contrary, the scriptures warn us of the red 'possum[95].

Without the renewing of the mind and heart, relapse is unavoidable. The lack of renewal of the mind and heart is also the reason many chosen fail. Failure is not due to a lack of faith or underestimating

---

[95] Matthew 12:45.

Satan. Failure in denying the wretchedness of our hearts[96] is the problem. If believers do not learn to see the problem for what it is, we will never be able to discern the change. If we do not recognize dirt, when the Spirit cleans up we will not recognize cleanliness either. Perhaps this is another reason faith is integral to our *'faith-walk'*. Since we do not understand goodness, truth, love, and freedom, we have to believe that God provides these things because He said He would. Without this type of faith, our eyes constantly drag us back to the depths of despair and fatalism. Without honest repair of the heart condition, playing possum is considerably easier.

Playing possum only works if the possum convinces the prey or victim that it is dead. For this reason, Satan offers absolutely no resistance during the perceived 'deliverance period'. Satan knows God is infallible; he therefore relies on the human heart condition for success. Satan knows just as he proved with pigs that God is not his greatest threat--it is the heart renewed by God's Holy Spirit. The renewed heart is Satan's greatest threat because it denies him followers and victory. One cannot build a kingdom without worshippers.

God gave Satan the abyss as an abode. The sanctified heart has no room for the fallen one. God's law mandates Him to deliver His People. God's decree as to when He binds Satan means that He cannot yet bind Satan yet. Because of this decree, Jesus cast Satan into the pigs. Because God promised to deliver us when we call upon His name, He does. God cannot lie. He declared that Satan is free to roam, until the appointed time of Satan's imprisonment. If God lied, even to Satan, He would be untrustworthy?

For this reason, God tells us two things to do in order to defeat the roaring lion;

1. *Submit to God first*-This allows God to close off the believers' heart to the wiles of Satan.
2. *Resist Satan*-This requires believers to heal themselves.[97] This does not mean that you cast out your own demon, yet in a sense it actually does. Believers you can heal yourselves if you follow the prescribed method set out by Christ. The method set out by Christ involves the three basic elements of a believer's life: Faith, prayer, and fasting.

---

[96] Mark 13:20.
[97] Luke 4:23.

We see that faith is not just the substance of things hoped for; faith is the element believer's control that enables God to function on our behalf. Our faith not only moves God it allows God to move in us. Faith is the way God accesses the earth. God gave dominion of the earth to mankind. Despite the fact that humans messed up the arrangement God keeps His word. God therefore needs our faith and our prayers to empower Him to function in the earth realm. There is a movie called the Santa Claus, the clause in the movie is a legal term. Faith and prayer are the clauses that allow God access to a region over which He relinquished control.

The reason submission to God offers so much power is because it is the proverbial Genie in the lamp. We must release God into our lives so He can save, control, maintain, and protect our lives. This is why Jesus submitted during His temptation by saying it is written. In the Lord's Prayer, He tells us to submit for the same reason. When we submit Satan has to combat God, this is why Satan flees. Satan will stay gone as long as we remain submitted to God. The instant we depart from submission, or get distracted Satan reappears in our life. This is how is seems, but the truth is that Satan never left, he was waiting on you to get bored with righteousness and open the doors so he could flood your heart again. Only those that try to live a holy life struggle. The beatitudes are about those that struggle for righteousness.

When you see a Christian with no struggle in their lives look out; the possum from hell is with them. There is no peace in the eternal warfare between spirits. The peace that God gives is because like the water Jesus walked upon God can calm the sea, right there and right then. Once Jesus left the water, the sea regained self-control. God only takes charge of situations. The battle is not your own because He can show up and deliver you in an instant. However, ask King Saul, God only delivers His own. He has mercy upon whom He has mercy upon. He loves mercy who He loves, He provides for whomever He provides for. Why is He like this - because He is King He too has *choice*.

Amen

Part V

How Does the Devil Do That?

"In whom the god of this world has blinded the minds of them which believe not, lest the light of the glorious gospel of Christ, who is the image of God, should shine unto them - 2 Corinthians 4:4."

Chapter Fourteen
Satanic Tools and Applications

"**In whom the god of this world has blinded the minds of them which believe not, lest the light of the glorious gospel of Christ, who is the image of God, should shine unto them** - 2 Corinthians 4:4."

Satan is the father of lies and the author of confusion, but he is not stupid. The book of Revelations informs us that God intends to punish Satan for deceiving the nations. How could Satan deceive nations without tools, vices, and applications? Satan has a plethora of tools and he has spent thousands of years perfecting their use.

    1. **SATAN'S USE OF POSITION** - One of Satan's tools is position. Believers are familiar with the concept of a right hand man from the many references in the scripture to Jesus sitting at the right hand of the Father. Everybody near the throne has some form of power or they would not be allowed to get near the King. This is not to say that it requires power to be near God. What happens is that those trusted--the elect few are bestowed with more power and responsibility than others. As in the story of Joseph and Pharaohs, there are four classes of people near the King:
1. The right hand man .
2. The magicians/advisers.
3. The emissary or steward of the king.
4. Workers.

What was lacking in Pharaoh's court was a *right-hand man*. The right-hand man has access to the power and is trusted to carry on in the king's stead. This is the position Pharaoh gave Joseph; chief, even over Potifar and the advisers in the court.

In our sin-filled lives, this right hand seat is Satan's favorite position[98]. They say whoever has the king's ear has the power. When Satan sits in your hearts right hand, he has the power. Not because he is powerful, but like pharaoh gave it to Joseph, we give it over to Satan.

---
[98] Ezekiel 28:2.

"**Set thou a wicked man over him: and let Satan stand at his right hand** - Psalms 109:6." In this Psalm, David speaks as a king would about the power structure in the court; the difference is that David refers to the evil workings of the kingdom. The different levels of power in the different kingdoms are as follows:

Position	Heavenly	Satanic	Human
Right Hand Man -	Jesus	The Beast	Holy Spirit
Magicians/advisers -	Archangels	Seraphim	Elders
Stewards of the King -	Cherubs	Cherubs	Deacons
Workers -	Angels	Powers Thrones Dominions	Believers

Another application of the power of position is apparent in **"And He shewed me Joshua the high priest standing before the angel of the Lord, and Satan standing at his right hand to resist him** - Zechariah 3:1." When God is in your life Satan will always be your adversary. God requires Satan to bow to His power exclusively. Zechariah 3:2 and Jude 1:9 remind us only the Lord has the power to rebuke Satan. Satan resists everything God does for humans. Remember, Satan is not actually resisting Christians; he is fighting the will and purpose of God. The only reason Satan is against you is he hates the God you follow. Without belief in the God with no name, you are nothing in either kingdom.

2. **SATAN'S USE OF SEED** - Yet another satanic application that we do not understand is that Satan also plants seeds. Matthew 13:38-39 says, **"THE FIELD IS THE WORLD, THE GOOD SEED ARE THE CHILDREN OF THE KINGDOM BUT THE TARES ARE THE CHILDREN OF THE WICKED ONE. THE ENEMY THAT SOWED THEM IS THE DEVIL; THE HARVEST IS THE END OF THE WORLD; AND THE REAPERS ARE THE ANGELS."** Did you think

that the words, "OUR FATHER WHICH ART IN HEAVEN…" are arbitrary? This distinction is necessary because *God only answers His children*. Moreover, we should only speak and pray to our Father, which is in heaven.

The pool of satanic offspring has increased to such an extent that Hell hath enlarged itself[99]. This not only means that Satan's kingdom spread and bore children, but that the power therein also increased. Satan's kingdom is now the largest kingdom in the universe. I am not saying that you can lose salvation that is a separate discussion. What I cite with authority is two separate instances that definitely prove that you can fall out of favor with God.

1. **"And Samuel said to Saul, 'Why hast thou disquieted me, to bring me up? And Saul answered, I am sore distressed; for the Philistines make war against me, and God is departed from me, and answereth me no more, neither by prophets, nor by dreams: therefore I have called thee, that thou mayest make known unto me what I shall do'. Then said Samuel, 'Wherefore then dost thou ask of me, seeing the Lord is departed from thee, and is become thine enemy**?'- I Samuel 28:15-16"

2. **"THE SON OF MAN GOETH AS IT IS WRITTEN OF HIM: BUT WOE UNTO THAT MAN BY WHOM THE SON OF MAN IS BETRAYED! IT HAD BEEN GOOD FOR THAT MAN IF HE HAD NOT BEEN BORN** - Matthew 26:24"

3. **"For rebellion [is as] the sin of witchcraft, and stubbornness [is as] iniquity and idolatry. Because thou hast rejected the word of the Lord, He hath also rejected thee from [being] king** -1 Samuel 15:23"

Remember, John 14:15 reminds that if we love the Lord we obey His commandments. Exodus 20:4 reminds us that God punishes all those that hate Him. The disobedient always fall victim to Satan. The disobedient; like Adam and Eve, do not fall prey to a lie they fall prey to the desires of their own wretched, disobedient, fleshly, carnal hearts[100]. The disobedient fall prey to their bad *choices*.

---

[99] Isaiah 5:14.
[100] Genesis 3:6.

3. **SATAN'S USE OF TIME** - They say time heals all things, but time can also work against you. "**And when the devil had ended all the temptation, he departed from Him for a season** - Luke 4:13." Like the Terminator; the devil never quits, never gives up, never relents, gets tired, or is satisfied. Here is something that almost every believer, pastor, or minister seems to forget. We love to cite seasons as indicators for blessings, but as is plain to see season also applies to temptation. Satan may go away for a while, or he may stay silent for a moment. Our issue and sin may lay dormant for years...but it is just SEASONAL. Although Jesus quoted scripture, prayed, and fasted Satan left when he was ready, and he only left for a season. If Satan the lion is brash enough to tempt Jesus, next season what chance do you have?

4. **SATAN'S USE OF UTILITARIANISM** "**And Jesus rebuked him, saying, 'HOLD THY PEACE, AND COME OUT OF HIM'. And when the devil had thrown him in the midst, he came out of him, and hurt him not** - Luke 4:35." All demons, including the head demon are subject to the authority of Jesus the Christ[101]. As we see in Luke 4:35, the devil had his way with the victim before releasing the victim to the power of Christ. The scriptures say no weapon formed against you shall prosper. As we see here, the weapons formed against you may control you for a while.

As we see in Luke 4:35, there is a brief moment in the struggle where it appears that Satan is defying the might of God. THAT IS NOT THE CASE. What actually occurs is that the possessed person has the *choice* to resist Christ the demon however does not. What demons rely on is the carnal nature of the victim. Jesus informed us that the demons go away and return to the place they called home. They will again take up residence immediately if God's Holy Spirit does not displace the demon.

God does not allow His children to suffer needlessly He will deliver you. God delivers His children from the devil regardless of a child's desire. Despite popular belief, the victim does have *choice* in the matter of demon possession. No one has to be possessed; demons

---

[101] Matthew 28:18.

come in by invitation only. We may call the invitations open doors, chinks in the armor, multi-generational curses etc. Whatever title you use for demonic activity demons are subject to Godly laws. Although Satan cannot empty a vessel, much as he did with Peter and Judas he can enter into any heart made available. If there is an empty vessel, they may inhabit that vessel. Satan masters the art of creating opportunities, God called this characteristic *merchandising*.

5. **THE SATANIC USE OF BONDAGE** - Satan is not in the business of freeing anyone. Consequently, Satan does everything he can contrive to keep you in chains. Luke 8:29 says, "**For He had commanded the unclean spirit to come out of the man. For often times it had caught him: and he was kept bound with chains and in fetters; and he brake the bands, and was driven of the devil into the wilderness.**" God will give you the strength to break your own bonds; but did He free you from Heroin or did you become addicted to Methadone? Pharisees once accused Jesus of casting out demons by the power of Satan[102]. Satan uses many tricks, one of which is to appear to do miracles. Since we do not spend enough time in intimate sessions with God, we cannot readily discern the genuine miracles.

6. **SATAN'S USE OF SERVITUDE** - "**YE ARE OF [YOUR] FATHER THE DEVIL, AND THE LUSTS OF YOUR FATHER YE WILL DO. HE WAS A MURDERER FROM THE BEGINNING, AND ABODE NOT IN THE TRUTH, BECAUSE THERE IS NO TRUTH IN HIM. WHEN HE SPEAKETH A LIE, HE SPEAKETH OF HIS OWN: FOR HE IS A LIAR, AND THE FATHER OF IT** - John 8:44" **Jesus** points out another way Satan controls our lives. By following Satan's commands and concepts, Satan becomes our father. When we emulate evil, we are Satan's seed. God did not bar Adam and Eve from Eden as punishment, but for our sakes. Therefore, when we spend our lives lying to ourselves about our true nature we spend countless hours in fellowship with the father of lies. This is where addiction rears its ugly head. The basis of all addiction is lies. The lies of addiction are; I do not have a problem, and I do not

---

[102] Matthew 8:28-29, 12: 24-27, Mark 3:15, 5:6-7, James 2:19.

need help. After all Satan is the father of confusion, who else but the confused would *choose* to hurt needlessly?

A short lesson on the word addict, the term *Addict* originated in Rome. When Rome conquered, the captives from the vanquished tribe called Addicts, were slaves to Rome until death.

7. **SATAN'S USE OF BRASHNESS** - "**And supper being ended, the devil having now put into the heart of Judas Iscariot, Simon's [son], to betray Him** John 13:2." The devil is not afraid of God. Satan obeys God because he too has to obey the Creator of the universe. Satan is not afraid of church, pastors, evangelists, or armor-bearers. I am not familiar with any scripture that indicated Satan's fear of the Lord. Jesus reminds us to fear He that can destroy the body and the soul. Satan will attack you at will, even in the presence of God. This is not because God is weak, but because, we have *choice*. A reassuring fact is that God, the everlasting Father is there to deliver us from the evil one. Who knows what humans would unleash if it was not for the hand of God.

8. **SATAN'S USE OF GUILT** - Guilt is another one of the Satan's special tools. There is no greater pleasure to the evil ones than to accuse us to ourselves. Revelations 12:10 says, "**And I heard a loud voice saying in heaven, Now is come salvation, and strength, and the kingdom of our God, and the power of His Christ: for the accuser of our brethren is cast down, which accused them before our God day and night**." How many times has the evil one whispered in your ear the details of your sin? For many years, the children of God let their evil Romeo serenade us with, "Oh what wonderful sins shine in your hearts." At the risk of sending the wrong message: Who cares what wonderful sins shine in your hearts. The shed Blood of Christ covers all sins in His children.

9. **SATAN'S USE OF ACCUSATION** - Satan uses these accusations against believers before the throne trying to persuade the Father to hand us over as unworthy because of our lifestyles or mistakes. "**And I heard a loud voice saying in heaven, Now is come salvation, and strength, and the kingdom of our God,**

and the power of his Christ: for the accuser of our brethren is cast down, which accused them before our God day and night - Revelations 12:10."

    10.   **SATAN'S USE OF ANGER** - Satan's anger stems from two places:
- a. Satan's rage about his demotion is the primary cause of his anger.
- b. The secondary cause of Satan's jealous rage is God's new wine[103].

The human heart provides a means to express this anger. For it is written that out of the human heart comes evil (Matthew 15:18-20). Although Satan does not create evil things in men, he most certainly uses them[104].

    11.   **SATAN'S USE OF PERSONAL ATTACKS** - The last manifestation of fiery darts is Satan's personal attacks[105]. The greatest example or illustration of the personality of Satan comes from the book of Judges 9:15. This passage in my humble opinion shows two things;
- a. This passage shows the true personality of Satan.
- b. This passage shows the futility of serving the dark lord.

Regardless of what Satan does, he has no direct power over humans, this he must gain by means of deception or greed[106]. Regardless of what Satan can do, he has no direct control over us but he can act by permission. Although seemingly complex, the three types of permission are simple.

THE THREE TYPES OF PERMISSION

1.   **GODLY PERMISSION** - Satan has to have God's permission to attack those that belong to Christ - John 6:37, Job 1.

---

[103] Judges 9:20.
[104] Ezekiel 28:16.
[105] Job 2: 1-7, Jude 9, Romans 10:13, Hebrews 11:34-37, Revelations 12:12.
[106] Judges 9:8, Luke 4:8.

2. **HEART PERMISSION** - Those in Christ are not exempt from their own hearts[107]. It is through the sin in the heart of men that Satan enters and controls this world[108]. Matthew 12:29 tells us that the strong man must first be bound before Satan can seize power. 1st John 1:8-9 reminds us of the contents of the human heart, and that we all have sin in our hearts and/or lives. This beloved, is how we allow Satan to bind us via the use of our sin. This is why we are told to be sober minded, to flee even the appearance of unrighteousness, to pluck out or cast off anything that will cause us to sin. It is because sin is the sole province, domain, and haven, of the fallen angel. It is in the *shade* (darkness, unrighteousness, a region without Light.) that Satan wields his power. Therefore, when we elect to live in darkness we elect to live under the rule of our father the devil.

3. **CITIZEN'S PERMISSION** - The last type of permission is *choosing* to be citizens of darkness forever. Citizens forever *choose* to live in the shade; therefore, Satan has full time access to them[109]. This is the danger spoken of in 2 Peter 2:20-22 and Hebrews 10:26. Satan is the elected ruler of the shade. Consequently, when you walk in the shade you are in his area of control.

The wages of sin (fellowship with Satan) are still death. This means the Lord our God is against your actions. Satan however, says that you may live in his shade (die). If however you do not wish to live in Satan's shade, his unquenchable fire he intends to use, against you. With Satan, *"You are damned if you do and damned if you don't."*

The Bible states unequivocally that Satan transforms himself into a being of light. In the garden, a snake would have been useless. Adam just finished naming the animals and therefore the relationship with the animals was not conversational. Adam's relationship with the animals stemmed from Adam's dominion over the animals. Moreover, Adam still had dominion over the earth. Satan had to enter through the human heart.

If you look at the communication between Satan and the wife of Adam, it consisted of one concept. The concept was simple; Satan offered the woman what appeared to be truthful. The fact is that Satan told Eve

---

[107] Matthew 15:1 8-20.
[108] Luke 4:6.
[109] Romans 1:24.

the truth both times. Satan's truth however, is always incomplete. For example, if Satan said, *fornication feels good*, that is true. The whole truth however is that *fornication feels good but fornication is a sin punished by hell*.

What Satan offered the woman is what he always offers people; that which we most desire. In Eve's case[110], she desired knowledge. In other cases we desire, drugs, another man's wife, the prosperity lie, or other vices. In the case of Christ, Satan had nothing of value to offer because Christ sought only Heaven. As long as we still seek the vain treasures of this world, we will be under Satan's feet. The beauty of God's mercy is that He commanded us not to covet these things for this very reason. Not because the things of this world themselves are bad but because the desire for them causes humans to do bad things.

The desire for knowledge is a worthy goal, but we see, centuries after Eve's mistake that the wisdom that God offers and the wisdom we can obtain are not the same. Wisdom, Godly wisdom comes from God. This means that true wisdom is receiving, assimilating, and understanding the things, and only the things God wants us to understand.

By what Jesus suffered, he learned obedience. If what Jesus did prior to age 30 did not qualify as obedience, it makes sense that what He learned prior to 30 is not wisdom. At the end of the three years, He ministered; prayed and fasted Jesus was obedient, and wise according to Godly standards.

God's standards are exacting and unyielding. What he gives He alone has. All good and perfect things come from God. Anything you get from anywhere else is neither good nor perfect. College is wonderful, Einstein was a genius, but neither was good nor perfect. We know this by whet the fruits of college and Einstein produced. Far more evil has transpired as a result of Einstein's genius and college than good. This is why God withhold both information and power. Since humans are neither good, nor perfect and most are unwilling to suffer what Jesus suffered to become so, we are not trustworthy.

A student that is unwilling to learn the discipline that accompanies power should never have power. Many human kings withheld thrones because their sons were unworthy, does not God have that right. Who better to know what the outcome of a reign than God? Who better to

---

[110] Genesis 3:6.

protect the sheep from the Po' Pots, Hitler's and Custer's of this world than God? Who better to know God and evil than the only person in the universe the Bible describes as good?

I once chose to steal a book from the bookstore. I did not steal from need or poverty, I did not even want the book, I just took it. I was not under the influence of a demon, I was just being stupid. Had God sent me to hell, it would have been just. You may not think it to be fair, but that is not His concern. Justice is of God, fairness is a human design. God weighs all things and knows all things, and is just. Godly exemption of a hungry man from the penalty of a thief is the only sin of *choice* sin listed. Demonic possession is not punished in the Bible, but demonic influence is punished. The issue again is *choice*. A person once possessed will incur judgment if they return to the old ways. Mary the prostitute had seven demons, but after Christ, she sinned no more.

This is the *choice* we must make in our own lives. Despite what areas of our lives we gave to Satan with God's help we must take them all back. It does not matter where Satan seems to hide in your life he is only after three things; you heart, your imagination or you soul. God is the guardian and protector of our souls so there are only two other places. All the work Satan does gets him closer to your destruction. This is why you must *choose* to walk away from the darkness. God will not leave you shipwrecked and alone, but if you follow Satan's beacon you will end up on a distant shoal or reef, lonely, broken, and empty.

The prudent thing for the ships captains to do was either not to land at night or to set out their own long boat to guide them through the shoals. They had maps of the harbor; there was not need to constantly wreck in the shallows. Unfortunately, Satan still wrecks lives for the same reason. The captains deemed landing their cargo more important that their lives. Nevertheless, as we know, a bad *choice* results in losing both our cargo and our lives.

When you wreck a vessels the contents of the vessel are fair game and the vessel itself remains exposed ot he elements. Our choices have the same effect on our lives. Sin not only allows Satan access to our soul, it exposes our hearts, and imagination to more debase things in our world.

The church is called to preach to the lost, only God can help the wrecked. Satan attacks children because he can wreck lives by poisoning their foundation. Youth ministries and children's ministries are more important that we realize, they not only set the tone for the lives of the children, they effect the next generation of decisions and choices--choices that affect everybody.

Maybe people do not really believe in hell, I shudder to think people really want to go to hell. However, believers, you do believe in hell, it is part of your belief system. Since Jesus always told the truth, there must be a heaven and a hell. Since Jesus always told the truth you must *choose* where you want to spend eternity, no one makes that decision for you.

Amen

Part IV

Living
in
the
Shade

"And the bramble said unto the trees, If in truth you anoint me king over you, then come and put your trust in my shade... - Judges 9."

Chapter Fifteen
Spheres of Demonic Influence

"**And the bramble said unto the trees, If in truth you anoint me king over you, then come and put your trust in my shade shadow: and if not, let fire come out of the bramble, and devour the cedars of Lebanon** - Judges 9:15"

Once I had a minister said of my writings that I used too many scriptures. He said he felt like he should have simply read the Bible. I agreed with him, he should. If believers actually studied their Bible, spoke to God, and listened to what God had to say I would be unnecessary.

The scriptures list several interactions between Satan and humans. In reference to the interactions the scriptures use the word *POSSESS*. There appear to be seven spheres of demonic possession. Seven is the number of completion, therefore these seven spheres comprises the total spectrum of demonic possession. The main reason demons do well at demonic encounters is that the church constantly attacks the symptoms (demoniacs) and not the demon. Perversion is not a spirit it of evidence of a spirit. You cannot rebuke or bind the spirit of perversion or pornography, because there is not one. You would do better to rebuke the spirit of whoredoms or uncleanliness, than the spirit of homosexuality.

Demons have names but there appear to be seven areas in which they operate.

1. **THE SPHERE OF SICKNESS** - Matthew 4:24 says, "**And His fame went throughout all Syria: and they brought unto Him all sick people that were taken with divers diseases and torments, and those which were** *possessed with devils***, and those which were lunatic, and those that had the palsy; and He healed them**." This type of demonic possession is easy to explain. We do not realize the simplicity of kingdom answers. Like any contagious disease, demons need a place to spread to, or a healthy organism to infect. The Gospels write about all manner of plagues upon the people and Jesus healing them. Sick people fall into complacency easily because we forget

about the Lord when we hurt. Therefore, when we take sick people and group them with demonized people the demons find new ground.

This is why scripture tells us to avoid the ungodly, because their ungodliness spreads to our hearts and minds. This is why Jesus pointed out that evidence of forgiveness from sins was healing in the body, not because sin caused the disease, but because the DISEASE IS SIN. This does not mean that all that are sick are sinful. In a restaurant with a smoking section, you do not have to smoke a cigarette to breath in the smoke, smell like the smoke, and depending upon what they smoke be affected by the smoke.

2. **THE SPHERE OF CAPTIVITY** - Matthew 8:28 says, **"And when He was come to the other side into the country of the Gergesenes, there met Him two** *possessed with devils,* **coming out of the tombs, exceeding fierce, so that no man might pass by that way.**" Here is yet another example of simplicity; the two *possessed* with the demons came out of the tombs. In the history of humankind, there has only been one use for tombs--tombs are houses for the dead.

Many of us that commit sins that lead unto death. In addition, there are those of us that dwell in sin. Both heart condition lead to death. Why would the living be among the dead? The living only confer with the dead when they share the same spirit. It is a simple concept; the men were among the dead because they too were dead. We forget that we only found Jesus near or in the tomb when He was dead. As soon as He resurrected[111] He vacated the tomb and never looked back. I believe the angels asked at that point, why the humans looked for the living among the dead?

3. **THE SPHERE OF SENSORY MANIPULATION** - In these two scriptures, we see both men suffer from sensory deprivation.

1. Matthew 9:32 says, **"As they went out, behold, they brought to Him a dumb man** *possessed with a devil.*

---

[111] Resurrect means to *raise again to activity*. Another meaning of resurrection is material belief that yields to spiritual understanding. With the Master's spiritual understanding, the physical laws yielded to His authority and He was able to resurrect Himself after three days under the earth. From a Fishing Trip in Patmos: The Disciple Maker's Edition.

2. "**Then was brought unto him one** possessed with a devil, **blind, and dumb: and He healed Him, in so much that the blind and dumb both spake and saw** - Matthew 12:22." In simple terms, this means that the men lost the ability to perceive the truth. The human creature discerns what reality using the five senses.

This particular type of possession is most troubling. Unlike other types of possession, the victim of their inhabitation can actually cry out or ask for help. However, in this state, sensory manipulation denies the victim the ability to reach out or perceive aid. Although this is not the most desperate level of demonic influence, it is one of the most common and leads to worse states. Sensory altering effects often leads the victim to despair, anger, or insanity. Sensory manipulation occurs in two forms; depravation and excitement.

DEPRIVATION - Sensory deprivation is most commonly associated with demonic influence. This tradition is not accurate. Demons more often than not use excitement to manipulate a person. The reason demons use excitement is that is far easier to create desire in human flesh for pleasure than for pain. In extreme cases, pain is pleasure, but the person still seeks the pleasurable effect caused by the pain. Depravation can drive a person towards or away from a thing. Both heaven and hell use this technique. God calls it a test and Satan calls it temptation. The methods are similar, although the desired effect differs greatly.

God promises in Isaiah 45 that He would give you affliction and oppression before pleasure. Satan promises in Judges 9 that he would give you pleasure before he gives oppression and affliction. If you cannot see the subtle differences, allow me to point them out to you. As with all traits between God and Satan, they are antithetical. God offers you the rewards of a life of sacrifices and servitude at the day's end. Satan, like the prodigal son asks for the rewards upfront then settles for whatever bondage is required to repay.

EXCITEMENT - Excitement is a peculiar use of sensory manipulation. Excitement manifests as lust or zeal depending upon whom you serve. There is no difference between lust and zeal. We use them to different the heart condition making it easy to differ. Samson, Peter, and John the Baptist are great example of this concept. Was it zeal or lust when Peter attacked the guard? Was it zeal or a lust to serve God that caused John to insult Herod? Was it zeal or lust, which caused Delilah to betray Samson? Was it zeal or lust, which caused Samson to follow Delilah?

Either way the senses make the flesh seem alive. Demonic possession does not crave destruction of the flesh Satan craves your soul. Satan cannot directly access your soul so he entices the flesh in such a diverse, vigilant manner he cause eternal damage to your soul.

4. **THE SPHERE OF DISEASE** - Mark 1:32 says, "**And at even, when the sun did set, they brought unto Him all that were diseased, and them that were** *possessed with devils.*" People under demonic influence not only congregate, but their demoniacs often manifest as disease. Remember demoniacs always manifest somewhere in the victim's flesh. Evidence of demonic activity is readily apparent in terms of health. Jesus taught that saying your sins are forgiven is easier than forgiving the sin. He continued to tell us that evidence of forgiveness is health a return to health.

It is a simple concept, people who commit suicide are not healthy, people that use drugs are not healthy, abusive people are not healthy, etc. Evidence in these people lives that they have a relationship with God is a change from the former diseased state that caused so much pain.

Let me explain one thing regarding disease, sin causes all disease. This however does not mean that everyone with a disease is engaging in a sin-filled life. Remember all human flesh was born in sin. There is one other reason that disease exists in the body, the human body has decrepitude built into the design. It is not clear if decrepitude is a result of sin, but the fact is that the body MUST die of something. Death is a natural result of life; it is the second death that we must fear.

5. **THE COVERT SPHERE** - John 13:27 says, "**And after the sop Satan** entered **into him. Then said Jesus unto him, THAT THOU DOEST, DO QUICKLY**." In twelve years of making disciples and instructing spiritual warfare, I believe that there is no more insidious sphere of possession than the covert sphere. Hollywood with its Omen, Exorcist, Jason, and Freddy Kruger movies have tricked us into seeing all demon possessions as tawdry, violent, and morose. Many people believe that foaming at the mouth, tearing chains, and scaring babies are the true manifestations of demons. Nothing could be farther from the truth.

THE SECRET PASS - The covert type of possession occurs in the hearts of believers. Satan entered into the heart of Judas because it was open. The scriptures give us the secret pass Satan used to enter Judas's heart. **"Then saith one of his disciples, Judas Iscariot, Simon's [son], which should betray him, Why was not this ointment sold for three hundred pence, and given to the poor? This he said, not that he cared for the poor; but because he was a thief, and had the bag, and bare what was put therein."** John 12:4-6 explains to us that Judas gave Satan an open invitation because even after three years with Jesus Judas' heart never changed. The fact is that Judas was a thief when he met Jesus, a thief when he betrayed Jesus, and a thief when he hanged himself. Judas still was a thief in his heart, if not in deed. Satan was therefore able to walk in and out of Judas's heart whenever he desired.

Even in the midst of God's Holy Spirit, an unsubmitted heart is viable territory for demons. The unsubmitted heart is the secret pass Satan's uses to access saints of all descriptions. People think that because we accept salvation we automatically change, change is a process. Submission is also a process. Unlike change, submission requires a completely new way of thinking before the changes take place. The unsubmitted heart therefore allows Satan to access the former state the person lived in, the former state the Bible calls darkness.

6. **THE SPHERE OF DISABILITY** - Acts 8:7 says, **"For unclean spirits, crying with loud voice, came out of many that were** *possessed [with them]*: **and many taken with palsies, and that were lame, were healed."** Like the victim of sensory deprivation, those disabled by possession cannot move from their condition. There is no way for me to determine which is worst; blindness and the need for a guide dog, or paralysis but having all of your senses. In one instance, you can compensate for your ability to perceive life. In the other case, you can perceive everything but you cannot enjoy anything. What is clear is that health issues create a black hole in believers. The spiritual Bermuda Triangle envelops years of righteousness, fasting, praying, and sacrifice. It happens all too often in the lives of believers; because, we are human the trouble in our bodies drives us away from intimacy with God.

7. **THE SPHERE OF DIVINATION** - Acts 16:16 says, "**And it came to pass, as we went to prayer, a certain damsel** *possessed with a spirit* **of divination met us, which brought her masters much gain by soothsaying.**" This sphere is most easily explained as the *Cleo* state. We all saw *Cleo* on the Psychic Friends Network. Although many manifestations exist, the majority of people under the influence of the spirit of divination are quiet and reserved. Satan's most useful persons are never loud and obnoxious. The way demon possessed people serve Satan best is subtly from positions of power. What is important to understand is that diviners; all diviners, have masters that they have to pay. There are no free rides in Satan's kingdom. If Satan gives you, a power or position there is always a price. Not only are the wages of sin still death: Satan's favors ALL rely on servitude and worshiping him.

Demons in our lives are in our lives by invitation. There are NO demons, ghosts, ghouls, or paranormal entities, that believers cannot control. Despite television shows the living and the dead do not speak. Despite television shows, demons are not the released souls of disgusting dead people. On the contrary, disgusting dead people are the result of demonic influence. There is and only has been one ghost buster in all of history. Jesus did not use electronics, séances, nuclear weapons, or Tarot cards to defeat the demons. Jesus conquered the demons by *choosing* to serve the Living God. Jesus conquered the demons with His *choice* to love. Jesus conquered demons to come. Jesus conquered demons by *choosing* to heal the sick. Jesus conquered demons by *choosing* to forgive sin. Jesus conquered demons by *choosing* to die. In addition, it is His *choice* to return and judge the world, and He will judge demons, demoniacs, rebels, and those who *choose* to serve Satan.

Amen

Chapter Sixteen
Object Possession, Animal Possession, and Natural Disasters

"And they shall no more offer their sacrifices unto devils, after whom they have gone a whoring. This shall be a statute forever unto them throughout their generations - Leviticus 17:7."

Many people unjustly contend that demons have the ability to possess inanimate objects. There is neither evidence nor any reason for demons to possess inanimate objects. Demons create death they do not function well in dead things or inanimate objects. In the entirety of the scriptures, there is no reference to demons inhabiting dead bodies. On the contrary, demons torment and manipulate the living. Demons need to use the living because the only way to accomplish their task is to use the living.

Demons are not alive, demons lack the Life of the Father who is in heaven. Demons, therefore, need humans to act as their agents in the earth realm. What demons do not do is inhabit dead things. Dead things cannot move nor can they reproduce. Dead things cannot perform any of the seven traits required for living creatures. Inanimate objects also have no power. If a demon wants to control a country; for example, it uses the king--not the throne. The throne maybe called the seat of power, but it is powerful because a powerful being sits on the throne. There is no inherent power in any chair or bench made of marble, wood, or gold.

The best example of demons creating death and not functioning well in dead things or inanimate objects would be the tomb in which Jesus' body laid. When the angel spoke, he asked a poignant question. The angel's question was intriguing because it spilt for all time the concepts of life after death, ghosts, and séances. ONLY DEAD THINGS REMAIN IN TOMBS.

What God means by Life and what we mean by life are not the same thing. Things that are alive live because of the Spirit of Life that is in them[112], the grave only has control of those not in Christ[113]. I remind

---

[112] Revelations 11:11.

you that in Matthew 12:43 the demon returned and inhabited the house. The demon desired to return to the place of rest it once occupied. The demon never speaks of the house as a place of power; the house is a safe place for the demon to hide from God.

THE ACHAN THEORY

A man named Achan stole a cup and hid it in his encampment. As a result of the theft all the camp's inhabitants were cursed. The story of Achan's theft might lead one to believe in accursed objects. I counter the Achan Theory with the evident truth in scripture. David and his men moved the Ark of the Covenant via ox cart in the Old Testament. Despite God's explicit instructions, one of the men touched the ark intending to stop the ark from falling. The man in the story was smitten, not because of a curse but because of disobedience. In Achan's story the reason was the same, the cup was not cursed Achan's thieving behavior was cursed.

To minds that cannot reason, the inescapable conclusion is that the Holy One that inhabits the praises of Israel also inhabits inanimate objects. Much like the Pharisees, we have ears but cannot hear what God says, minds that do not think as God does, and hearts that do not share in God's love. Jesus spoke of rebuilding the ruined temple in three days. People laughed at Jesus because those laughing did not understand that Jesus the Living only dealt with the living. Even when Jesus raised people from the dead, it was a simple matter of sweeping the *house* clean and moving into the heart.

The way demons inhabit houses, countries, and palaces is through the hearts of people. Someone once said that before a kingdom can change men must change. Therefore, before demons can take over a house, country, or palace they must influence men[114]. If you want to influence a household or inhabit the house, you do it by influencing the people that live in the house. The reason demons DO NOT possess inanimate objects is because demons are unable to influence inanimate

---

[113] 1 Thessalonians 4:16 - "**For the Lord Himself shall descend from heaven with a shout, with the voice of the archangel, and with the trump of God: and the dead in Christ shall rise first**."

[114] Matthew 12:29.

objects. How can a spirit influence a rock, something with no spirit? In order to manipulate physical laws

ANIMAL POSSESSION

When we look at Creation through God and not because of science, we see something interesting. We notice that through the hands of God All creatures (Expressions of the Creator {Romans 1:20}) were created within the first six days of creation. This means that Adam had complete control of the animals created during the six days[115].

In the story of Balaam, the Lord God gave the gift of speech to an animal to curtail Balaam's wrath. In the book of Matthew, when the Lord deals with the demons of Gergasene the demons spoke to Jesus through the boy, the pigs never spoke. In Mark 1:24, the man spoke through the demons inhabited him. When Satan entered Peter, the voice of Peter spoke and Judas spoke in his own voice. In the case of the temptation of Jesus, there is no description given of the appearance of the person that tempted Jesus the Son of God.

There is no case or example of the devil giving the gift of speech to inanimate objects or beasts of the field. The reason for this is simple but paradoxical; Lucifer cannot create life nor can he alter creation components. It is like renting a car, no matter how much you paint the car, put new tires on the car, or change the interior the shape. The number of doors and size of the car does not change; all you can do is ride.

In other words, Satan can destroy things. He is the prince of the power of the air, which allows him to manipulate air. He cannot however add to or take away from the word of God. The creation account is an account of 'the words of God' therefore Lucifer cannot add to or take away from what God has put into place. Jesus says in Revelations that Satan uses deceit and confusion to destroy, not demon possession.

Despite fables of Baphomet's Goat, animals everywhere have and always will do exactly the will of God. Although we may wish to believe animals have souls, there is no evidence of this in scripture. The sacrifice of the animals was not because their blood was cleansing but because it was symbolic and prophetic. The blood of animals symbolized the impure attempt of fallen man to offer something to God for atonement. The reason God required the useless, less than pure animal was that the

---

[115] Genesis 1:24.

animal's filth represented the sin in humankind. There is only one Christ, and one shedding of Blood. Until Christ's time animals were tools to accomplish the will of God. After Golgotha there was no need to sacrifice animals, the shed blood of Christ paid it all.

Numbers 22:28 is the only example in the Bible of human attributes existing or being given to animals. **"And the Lord opened the mouth of the ass, and she said unto Balaam, What have I done unto thee, that thou hast smitten me these three times**?" God brought about this episode for His purpose. Satan does not have control over the animals; he is the prince of the power of the air. Review your scriptures. The Bible calls animals beasts of the field. Genesis 3:17 & 21 explains why Satan has no control over animals. God revoked control from the man. Remember, Satan only obtained dominion over what God gave the man dominion over. God expelled Adam and for Adam's sake, God cursed the earth, revoked dominion over the earth, the beasts thereof, trees fowls of the air, fish in the sea when He expelled Adam. When the Lord cursed the earth for our sake, He barred Satan from the animals as well.

In Jonah 1:17 we see that God using His supreme power to create or at least modify a great fish to swallow Jonah, **"Now the Lord had prepared a great fish to swallow up Jonah. And Jonah was in the belly of the fish three days and three nights**." Whatever the creature was that swallowed Jonah it obviously did not exist before or after Jonah's episode. This is yet another example of Godly intervention.

Leviticus 17:7 may confuse you but the explanation comes from Exodus 32. The Golden Calf the children of Israel fashioned did not have demons in it, but it represented the chief demon. The Goat demon is not a reference to an idol that is possessed. The Goat demon is the demon, the deity, the fallen angel that Satan's followers make idols and to worship. The Goat demon or the demon of the goat is none other than Satan, the adversary of mankind. I cite the scriptures to verify this point, and to show you that even the idols the Bible refers to as demons are demonic in their purpose not in actuality.

1. Exodus 32:8 - **"They have turned aside quickly out of the way which I commanded them: they have made them a molten calf, and have worshipped it, and have sacrificed thereunto,**

and said, These [be] thy gods, O Israel, which have brought thee up out of the land of Egypt."

2. Deuteronomy 32:17 - "**They sacrificed unto devils, not to God; to gods whom they knew not, to new [gods that] came newly up, whom your fathers feared not.**"

3. 2 Chronicles 11:15 - "**And he ordained him priests for the high places, and for the devils, and for the calves which he had made.**"

THE NEPHILIM, REHAIM, AND ANAKIM

We know that the Nephilim, Rehaim, and Anakim, were not *creatures*, because the Creator did not make them. They therefore could not reproduce themselves nor maintain their lifestyle. I am unsure what these entities were, although listed as giants. Goliath and the Philistines are of the lines of these things, but that would then beg the question, was Goliath the son of an angel. We laugh at Greek mythology and there celestial sibling rivalry-but one has to wonder, did they fill in the blanks in our Bible, or where they just trying to make the scenario easy to understand.

Many times in the scriptures, demons showed strokes of evil genius. *Prima Nocturne* was a stroke of brilliance from the evil ones. The rationale behind *Prima Nocturne* was to stop or at least delay the birth of Christ. Remember, prophecy required a clear, traceable line from the House of David. *Prima Nocturne* first occurred in Genesis 6:1-4 - "**And it came to pass, when men began to multiply on the face of the earth, and daughters were born unto them, that the sons of God saw the daughters of men that they [were] fair; and they took them wives of all which they chose. And the Lord said, MY SPIRIT SHALL NOT ALWAYS STRIVE WITH MAN, FOR THAT HE ALSO [IS] FLESH: YET HIS DAYS SHALL BE AN HUNDRED AND TWENTY YEARS. There were giants in the earth in those days; and also after that, when the sons of God came in unto the daughters of men, and they bare [children] to them, the same [became] mighty men which [were] of old, men of renown.**" When Satan cheats, God always intervenes and spares humanity from their vile actions. There is no other references to mating between humans and demons or any resurrections caused by demons.

NATURAL DISASTERS

Many people cite scriptures concerning weather changes as indicators of the return of the King. They are correct; God did give the seasons for signs. What Jesus wanted the fishermen and farmers to understand was not impending doom, but signs of change. When Jesus asked could they not tell the signs, He referred to the kingdom of heaven being at hand. The point Jesus made was that the old regime of Satan no longer controlled God was King again.

The earth is a living creature. Every living thing created by God is a creature. The earth therefore has natural processes that occur to maintain balance. What humans call natural disasters, God calls natural order. Do people die during natural disasters? Yes, many people die, but they do not have to. Every year we have tornados, typhoons, monsoons, and hurricane seasons. Like crop seasons, we call these events seasons because they occur the same time very year and the same places.

I live in a rural area. Having tended the land I learned a great deal about the order of Gods creature. Thunderstorms are vital to maintain plant life, remove dead and dying trees and to nitrify water for fertilizer. Snow is a wonderful way to replenish water in the soil. Termites are vital, otherwise the dead trees and leaves would stack up and overrun the earth. It is by design that termites live in the ground, what an efficient way to get the minerals needed for new trees back into the earth.

Natural disasters are a wonderful example of the spiritual dichotomy between man's desires and God's will. God set in motion a series of interdependent systems design to sustain all life in and on earth. Despite the necessity of nature, it is an inconvenience to our way of life. We desire cities, airplanes, immense towers, large floating cities, and space ships. What humans refuse to abide by is to one of their own laws of physics. *For every action there is an equal and opposite reaction.*

Everything we introduce into the human body, the human body has an equalizing effect. In a no less ingenious plan, the earth responds the same way. This mentality is what displeases, saddens, and angers God. How stupid a people that can fly in space, but refuse a subdue themselves to sustain themselves or refrain from sin. How stupid a people, who would rather anger God and go to hell than turn away from sin. The loss of souls to greed, fear, and selfishness is the greatest natural disaster in history.

Amen

Part III
The Garden of Secrets

"And the Lord God planted a garden eastward in Eden; and there He put the man whom He had formed. And out of the ground made the Lord God to grow every tree that is pleasant to the sight, and good for food; the tree of life also in the midst of the garden, and the tree of knowledge of good and evil - Genesis 2:8-9."

Chapter Seventeen
The Dusty Secret

"IN THE SWEAT OF THY FACE SHALT THOU EAT BREAD, TILL THOU RETURN UNTO THE GROUND; FOR OUT OF IT WAST THOU TAKEN: FOR DUST THOU (ART), AND UNTO DUST SHALT THOU RETURN - Genesis 3:19[116]."

Throughout the Bible, *dust* almost exclusively refers to the ashes of dead life forms. The planet Earth has on it Carbon based life forms called Human or Terrestrial beings. All living things on the Earth are Carbon based. When these living things die, they not only release Carbon dioxide helping to sustain the ecosystem, they decompose and turn to dust or ashes. Blackness caused by burning is because Carbon is a black element. Subsequently, when burned humans give off the dark gray ashes.

In short order, we explore what *dust* means to Satan and his followers. In the chapter *The Stones of Fire* we discussed, the angels of God. Have you ever wondered what angels eat? The answer is not only scriptural but simple: spirit beings eat spirit food **"Jesus saith unto them MY MEAT IS TO DO THE WILL OF HIM THAT SENT ME AND TO FINISH HIS WORK** - John 4:34."

Remember, spiritual beings are super (above)-natural; consequently, their food is super-natural. If you will, take the time to refer to Fig 3[117], Lucifer falls just below the Father. In terms of earthly food, the closer you are to the King, the sweeter the food and fragrance. Lucifer, therefore, ate the sweetest of all the angels because he was the closest to God. Ezekiel 31:16 tells us that Lucifer and all the angels ate the same thing; the one thing fleshly beings do not, the Living Water of God. After God cast Lucifer down[118] God told Satan that he would have to eat dust from then on. This meant two things for Satan:

---

[116] Related scriptures: Genesis 2:7, 3:14, 3:19, 18:27, Deuteronomy 28:24, 32:24, Job 10:9, 13:12, 20:11, 21:26, Psalms 22:15, 103:14, 104:29, Ecclesiastes 3:20, 12:7, Isaiah 26:19, 29:4, 61: 3, Jeremiah 31:40, Daniel 12: 2, Micah 7:17, Matthew 10:14, 2 Peter 2:6.

[117] Page 50.

[118] *Cut* is the actual term used in Ezekiel 31.

1. Satan no longer ate super-natural food--Living Water.
2. Satan was therefore no longer exalted above natural things.

POINT ONE - is self-explanatory and requires no in depth discussion. The jest of it is as follows; God cast Satan down so Satan no longer enjoys the taste of God's sweet Spirit.

POINT TWO - God told Adam that he came from dust and he would return to dust. Some contend that this means God designed humans to live forever. This scripture does not support this. What is clear however is that humans were not supposed to have to toil and suffer. Toil and suffering came about as a part of Adam's sin.

When life forms die, they disintegrate into dust/ashes. A decomposing body is not *dead* (Not having the capacity to produce or sustain life, barren), until it has completely decomposed. Until the body completely decomposes, animals and bacteria feed on the carcass. When the corpse finally becomes *dust,* it is of little use to anyone except as fertilizer/ raw minerals. This is why the Old Testament required burnt offerings before God spoke. When the flesh charred to dust/ashes God knew that the flesh was dead. This is the desired result of righteousness, *death to our flesh.* The sweet smell of dead flesh alerted God that the spirit was free to commune with Him.

If you understand this, you will also understand that Jesus conquered death and the grave on the cross, before He arose. Jesus conquered Satan's kingdom the second His Spirit leased from the rotting carcass on the cross[119]. The body that walked the earth and ate with the twelve no longer sustained Life, it was useless to Jesus. However, it was NEVER *dust,* so SATAN NEVER GOT TO FEAST ON IT. This is yet another subtlety of God's plan, which denied Satan any chance of glory.

Fire breaks down carbon based forms. We live because God is Life and we are the cells/members of His body. Therefore, we have the power not to become dust for Satan's pleasure. We become dust when we do not live up to or perform the will of God. The dead Christians are the cancer that Jesus spews out, that He describes as passing out into the drought; something that defiles His body. Dead piece of non-fruit bearing wood Christ bore to Golgotha best symbolize dead Christians.

---

[119] Matthew 27:50.

Why is this death important? Satan now has to wait until we rot and denitrify before he can eat. Satan no longer has the ability to digest Living food. Not only does Satan now have to wait to eat, he has to watch and wait for sinners to decompose. This conception of death also explains Proverbs 30:15-16, which lists four things that are never satisfied. "**The Horseleach has two daughters crying, Give give. There are three things that are never satisfied, yea four things say not, It *is enough:* The grave: and the barren womb: the earth *that* is not filled with water; and the fire saith not it is enough**." Let us explore the four things that are never satisfied.

1. **THE GRAVE IS NEVER SATISFIED** - The grave[120] is the place the dead all end up. The grave is a pit or tomb. The purpose of the grave is twofold;

    i. The grave stores dead rotting bodies and keep them away from the living.

    ii. The grave allows the decomposing body to re-enjoin its elements to the earth.

The grave is always hungry because the grave exists only to service death. The grave thrives and exists to eat death and is therefore never satisfied. This is why Christ had to conquer the grave. If you conquer death but not the grave, the grave will still try to find a way to eat. Why do I give living attributes to the grave? Because the angel of the grave (Revelations 9:11) is alive and will never be satisfied. Any place that deals with death is the domain of Satan. That is why the angel asked Mary, "Why do you look for the living among the dead or why do you look for the Living (those alive in the Spirit) where Satan reigns?" Conquering the grave was simply another facet of Satan's ignominious defeat. In order to crush Satan's head Jesus had to crush all of Satan's strong holds. Imagine how hungry Satan must be since Jesus retook the grave and destroyed Satan's cupboard--the place Satan stores his food.

---

[120] Hades, Sheol, 'the place of the holding'.

2. **THE BARREN WOMB IS NEVER SATISFIED -** A mother will tell you that no matter how troubled a pregnancy she would conceive of aborting the child. It is the nature of women to bear children that is part of God's design. Although this topic is touchy, believers must learn to walk in the truth, regardless of the cost to our pathetic egos. To women, children are as natural and necessary as air. God designed women to bear children and part of that design requires desire. In the case of motherhood, when I use the term *design* I mean God's order. Consequently, women yearn for kids not because they are from Venus but because they are from God. It is the desire for kids that causes the barren or unused womb to yearn for children. What does this have to do with never being satisfied? Believers, the Bible says that God made man His image; and the woman God made from the man. Therefore, if God made the woman from man, God also made women in His image. This is not rocket science. It is simple fact, if God makes a product in His image the elements of the product must be also be made in God's image.

The womb--the barren womb, will never be satisfied because it was designed to produce life. Therefore, a dead zone creates discomfort. An entity designed to produce life can never be satisfied not producing life. This is why a woman that is barren or without a child feels there is something missing. That thing that is missing is her purpose. This is why I say this topic is touchy. This is no insult, if you understand who God is you know that. According to Genesis, God gave woman three purposes in her great design (life):

i. To please God.

ii. To complete the man.

iii. To be bear children.

Of the three purposes set aside for women, the production of life is the most God-like. Any woman in the will of God accepts that her greatest prize in this life is to be able to create, carry, and birth life. To disdain gift, this is to be outside the design of God.

Jesus' bride; the church, also has a womb. This womb is NEVER satisfied with, or supposed to be barren. The church's womb should never be empty. The church must never settle for barrenness. The yearning and the emptiness the church feels is not due to lack of prosperity but because the church is BARREN.

3. **THE EARTH THAT IS NOT FILLED WITH WATER IS NEVER SATISFIED** - "**MY GOD, MY GOD; WHY HAST THOU FORSAKEN ME**?" are words uttered by the Lord and Savior Jesus Christ at the lowest and the highest point in Jesus' life. This was the only time in life that Jesus was cut off from the Father. The separation from Living Water Jesus describes in the same manner Jonah describes the whale, and Joseph describes prison. In all three cases the thing that separated them from God was this corporeal (confined by a corpse) life.

In the whale, Jonah was in prison. Joseph was in prison. Jesus was in the prison of that dying body. True freedom only when God is present. When all three men found themselves cut off from Life, they realized the need to rejoin themselves to God.

In Jesus' request for water, "I thirst," He did not need a drink. He wanted God's Living Water, but He was given vinegar; a bitter drink. Why was the drink bitter? As in Exodus with the golden calf, God made the children of Israel drink of the bitterness of their *choice*. Jesus too had to drink from the cup of this life. The fact of the matter is that the source of water in this life is a bitter wellspring that emanates from hell. Bitterness is the distinct taste and flower of death. The only water worth drinking is that water which gives Life. The next time you make a *choice*, consider which cup and the source of the water.

The dry, chaffed, earth constantly groans for the presence of God's Holy Spirit[121]. Before God's Holy Spirit came and permanently dwelt among us there was no Water in the earth realm. I believe a man named Noah was the only person to see what God's Holy Spirit looked like when He moves. God spoke to Noah and instructed him to build an ark. A boat was unheard of so God had to give the instructions as He always does. Noah was

---

[121] Genesis 2:1.

obedient and one hundred years later, he saw a physical manifestation of God's Holy Spirit. After forty days and nights of rain (reign), God filled the earth with water (the Glory of God.) All those God set aside He saved all those without the safety of His hand perished. God's Holy Spirit has filled the earth with His awesome fragrance, much like the floodwater. Like those in the ark, those in the shed blood survive. Those outside the shed blood of Christ perish.

The earth without Water is never satisfied for the same reason the barren womb is not; God designed it to produce life. The earth; like any creation, has a Creator for whom it yearns. Although the earth is not human, it is alive; God created it even before man. Man became a living soul when God spoke. Romans 1:20 [122] reminds us that evidence of God's is not only ever present but obvious. The lack of Living Water is also evident--the Bible calls this a famine.

4. **THE FIRE IS NEVER SATISFIED** - We return to the false light in Patmos, the burning, evil ways of Satan, the Gates of hell. Lucifer at one time ate and thrived on Life. When God cast Satan out, part of the curse was that Satan now has to eat dust. The dust Satan eats is the ash or dust of the dead. This means two things for believers;

    i.   Satan must wait until we die to feast on our ashes.
    ii.   Satan must create death in us so he can eat.

Because Satan is darkness and desires your company, he spends his time making traps for you. Although Satan cannot make you fall, he certainly makes standing upright more difficult. The main way in which he does this is by appealing to what your hear sees as a thing to be desired. Whatever pleases your lust Satan will make available to you. Amazingly enough, at the height of pleasure death is most prevalent. Study the history of mankind, the greatest societies in history fell prey to the flesh. The final social values of all fallen empires reek of death and decadence.

---

[122] Romans 1:20, "**For the invisible things of Him from the creation of the world are clearly seen, being understood by the things that are made, (even) His eternal power and Godhead; so that they are without excuse**."

Contrary to popular teaching people are not miserable because times are hard, people are miserable because sin make things hard. The world is only violent because we live here. The flesh only reigns in places we withhold from God. In these places, places which Satan calls the shade death abounds.

If it we not for sin this world would be a garden. Perhaps that was the ultimate secret in the garden. Perhaps the thing we do not understand is that there was no way for Adam to succeed. Perhaps the garden was a lesson to Satan and the angel--Nothing that worships itself thrives. Perhaps we should stop looking for the cause of sin in the trees and in the stars, lust starts in our hearts. Sin is not the fruit of Satan; sin is the fruit of our unrighteous hearts. We conveniently blame Satan for all the evil in our hearts. Even if Satan is responsible for the evil in our hearts, the sin in the world and the horrible conditions that exist, we still have to make the *choice* to participate. Not only is this not a viable excuse, it still does not override the fact that God judges the *choice* not the effect. Jesus said that you committed adultery in your heart, before it ever comes to life. The Bible says you murder a man in your heart before you ever put him to the sword. It is always a *choice* to sin.

There are examples in God's laws (i.e theft of food) that allow Him to be just. However, God never said the man was not a thief, He said He simply exempted the man from the penalty of a thief. When the two thieves hung on the cross on went to hell for his crimes and the other was forgiven his sins. This is what makes God just, He judged the man not for his deeds but the content of his heart. The man was a thief, but in his heart, he repented. The other thief may have stolen less, we do not know. What is clear is that he was not repentant for his deeds, which means he was never going to stop thieving.

Man's sin did not repent God; it is the fact that we *choose* not to change that saddened Him. The thing that He promises not to strive against continually is not sin; it is man's *choice* to sin. The *choice* to keep sin in our hearts is evidence of what type of actions we will engage in. Therefore God knows what we will invariably do by what we keep in our hearts. The pure heart produces pure deeds. Actions themselves do not justify men unto God, but a pure heart draws Him close. Even Paul said he did thing that were inconvenient to do. Righteousness is by no means convenient, easy, or readily attainable--but it is worth your while.

Although I cannot guarantee you heaven, I can unequivocally guarantee that if you do not train yourself to walk away from sin, and you do not foster a relationship with God you will see that other thief.

Amen

Chapter Eighteen
The Edible Secret

"AND WHEN HE HAD GIVEN THANKS, HE BRAKE [IT], AND SAID, TAKE, EAT: THIS IS MY BODY, WHICH IS BROKEN FOR YOU: THIS DO IN REMEMBRANCE OF ME -1 Corinthians 11:25[123].**"**

Another important term from the garden is *Eat*. The term *Eat* is pivotal in understanding what went on that day in the garden. As always, let us look at this term via scriptural analysis. For too long have we tried to put God in a box, making His word of little value. It should not be surprising to double-natured creatures, such as humans, that God's words have at least two applications. The application is dual because we are dual-natured; spirit and flesh.

1. Proverbs 13:2 - **"A man shall eat good by the fruit of [his] mouth: but the soul of the transgressors [shall <u>eat</u>] violence."**

2. Matthew 26:26 - **"AND AS THEY WERE EATING, JESUS TOOK BREAD, AND BLESSED [IT], AND BRAKE [IT], AND GAVE [IT] TO THE DISCIPLES, AND SAID, TAKE, <u>EAT</u>; THIS IS MY BODY."**

3. Revelations 2:7 - **"HE THAT HATH AN EAR, LET HIM HEAR WHAT THE SPIRIT SAITH UNTO THE CHURCHES; TO HIM THAT OVERCOMETH WILL I GIVE TO <u>EAT</u> OF THE TREE OF LIFE, WHICH IS IN THE MIDST OF THE PARADISE OF GOD."**

As we read the Bible, we must learn to look at it as a painting more so than a book. The Bible is obviously canonized[124] text, but it is far from being a book. The Bible is a picture, a painting comprised of small dots we call words. God arranges and rearranges these words just like the dots

---

[123] Related Scriptures: Ezekiel 5:10, 12:18, 22:9, 33:25, 34:19, Hosea 4:8, 4:10, Nahum 3:15, Psalms 22:29, 102:24, 127:4, 141:4, Proverbs 1:31, 13:2, 18:21, Songs 4:16, Isaiah 3:10, 55:2, Jeremiah 15:16, 22:22, John 6:50-53, 6:58, 1 Corinthians 11:24, 11:26, 11:27, 11:28, Revelations 2:7, Revelations 2:17.

[124] The name *Bible* comes from the parchment people wrote the scrolls on called *biblios*.

in television. God arranges and rearranges to make different pictures. The beauty of this is that the same dots show different levels of the same God. By use of the tool, we have come to know as 'Revelation' the Master is actually rearranging the dots and showing different levels of Himself[5].

The most beautiful portrait in the history of humankind does not hang in a museum; it hung on a hillside called Golgotha 2008 years ago. The reason the Bible is so beautiful is that it is a portrait of God. How sweet it is to know that the Lord painted a self-portrait and give it to those He loved. The reason the Bible is so sacred is not because of the words but because of whose words they are.

Jesus tells us that, "**MAN CANNOT LIVE BY BREAD ALONE, BUT BY EVERY WORD THAT PROCEEDS OUT OF THE MOUTH OF GOD.**" The words are clear there can be no mistake. If you insist that the words of God are only contained in the Bible, then throw away the first verse in the Gospel of John, "**In the beginning was the Word, and the Word was with God, and the Word was God.**" If you insist that God's words are the only elements of creation then you will have to throw away Genesis 2:7, "**And the Lord God formed man [of] the dust of the ground, and breathed into his nostrils the breath of life; and man became a living soul.**" It was not the 'words' of God that made man a living soul it was the breath of God that made man a living soul.

Remember, we are dealing with a portrait comprised of words. I say this because the words are not arbitrary; they are the ingredients of God. The Breath of God is where all words begin. It is not the fact that they are God's words that give life, but the fact that God is speaking that creates the life. What this means is that God is Life. As such, whatever He touches, speaks, wills, or wants instantly becomes Living. Consequently, to eat God's words means any or all of the following;

1. To eat God's words means to do God's will - John 4:34.
2. To eat God's words means to partake of God's Holy Spirit - John 4:10.
3. To eat God's words means to live righteous and be written in the Lamb's Book of Life - Revelations 20:12.
4. To eat God's words means to be righteous and have peace, and joy in God's Holy Spirit - Romans 14: 17.

Consequently, it should be understood that the spiritual term *eat* means - *side with, become like, enjoin, ingest, partake of, or learn from*.

God's command in Genesis 2:16 would then mean that the man MUST NOT *side with, become like, enjoin, ingest, partake of, or learn from the tree of the knowledge of good and evil.*

God told Adam he could eat of the Tree of Life. We must ascribe the same characteristics to the word eat and apply it to both trees. It is unworthy of believers to assert the eat means make a meal of when applied to one tree but something different to the Tree of Life in the same passage. Therefore, God said that man had permission to *side with, become like, enjoin, eat, partake of, or learn from the tree of life or the tree of the knowledge of good and evil.*

In man's vain attempt to understand God, they alter the meaning of God's words. This is not always intentional, more often than not it is done out of ignorance. The paradox is akin to the concept of going to the club looking for a *soul mate.* What makes this concept so humorous when I hear it is that those who most often say it search for their soul mate with the flesh. You cannot understand God in the flesh. God does not speak to the flesh. To understand spirit you must be of the Spirit, or at least in the spirit. What is the difference? The difference is the same as being in a Chinese temple. Anyone can go into a Chinese temple, but a Chinese person is Chinese all the time.

Definitively we look to Strong's to see and hear what the word eat means in the Garden of Secrets. We include the two Strong's entries for this verb. The one that is the most intriguing is 5315. If you look at all the applications, you see how many different possible meanings this word can have. The Strong's numbers used are 0398, and 5315.

A SECRET OF THE GARDEN

Strong's 0398 Akal {Appears in Old Testament only}
1. *To eat, devour, burn up, feed, to eat (human subject).*
2. *To eat, devour (of beasts and birds).*
3. *To devour, consume (of fire).*
4. *To devour, slay (of sword).*
5. *To devour, consume, or destroy (inanimate subjects).*
6. *To devour (of oppression).*

A SECRET OF THE GARDEN

Strong's 5315- **Phago** (Greek) / **Nephesh** (Hebrew) {Appear in Old Testament and New Testament }
1. *Soul, self, life, creature, person, appetite, mind, living being, desire, emotion, passion.*
2. *That which breathes the breathing substance or being, soul, the inner being of man.*
3. *Living being.*
4. *Living being (with life in the blood).*
5. *The man himself, self, person, or individual.*
6. *Seat of the appetites.*
7. *Seat of emotions and passions.*
8. *Activity of mind.*
9. *Activity of the will.*
10. *Activity of the character.*

Technical jargon and word study bore most Christians they are however, necessary. *Eat* is singularly the most important, of all the words in the story of the fall of man. *Eat* is important because whatever the tree or its fruit was, the way in which the tree affected man is key. We see that the woman saw the tree to be desirable and then ate. The man did not see the tree as desirable. It was not until the woman gave it to Adam, did Adam eat.

If we look together at Genesis 27:4, we see the perfect example of what the garden schemata describes. Both Hebrew terms for *eat* 0398 and 5315 appear in Genesis 27:4. In this passage Jacob is about to bestow a blessing, so he requests his son to slay a deer and bring the meat of the animal to him. **"And make me savoury meat, such as I love, and bring [it] to me, that I may eat** ^{0398}**; that my soul** ^{5315} **may bless thee before I die**."

Obviously, Jacob could not find a blessing for his soul in deer meat. Under normal conditions, the best veal cutlets are not savoury enough to cause one to welcome death. What then was it that affected Jacob that brought about blessing? Turn to Genesis 4:4, **"And Abel, he also brought of the firstlings of his flock and of the fat thereof. And the Lord had respect unto Abel and to his offering**." It is obvious what pleased both God and Jacob, was the intention of the person, not the food. Veal may please, and excite, but it has no effect whatsoever on the soul. Adam and Eve ate (*sided with, become like, enjoin, ingest, partake of, or learn from*) something that not only directly affected their flesh; it also instantly and eternally effected their soul.

I love Cheesecake. My mother says it was my first solid food. I pay a great deal of money for food, but it has never affected my soul. As wonderful an experience Cheesecake it pales in comparison to the presence of God's Holy Spirit. If I could pick my ultimate meal, it would consist of Lobster, garlic/buttered Asparagus and of course Cheesecake. Adam and Eve had a peculiar diet; they were fruitarians according to Genesis 1:29. The fact that they were fruitarians would lend itself to suggest that they did indeed eat (0398) fruit. Nevertheless, if you look at the reference to fruit as meat they all indicate nourishment instead of flesh[125].

For argument sake, let us agree that the fruit was indeed an Apple. Again, we go back to the garden and see that whatever they ate did indeed go into their bodies. Had whatever they ate been an apple, it would have passed into the draught[126]. Even if the food were poisoned, it would have passed out into the toilet according to Jesus. The word of God does not change. This means that at no time in our lives can the food we eat defile us. The consumption of edibles did not defile Adam and Eve it was the contents of their hearts. The thing that they ate of indeed did nourish them but it nourished or encouraged the disobedience already in their fleshly hearts. If eating means; *Side with, to become like, to enjoin, ingest, to partake of or to learn from* whoever Adam and Eve ate with gave them bad advice.

God did not punish Adam for eating of the tree but for disobedience[127]. Surely, God must know why He punished the man. God says He punished the man because Adam listened to the woman instead of listening to Him[128].

---

[125] Genesis 1:29, Ezekiel 41:12, Daniel 4:12, 4:21, Habakkuk 3:17, Malachi 1:12.
[126] Matthew 15:17-20.
[127] Genesis 3:17.
[128] Please read Exodus 20:3-4.

THE APPLE THEORY

Since tradition has the fruit as an Apple, eating from an Apple tree should have created Applesauce. There are three problems with the Apple theory;
1. Were the fruit an Apple, would the tree not have been called an Apple tree instead of the Tree of the knowledge of good and evil?
2. Would a tree that grows the knowledge of good and evil actually bear apples as well?
3. Is the knowledge of good and evil good for meat?

THE LILLITH THEORY

"Adam's first wife was a relic of an early rabbinical attempt to assimilate the Sumero-Babylonian goddess Belit-ili, or Belili, to Jewish mythology. The Canaanites, Lillith was Ballat, the 'Divine Lady," she was addressed Lillake. Hebraic tradition said that Adam married Lillith because he grew tired of coupling with beasts, a common custom of Middle-Eastern herdsmen...Adam tried to force Lillith to lie beneath him in the missionary position. But Lillith was neither Moslem nor Catholic. She sneered at Adam's cruelty, cursed him, and flew away to make her home by the Red Sea...God sent angels to fetch Lilith back, but she cursed them too, ignored God's command, and spent her time coupling with demons[129].

Here in The Lillith Theory exist the makings of many myths. We see the feminist undertow heralded in Lillith Fair. One must wonder what type of people celebrate the *choice* to rebel against God and mate with demons[130]? We also see the inescapable beginning of the deity in the Arthurian tale, the Lady in the lake (*Lady Lillake*). We also see a subtle, intricate ingenious deceit by Satan. In the story of Elijah, we see the reappearance of the combination of this Lucifarian lie in Baal (*Belili*) and his female cohort Jezebel.

I started this chapter with a scripture from Corinthians; it is now time to look at it in depth. If you can look at Jesus' words and you still contend that Adam and Eve ate an Apple or some other type of flora I

---

[129] The Women's Encyclopedia of Myths and Secrets. Harper San Francisco, New York, NY 1983, (page 541).
[130] The mentality behind Bestiality originates here.

implore you NOT TO PARTAKE OF COMMUNION. Look at these scriptures dealing with the consumption. Nowhere in these scriptures does the Bible indicate anything special about the preparation of the food. Christ is the Tree from which the disciples ate.

1. Matthew 26:26 & 28 - "**And as they were eating, Jesus took bread, and blessed [it], and brake [it], and gave [it] to the disciples, and said, 'TAKE, EAT; THIS IS MY BODY ...FOR THIS IS MY BLOOD OF THE NEW TESTAMENT, WHICH IS SHED FOR MANY FOR THE REMISSION OF SINS'.**"

2. Mark 14:22 & 24 - "**And as they did eat, Jesus took bread, and blessed, and brake [it], and gave to them, and said, 'TAKE, EAT: THIS IS MY BODY...', And He said unto them, 'THIS IS MY BLOOD OF THE NEW TESTAMENT, WHICH IS SHED FOR MANY'.**"

3. Luke 22:19 & 20 - "**And He took bread, and gave thanks, and brake [it], and gave unto them, saying, 'THIS IS MY BODY WHICH IS GIVEN FOR YOU: THIS DO IN REMEMBRANCE OF ME...LIKEWISE ALSO THE CUP AFTER SUPPER, SAYING, THIS CUP [IS] THE NEW TESTAMENT IN MY BLOOD, WHICH IS SHED FOR YOU'.**"

The disciples did not partake of any flesh and they most certainly were not cannibals? How can you see the beauty of breaking the Bread of Life and not see how the partaking of nourishment (commonly called eating) of Christ bestows the eater of His characteristics? More important that the flavor of the food is the effect it had on the disciples. Can bread or any fermented alcoholic beverage remit the sins of the world? Perhaps John 3:16 should read - For God so loved the world that He served as food His only begotten Son, that whosoever eateth of Him shall not perish but have everlasting life. If God wrote it this way, it would be easy to understand but everybody would think Christians to be crazy Cannibals.

There is no way to escape the fact that both the *Apple Theory* as well as the *Lilith Theory* are unable to explain the episode in the garden in Eden. I close this chapter because the Bible admonishes not to bandy words for the sake of argument. We leave the chapter with this thought. If the body and blood spoken of in Matthew 26:26-28, Mark 14:22, Luke

22:19 and 20 are just bread and wine, how could they change your soul and wash your sins?

Amen

Chapter Nineteen
The Secret Fruit[131]

"But the *fruit* of the Spirit is love, joy, peace, longsuffering, gentleness, goodness, faith, Meekness, temperance: against such there is no law - Galatians 5:22."

The next word needed to complete the picture of God's Garden of Secrets is the word *fruit*. This word like the others is an integral part of the creation schemata. The *fruit* in Eden becomes the pivotal point of all of man's history. The church is much slower to change than the world. The traditional church is afraid of change. The church should be stable, but when wrong should repent immediately. Though God's people had God's law, they adopted 611 other laws that were contradictory to the will of God.

Men forced Native Americans to live with the stigma of the word 'Indian' for over 300 years. However, for whatever reason the American government refuses to allow these people any hint of the dignity they once possessed. In much the same manner as the American government refuses to change, the church promulgates antiquated teachings to the children of God as truth and irrefutable facts. When new information or Revelations are unearthed, like the ultimate Revelation Himself, they are crucified and buried; often without due cause. To this end, I submit the following information on fruit as component of spiritual warfare training.

For our purposes, we define *fruit* thusly.

1. (1.a) *The ripened ovary or ovaries of a seed bearing plant, together with accessory parts, containing the seeds and occurring in a wide variety of forms.*

2. (3) *A plant crop or product.*

---

[131] Other Scriptures dealing with this concept: Genesis 3:6, Exodus 21:22, Leviticus 19:23; Deuteronomy 7:13, 28:4, 28:11, 28:18, 28:53; Judges 1:12, 9:11, 2 King 19:30, Psalms 21:10, 92:14, 127:3, 132:11: Proverbs 18: 19, 10:16, 11:30, 12:12, 12:14, 13:2, 18:20, 18:21, Isaiah 27:6, 57:19, Jeremiah 6:19, 11:16, 17:10, 21:14, 32:19, Ezekiel 17:8, 17:9, 19:12, 19:14, Hosea 9:16, 10:1, 10:13, Amos 2:9, Matthew 7:17, 7:18, 7:19, Mark 4:20, 11:14, Luke 3:9, 6:44, 19:9, John 4:36, 12:24,15:2, 15:4, 15:5, 15:8, 15:16, Acts 2:30, Romans 1:13, 6:21, 6:22, 7:4, 7:5, 15:28, Ephesians 5:9, Philemon 1:22, Colossians 1:6, Hebrews 12:11, James 3:18.

3. (4) *Result; outcome.*
4. (5) *Offspring; progeny*[132].

In addition, we use information found in Vine's, wherein the various uses of the term fruit are exposed. *"Karpos fruit, is used;*

    1. *Of the fruit of trees, fields, the earth, that which is produced by the inherent energy of a living organism,*

    2. *Metaphorically, (a) of works or deeds… 'fruit' being the visible expression of power working inwardly and invisibly".* I use this excerpt to show that of the 208 times the term fruit is used it does not always refer to edible, physical fruit like peaches, pears, and plums. Here are some of the scriptures that illustrate this concept.

1. John 15:4-5 - "**ABIDE IN ME, AND I IN YOU. AS THE BRANCH CANNOT BEAR *FRUIT* OF ITSELF, EXCEPT IT ABIDE IN THE VINE; NO MORE CAN YE, EXCEPT YE ABIDE IN ME. I AM THE VINE, YE (ARE) THE BRANCHES: HE THAT ABIDETH IN ME, AND I IN HIM, THE SAME BRINGETH FORTH MUCH FRUIT: FOR WITHOUT ME YE CAN DO NOTHING.**"

2. John 15:8 - "**HEREIN IS MY FATHER GLORIFIED, THAT YE BEAR MUCH *FRUIT*; SO SHALL YE BE MY DISCIPLES.**"

3. John 15:16 - "**YE HAVE NOT CHOSEN ME, BUT I HAVE CHOSEN YOU, AND ORDAINED YOU, THAT YE SHOULD GO AND BRING FORTH *FRUIT*, AND (THAT) YOUR FRUIT SHOULD REMAIN: THAT WHATSOEVER YE SHALL ASK OF THE FATHER IN MY NAME, HE MAY GIVE IT YOU.**"

4. Proverbs 8:19 - "**My *fruit* is better than gold, yea, than fine gold; and my revenue than *choice* silver.**"

5. Proverbs 10:16 - "**The labour of the righteous tendeth to life: the *fruit* of the wicked to sin.**"

6. Proverbs 11:30 - "**The *fruit* of the righteous is a tree of life; and he that winneth souls is wise.**"

---

[132] American Heritage Dictionary, Houghton Mifflin Corp. 1982, Boston (p.537).

7. Proverbs 18:21 - "**Death and life (are) in the power of the tongue: and they that love it shall eat the *fruit* thereof**."

There is a distinct and desperate need for believers to understand that the term *fruit* when used by Eve had nothing to do with edible fruits[133]. It is imperative for believers to know what Eve and then Adam partook of did not go into their mouths it went into their hearts[134]. The scripture refers to eating of the tree, and of the effect, the 'meal' had the two participants. The two participants ate of a tree that defiled them. According to Jesus, this meant that the meal affected their hearts. The Scripture says that what a man eats passes out into the drought and does not defile the man. Whatever Adam and Eve ate was not food; it stayed in their bodies and caused instant death.

Obviously, the *'Tree of Life'* only bears one type of *fruit--Life*. Similarly, the tree of the knowledge of good and evil only bears knowledge. Much as an apple tree only bears apples and fig tree only figs, the tree Adam and Eve partook of bore death. As far as I am aware, there is no tree on earth that bears a *fruit*, which when eaten kills the soul. Let us examine the two sides of evil.

Is this to say that the knowledge of God and evil results in death? The answer is both yes and no. This answer is bifurcated not because I wish to confuse but because evil like most issues, has two sides of the knowledge of good and evil.

KNOWLEDGE OF GOOD AND EVIL SIDE ONE

Believers, we must use this word *natural* in context. Natural simply means *of this world.* God; as we discussed earlier is Super-natural. What does any of this mean? In God's will, there is no evil and in God's way, there is no evil. Nothing God does is either evil or good; it is simply His will. Let us explain it this way. No matter how late you desire to sleep, the sun will always rise due east exactly when God designed it to rise. We invented daylight savings time and different time zones, yet the sun's schedule never changes. We do not call the sun evil in the heat of summer, or good in the beautiful setting of the horizon. We accept these

---

[133] Genesis 3:1.
[134] Matthew 15:23-25.

aspects of the solar cycle because we are powerless to change them. We can modify our response to the solar cycle but that is all.

As it also is with the Lord our God, we can modify our *choices* but that is all. Therefore, just as we accept the solar cycle, believers <u>must</u> accept completely and without question the will of God. We must do this not because we understand or agree but simply because HE IS GOD. The concept that God "**AM**" is involved not complicated. After all, of Solomon's escapades, sexcapades, and wealth, it took Solomon a lifetime to understand the 'I Am'. When Solomon finally did understand he realized our insignificance compared to the will of God.

KNOWLEDGE OF GOOD AND EVIL SIDE TWO

No, the knowledge of good and evil is not bad, at least not since expulsion from the garden. Since expulsion from the garden, the knowledge of good and evil is required to reconcile us to the Father. However, only the knowledge of God is good[135]. You must understand believer, that the Lord our God is a jealous God and does not share. God is not evil; therefore, a desire to know of evil means a desire to know something other than God. Parents you should understand this concept best. How do Parents feel when children do things other than what we teach or allow, or when our kids tell us that their friends' parents allow it therefore we are not being fair.

When I was a child, I had friends and schoolmates of all colors and cultures. I left home and attended college abroad for one semester. During that semester, I developed a prejudice against a specific group of people. I did not base my prejudice on personal feelings but on the atmosphere at the school and of the people, I frequented. Upon my return home, I bantered about this group of people and how much I hated them. My father sat at the head of the table serving dinner looked at me and spoke, "Wait a minute. I do not know where you got this hatred from; I did not teach you that. I know you did not learn it in this house. Take it back where you got it from and don't ever let me hear you speak that way again." My father was not being mean but the rules of his house (his will) did not allow such behavior, and my father also immediately recognized that the behavior was not of him.

---

[135] Matthew 19:17.

In the garden in Eden, God knew that Adam partook of the *tree* because there was something in Adam's behavior that the Father knew was not of God. The question the Father put to Adam was, "**WHO TOLD YOU THAT YOU WERE NAKED**[136]?" In other words, who else have you eaten of[137]; whose *fruit* are you?

In both the creation story and the fall of man, we see that the term *fruit* appears 7 times. The times God uses the term, we see something very important. We see that God uses the word to mean by-product, offspring, or result. This is extremely important in the understanding of what actually took place in the garden in Eden.

If we retain the philosophy that the *fruit* spoken of by Eve and then by Satan is a literalism, you will always miss the essence of Spiritual Warfare. Believers, the beginning of our walk away from God does not begin in the flesh it begins in the heart. It was not Eve's partaking of the *fruit* that began the fall--it was the fact that Eve saw in her heart that the *fruit* was desirable. UnGodly desire in the heart is always the beginning of the end. Whatever God calls off limits--**must be off limits**. It does not matter how desirable the item or items maybe, they must not become pleasing to our hearts, and thus desirable.

The Bible tells us in James 1:15 that whatever our heart dwells on long enough we will do. Couple that with the warning of the power that the eyes have to bring about our fall. This behavior is not unique to Adam and Eve nor is it a human trait--it is a trait of Satan's *fruit*. What does this mean? Simply put; despite the fact that the Book of Ezekiel falls late in the Cannon, the events Ezekiel speaks of proceed the fall of man. As it always is with sin in our lives, the sin has always taken place long before we see the physical result. What the scripture[138] reminds us of is that the unrighteousness always takes place in the human heart before our flesh gets a chance to manifest the darkness. This is why the Lord our God deals with the human heart. Not because the flesh is difficult to deal with it is because the flesh is acting out what is in the heart. If you allow God to renew your heart and mind, and the body will eventually follow.

---

[136] Naked means to be without covering. To be natural, not super natural as ADAM WAS WHEN God created him.
[137] Learned of, enjoined to, supped with, or partaken of.
[138] Matthew 15:18-20.

I point this out so that you can see and determine exactly when the sin took place? The answer consists of three tiers all found in Genesis;

THE FIRST TIER OF THE ORIGINAL SIN

1a. The first tier of the original sin we find in Eve's response to Satan. Notice her verbiage. **"And the woman said unto the serpent, we may eat of the _fruit_ of the trees of the garden** - Genesis 3:2."

1b. Let us compare Eve's statement to the actual command from God. **"BUT OF THE _TREE_ OF THE KNOWLEDGE OF GOOD AND EVIL, THOU SHALT NOT EAT OF IT: FOR IN THE DAY THAT THOU EATEST THEREOF THOU SHALT SURELY DIE** - Genesis 2:17."

1c. Next, let us compare that to what Satan said, **"And he said unto the woman, Yea, hath God said, Ye shall not eat of every _tree_ of the garden** - Genesis 3:1."   When we look together at these statements, let us analyze them in terms of righteousness and unrighteousness. We define righteous as God's will and unrighteousness as anything else. The difference between points a, b, and c, should be obvious, but let us compare them line by line and see the difference.

In example 1b God said clearly, do not eat of the _tree_. In 1c Satan clearly asks about eating of the _tree_. Eve changes the words, and the essence of what God says. IT IS NOT POSSIBLE TO CHANGE THE WORDS OF GOD AND NOT CHANGE THE MEANING. If you believe that this is possible, you do not understand what God means when He says I AM the same yesterday, today, and forever. How can God's words be the same yesterday and forever if we change them? Eve's _choice_ to change the words is integral to understanding where and why spiritual warfare actually begins.

In actuality Eve's heart already changed, we know this because unrighteousness flowed out of Eve's mouth. It is obvious that Eve's willingness and _choice_ to depart from righteousness was not without effect. To believe that this was simply a mistake and not a conscience _choice_ is to either be in denial of the account or proof that you have not read the account.

Matthew 4:4 is not an arbitrary scripture, it proves why we should neither add nor take anything away from His words. Solomon arrayed in all his splendor spent his life searching only to find that the greatest wisdom in the universe is righteousness. To this end in Ecclesiastes 12:13 Solomon writes, **"Let us hear the conclusion of the whole matter:**

Fear God, and keep his commandments: for this (is) the whole (duty) of man." Thus, we must conclude that had Eve, been righteous, feared God, and obeyed His words the fall would not have occurred. I am not exempting Adam from this fiasco, but we deal with him separately. God deals with Adam separately because at no time in this episode did Adam act in unison with his wife nor did Adam act like a husband. Adam and Eve are simply co-defendants.

The picture I endeavor to draw for you is simple. Had Eve responded as The Master did, "IT IS WRITTEN," and repeated God's words exactly, Satan would have had nowhere to go. This is why there is so much distortion and so many problems in the Christian religion. Biblical interpretation is a bastion for Satan's deception. Eve did not arbitrarily change a word she altered God's meaning.

No matter your intentions, only the Son of God saves. Look at it this way, there is only one Jesus and He never changed; neither, has God's Holy Spirit nor the Father. Consequently, believers, any scripture that changes is NOT OF GOD[139]. Trying to make the Bible easier to read is not evil, but it is unGodly. Words spoken by the Master fly directly in the face of interpolation and interpretation[140]. We are to raise the level of understanding, not dilute the message. Although I personally welcome discussion and debate, I do not recommend discussion and debate with the Father of Creation. God is and has the last word on all things. God's words exist the way they do because God gave His words this way intentionally.

THE SECOND TIER OF THE ORIGINAL SIN

The second tier is more obvious and more insidious. In the book How to Try a Spirit, M. Garrison writes something profound about spiritual dynamics. She asserts that the reason the church is unsuccessful dealing with demons is that the church attacks the symptom (fleshly manifestation) and not the actual demon. In terms of our topic, we express this as dealing with the fruit and not the tree. For example, let us look at

---

[139] Galatians 1:8 - "**But though we, or an angel from heaven, preach any other gospel unto you than that, which we have preached unto you, let him be accursed.**"

[140] "**And He said unto them, 'UNTO YOU IT IS GIVEN TO KNOW THE MYSTERY OF THE KINGDOM OF GOD: BUT UNTO THEM THAT ARE WITHOUT, ALL (THESE) THINGS ARE DONE IN PARABLES'.**"

the issue of fornication. "**BUT I SAY UNTO YOU, THAT WHOSOEVER LOOKETH ON A WOMAN TO LUST AFTER HER HATH COMMITTED ADULTERY WITH HER ALREADY IN HIS HEART. AND IF THY RIGHT EYE OFFEND THEE, PLUCK IT OUT, AND CAST (IT) FROM THEE: FOR IT IS PROFITABLE FOR THEE THAT ONE OF THY MEMBERS SHOULD PERISH, AND NOT (THAT) THY WHOLE BODY SHOULD BE CAST INTO HELL**[141]." In this scripture, we see the obvious but do not understand the actual. It is not the visual perception of the woman that causes the issue let us pause to explain why.

The way the human eye works is that it simply receives light. The way we see something is that an object reflects or absorbs light and our eyes pick up the results of the reflection. The only ways to stop this occurrence called *Vision* is to close the eyes, or to alter the image with some type of glass (sunglasses). For this reason, the actual viewing of the woman could not be a sin--God created eyes and vision. Some argue that I am contradicting scripture. Again, I say they see the obvious but do not understand the actual. What Jesus is doing is assisting those too weak to control their desires. It is clear what Jesus is saying is that if you cannot control your wretched heart; destroy the instruments that give rise to your sin. It is extremely difficult to steal without hands, to fornicate without genitals, or to lust without eyes. The organs are not the problem; they are simply the vehicle we use to execute our sinful will.

As we can now see clearly, Eve saw what her heart wanted her to see. Unrighteousness is desirable, Eve's heart was affected; the eyes after all are the windows for the heart. Eve's failing compounded the problem at even a lower level. The scripture states that she was a part of the man. In following the scriptural principle, concerning that which defiles a man-- Adam did What Eve desired to do.

Eve's heart contained one vital flaw; she had no real relationship with God. As is plain in the scripture, there is very little discourse between God and the woman. Adam clearly had a relationship with Eve. It was in the fellowship with God that Eve fell short. She was able to recite the words to the best of her ability but she had no relationship with God so the words meant nothing. Believers this is the difference between those who are in Christ they have council with Him. This is the danger of

---

[141] Matthew 5:28 & 29.

citing and quoting scriptures as catch phrases; yet, and not understanding or supping with God's Holy Spirit.

In the wilderness Jesus not only quotes the scriptures verbatim; But He used the appropriate scripture for the appropriate situation;
1. This required study.
2. This required understanding of the will of God.

Matthew 28 puts the onus on the believer, and admonishes the believer to, "...**TEACH WHAT I COMMANDED**..." This relationship with God also requires study and understanding. John 14:15 reads "**IF YOU LOVE ME OBEY MY COMMANDMENTS**." Surely, we must know God's commands before we can obey them. Had Eve repeated the actual command her fate would have been different.

John 14:15 must have a converse application to it. If you do not obey my Commandments, then you do not love Me. John 14:15 illustrates for us clearly the last three pieces of the original sin puzzle.
1. The heart condition.
2. The physical manifestation.
3. Unfamiliarity/ lack of relationship with God's Holy Spirit.

WHAT WAS THE *FRUIT*?

John 8:44 is a poignant scripture; it explains what God meant in Genesis regarding *fruit*. "**YE ARE OF (YOUR) FATHER THE DEVIL, AND THE LUSTS OF YOUR FATHER YE WILL DO. HE WAS A MURDERER FROM THE BEGINNING, AND ABODE NOT IN THE TRUTH, BECAUSE THERE IS NO TRUTH IN HIM. WHEN HE SPEAKETH A LIE, HE SPEAKETH OF HIS OWN: FOR HE IS A LIAR, AND THE FATHER OF IT**." Adam and Eve are the *fruit* of the fallen tree written of, in Ezekiel 31:9-11. Adam and Eve became Satan's fruit. Adam and Eve became a physical manifestation of the one who said, "**I am a god, I sit in the seat of God, in the midst of the seas**." Adam and Eve were the fruit of Satan's tree and the evidence of the content of Satan's heart.

From Ezekiel 28:15-17 you see it was the Satan's heart that God disdained first. God found evil in Satan before his deeds reflected what he desired to do. Look to Genesis 1:11 wherein God makes a phenomenal statement about the type of tree God plants. "**AND GOD SAID, LET THE EARTH BRING FORTH GRASS, THE HERB YIELDING SEED, (AND)**

THE FRUIT TREE YIELDING FRUIT AFTER HIS KIND, WHOSE SEED (IS) IN ITSELF, UPON THE EARTH: AND IT WAS SO." God plants *self-perpetuating trees*. *Self-perpetuating trees* differ from simple fruit bearing trees. The trees God plants give life because God made them in His image. The human creature therefore produces Godly fruit because we are Godly fruit. Since God is our Tree made in His image means that He created us to be His fruit[142]. The forbidden *tree* brings about death-spiritual death. As we know, the thief comes only to steal, kill, and destroy and like Cain we are like the tree from which we suckle. It is in our sin filled hearts and selfish ways that we are like Satan. The book of Hebrews explains the difference between the last Adam[143] and the fallen Adam. In Genesis, God made Adam the man in His image. Adam fell because he became a reflection of the tree that Adam ate of-Satan. The scriptures tell us why Christ is beloved of God. It is not only because He was His Son because Adam was also a son. It is because Jesus retained the image of the Father[144]; Jesus was the first fruit.

Obviously, trees bear fruit but that is far too small a scale for God. Jesus did not come to bear fruit but to plant trees; trees like the ones cut down from heaven[145]. Jesus came to plant self-perpetuating trees like Him, trees spoken of in Revelations as being for the healing of all the nations Satan deceived.

God is never complicated, but He is always intricate. Let us together understand that the flesh of a fruit is only useful as food. Only the seeds have any value as far as replenishing the earth. God does not want mere fruits devourable by life or by Satan. Unless a seed first dies it cannot bring forth life[146]. The same law of dying and growing applies to human flesh. Once the seed/flesh dies the life it contains releases into the soil and another just like it grows. This is why we must allow God to abide in us; otherwise, when we die the life that ebbs is not Godly but the sin-filled nature of Adam. God needs trees willing to bear seed-producing fruit like the ones He planted in Eden[147]. In other words, God needs

---

[142] James 1:18, "**Of His own will begat He us with the word of truth, that we should be a kind of first fruits of His creatures** - James 1:18."
[143] 1 Corinthians 15:45.
[144] Hebrews 1:1-6, John 14:7, John 14:9.
[145] John 15:1-6
[146] John 12:24.
[147] Genesis 1:29.

believers that are willing to die to sin so that God's seed will live on. The way to make the difference is not to make fruit but to plant seeds (The parable of the sower).

One apple is meal enough for one person but it can produce 10-20 trees. God's trees produce fruit that have His seed. When God's trees multiply, they make His seed innumerably. This is why God demands upright trees. Without righteousness or up-rightness, we are merely fruit upon which to feast. However, as His trees-upright and strong we can feed the fruit long enough for them to bear seeds. Once these seeds die, they can yield an orchard of Godly-fruit bearing trees.

HUSBANDRY/GARDENING

Let us look at the concept of Husbandry/gardening again briefly. John 15:1-6, "**I AM THE TRUE VINE, AND MY FATHER IS THE HUSBANDMAN. EVERY BRANCH IN ME**[148] **THAT BEARETH NOT FRUIT HE TAKETH AWAY: AND EVERY [BRANCH] THAT BEARETH FRUIT, HE PURGETH IT, THAT IT MAY BRING FORTH MORE FRUIT. NOW YE ARE CLEAN THROUGH THE WORD WHICH I HAVE SPOKEN UNTO YOU. ABIDE IN ME, AND I IN YOU. AS THE BRANCH CANNOT BEAR FRUIT OF ITSELF, EXCEPT IT ABIDE IN THE VINE; NO MORE CAN YE, EXCEPT YE ABIDE IN ME. I AM THE VINE, YE [ARE] THE BRANCHES: HE THAT ABIDETH IN ME, AND I IN HIM, THE SAME BRINGETH FORTH MUCH FRUIT: FOR WITHOUT ME YE CAN DO NOTHING. IF A MAN ABIDE NOT IN ME, HE IS CAST FORTH AS A BRANCH, AND IS WITHERED; AND MEN GATHER THEM, AND CAST [THEM] INTO THE FIRE, AND THEY ARE BURNED**." Eve was the fruit of an untended garden. This means her gardener failed to cultivate into her the righteousness to walk closely with God. Had Adam been the type of Husband described in John 15 Eve would never have had an opportunity to speak to Satan alone.

However, the fault was not Eve's; after all, Adam did not come from the woman. The man also had issues of the flesh for Adam harkened to Eve instead of to God. What the scripture says is clear, although the meaning is a mystery. The Master said it was not good that man should be alone. I cannot say with certainty, but it makes sense, that whatever the reason solitude was not good God tried to remedy it with the woman. This

---

[148] This by the way would make Jesus the *Tree*.

does not mean God failed. The creatures with *choice* had the ability to *choose* evil instead of good. The creation of the woman God intended to head Satan off at the pass. God knew Adam would make a *choice*. Instead of only two spiritual *choices*, God gave Adam a third fleshly alternative that Adam could understand. God gave Adam three *choices*:
1. The Tree of life.
2. The tree of the knowledge of good and evil.
3. The woman.

Satan did not have to be evil; it was his *choice* to be evil. The same selfish *choice* was the thing Satan relied on when he came to the woman. Some scholars assert that Satan and Eve had a sexual relationship, but there is no evidence to support this claim. There is ample evidence to support copulation between the sons of God and the daughters of men[149]. However, none of the scriptures dealing with human/angel sexuality point to Eve and Satan in result or deed. What we do know is that according to Romans 1 God actually gives people up to their own vile affections. As evident with Adam, to be spiritually dead does not mean cease to exist it means to be cut off from Life; cut off from God. In the book of Job, God placed a hedge about the Arab Job, which also protected Job's mind[150]. It is for this reason that God allowed Satan to afflict Job, but God forced Satan to stay away from Job's mind. In Romans, we see that God does not only give people up to reprobate hearts but to their reprobate minds. God's Holy Spirit renews the mind in believers. This term renew means to make new again or to put back to the original design. When Adam partook of the forbidden *tree*, God cut his spirit off, therefore, his mind God also cut off. When Adam tapped into Satan, he also tapped into Satan's vile attributes. Adam therefore viewed the woman's body in an ungodly manner.

Nudity is not vile; otherwise, God would cause humans to be born wearing clothes or a pelt. The vileness of Satan pervading through the flesh creates this condition. It was not Salome's dance that which vile it was the vileness in the King and her mother's heart that cost John the Baptist his head. Satan acting through Herodias saw the king's vile heart and simply appealed to what the king desired. In the garden in Eden with Herod, Satan's influence destroyed Adam, Eve, and Creation. Satan's

---

[149] Genesis 6:1-2.
[150] Job 2:7.

influence turned nudity into a relationship more like incest. The man no longer saw through innocent eyes, but through the evil, lustful eyes of Satan.

When unrighteousness fills the heart of a believer, unrighteousness fills their lives as well. Only God's Holy Spirit renews. You cannot simply dump issues and think they will stay gone. If you were smart enough to get away from it, you would have been smart enough to stay away from it in the first place. Jesus had to fast and pray not because He was sinful but because He lived in a sin-filled body. All fleshly creatures face the same dilemma--regardless of heritage or parent's influence in heaven. Had Adam kept his wife and himself in constant communion with God and stayed in righteousness they would have never fallen. Jesus conquered the flesh by letting one simple thought pervade His heart, **"JESUS SAITH UNTO THEM, MY MEAT IS TO DO THE WILL OF HIM THAT SENT ME, AND TO FINISH HIS WORK**[151]**."** He therefore was never interested in anything the great Red dragon had to offer.

WHAT WAS THE FALL?

Let us take a moment to pause and actually get a concise understanding of the *fall* of man. This concept is flawed. This book is about choice. I am unfamiliar with anyone that *fell* from grace. Isaiah describes Satan falling from heaven, but before he fell God threw Satan out first. Adam and Eve did not fall out of Eden God drove them out. The people in the flood drowned, Saul and Solomon walked away from God. David sinned, Judas betrayed Him, Caiaphas had Him crucified, but I Know of no one that actually *fell* from grace. God's grace is sufficient, it does not allow people to fall from it, that is why it is SUFFICIENT (ample, enough). God's grace stops us from *falling*. Many people have jumped or been thrown from God's favor but they did not fall.

Adam and Eve did not fall, they were abased. God was well within His rights to drive them out. God's law decrees;

1. **"Thus saith the Lord God; 'REMOVE THE DIADEM, AND TAKE OFF THE CROWN: THIS [SHALL] NOT [BE] THE SAME: EXALT [HIM THAT IS] LOW, AND ABASE [HIM THAT IS] HIGH'** - Ezekiel 21:26"

---

[151] John 4:34.

2. **"And whosoever shall exalt himself shall be abased; and he that shall humble himself shall be exalted** - Matthew 23:12"

Make no mistake, when it comes to grace no one falls. God cannot stand those that exalt themselves that is after all His job. Of grace: if God be for you who can be against you. Conversely, if God be against you who can be for you? Once you are turn over to yourself by God you will not return.

THE CAUSE OF THE FALL

It is important to realize that *eating the fruit is* not what caused the fall. It is also imperative to show that this eating the fruit concept is not accurate. Regardless of what type of reasoning, consider the sources of the information. The three inputs in the scripture come from:
1. The Father says, 'tree'.
2. Satan who 'tree'.
3. Eve; the sinner says, 'fruit.

If you refuse to believe this writer, believe the word of God. God never told Adam and Eve not TO EAT OF THE FRUIT, GOD SAID DO NOT EAT OF THE *TREE*.

I resist using science if possible but in some cases, the science of the thing sheds brilliant and clarifying light on a subject. The illumination of this information should make it clear. God told Adam and Eve in no manner should they follow Satan. God's will requires no involvement or contribution from Satan. God did not desire Adam and Eve to have anything that could harm them. God therefore put Adam and Eve in the safety of His garden and provided for their needs. The one thing God denied His children was the one thing that could hurt them.

Again, we must understand that it was knowledge Adam and Eve sought that was evil. It was the reason Adam and Eve wanted to *eat* of the *tree* that was evil. The fact of the matter is that fruit cannot feed itself. This is why fruit begins to rot immediately upon leaving the tree. All the sustenance to the fruit comes from the tree. The tree on the other hand thrives on a variety of sources of nutrition. The tree eats through both its roots and its leaves. Water and many trace minerals come to the tree directly from the soil. Trees photosynthesize sunlight and absorb gases from the air and through their roots in the form of rainfall. The sum of this chemical process results in what we call *fruit*.

The tree does interesting things when it creates fruit. It is common knowledge that most of the nutrients of the fruit are in the skin or epidermal layer of the fruit. If that is the case then what is contained in the seeds? What the seeds contain is the essence of the creative nature of the tree. The seed has the veritable DNA of the tree. **When planted in suitable soil seeds immediately try to reproduce. The seed however does not try to produce fruit. God did not design the seed to produce fruit the seed creates trees.** Much in the same way a clam produces the favored pearl, fruit is the result of many chemical processes but it is by no means the life of the tree.

THE TREE OF THE ACCURSED FRUIT

When Jesus cursed the tree in Matthew 21:19 it appears that the cause was the lack of fruit. Believers this is the immature saint's understanding of this event. The mature understanding is that Jesus cursed the tree because the tree did not adhere to the *fruit making process*. A tree is known by its fruit is about the seed, not the fruit. The tree's fruit enables a person to see what happened inside the tree. If a tree bears fruit in due season the inside behaves within the will of God. If however the tree bears no fruit, it becomes obvious as in the human that the heart of the tree is not in the will of God. **Trees that bear no fruit are of no use to the Kingdom, not because there is no fruit, but because there are NO SEEDS**[152]. The trees' disobedience angered the Master. Be fruitful and multiply is not a suggestion it is a command. The tree in Matthew 21:19 was therefore out of God's will.

Hydroponics is the science of growing fruit without soil. A hybrid such as a Tangelo man creates by cross-pollinating species of fruits. Despite soil-less or artificial breeding a SEED is necessary. In Matthew 21:19 the fruit was of no consequence. Jonah 4:6 shows that the fruit is a simple byproduct of a Godly seed. The fruit only served the man, the tree served God. Like sex, fruit gives pleasure but in both cases God's ultimate design for the seed is to produce life.

The wages of righteousness are;
1. Death to self.
2. Life in God's Holy Spirit.
3. Pleasure.

---

[152] Genesis 1:29.

4. Joy.

In Satan's twisted way of spreading carnage and death, he too makes fruit. Satan's nurturing process however brings about;
1. Pleasure.
2. Joy.
3. Death in Satan's shade.

The command to be fruitful contains in it God's mandate to make more of self. We understand that the fruit is of the tree it is not the tree. Consequently, we must understand that fruit is necessary so that there is seed. Without the seed, there can be no self-perpetuating trees. Without the trees, there can be no life.

Amen

Chapter Twenty
Trees with Secrets

"**The fruit of the righteous is a tree of life; and he that winneth souls is wise** - Proverbs 11:3."

We take this opportunity to move to another phase of the story of Creation that causes confusion. Again, the culprit is a word. The culprit is a common word, a word used every day. The word I referg to is *tree*.

For the purpose of this book, we use the following definition for *tree*. Tree-*A diagram showing family lineage*[153]. This definition becomes important to us as believers in Christ for two main reasons.

1. To authenticate Jesus.
2. To prove where offspring originated.

Some question, why this definition for *tree* matters to believers? The answer becomes apparent when we traverse the Bible as a whole. Of the 201 times the scripture uses the word tree many of the references do not refer to the wooden giants we use as firewood. Before we analyze the *tree* in the spiritual realm, we need to go into another word. The other word we need to exculpate is garden. The same dictionary offers a wonderful definition for garden, that being; '*a fertile, well cultivated region*' (p.548 {4}).

Creation deals with the origin of sin, actually it deals with the introduction of sin to this world. I use the term introduction because sin came to mankind from another type of being. Fear not brothers and sisters, this is not some ridiculous trip into outer space, sin came to the flesh by a spiritual creature. The concept of sin (evil, rebelliousness, disobedience came to human kind by a fallen angel. What does this have to do with trees? Well we have to recall the definition of tree that we agreed to use previously. It is not arbitrary that in Matthew 4 Jesus began each response to Satan with the words, "**IT IS WRITTEN**..." These three

---

[153] <u>American Heritage Dictionary</u>, Houghton Mifflin Corp. 1982, Boston p.1291-(8).

words have more power than we understand. These words set the Lord against Satan. Another way to understand the use of these words would be to use the phrase, 'In the name of Jesus.' The phrase, "It is written," has the same authority, as in the name of Jesus.

Now let us study the following scriptures to get a better understanding. It is only when we change God's words that the enemy has the opportunity to pervert them.

1. Genesis 2:9 - **"God made every tree to grow that is pleasant to the sight, and good for food; the _tree_ of Life in the middle of the garden, and the tree of the knowledge of good and evil."**

2. Genesis 2:16 & 17 - **"The Lord God commanded the man, saying, 'OF EVERY _TREE_ OF THE GARDEN YOU MAY FREELY EAT; BUT OF THE _TREE_ OF THE KNOWLEDGE OF GOOD AND EVIL, YOU SHALL NOT EAT OF IT; FOR IN THE DAY THAT YOU EAT OF IT YOU WILL SURELY DIE'."**

3. Genesis 3:22 & 24 - **"The Lord God said, 'BEHOLD, THE MAN HAS BECOME LIKE ONE OF US, KNOWING GOOD AND EVIL. NOW, LEST HE PUT FORTH HIS HAND, AND ALSO TAKE OF THE _TREE_ OF LIFE, AND EAT, AND LIVE FOREVER.' Therefore, the Lord God sent him forth from the garden of Eden, to till the ground from which he was taken. So He drove out the man; and He placed Cherubs at the east of the garden of Eden, and the flame of a sword which turned every way, to guard the way to the tree of life."**

I would like to point out that there is no known tree or fruit now or in the history of mankind that comes from the earth which when consumed gives Eternal life. Brothers and sister too long have we tried to squeeze the Almighty into our tiny lives and language. I assure you that Better Homes and Gardens could never picture the garden in Eden in any issue. This is because the concept of garden in our world consists of shrubs and flowers. However, we must understand that Eden and Paradise are fertile, well-cultivated regions. They are not fertile because of their ability to grow flora. They are fertile, well-cultivated regions because the Father dwells there. The fertility and cultivation of what we would loosely call soil, is as a place or condition favorable to growth.

The soil in the garden is Holy Spirit. It is only from this fertile condition favorable to growth that life sprung forth. The soil we refer to as being able to grow things is actually the bosom of God. The reason that it is fertile is because God is good and His goodness abounds. Even the Tree of Life God planted in this soil. The tree of Life sprang forth from a fertile, well-cultivated region, a veritable garden of Love.

Now we delve further into trees and what they represent using the following scriptures pertaining to trees.

1. Ezekiel 28:13 confirms that the fallen angel was in Eden, and explains while he was there he was still beautiful. It also explains in my opinion why Eve was beguiled so easily, **"YOU WERE IN EDEN, THE GARDEN OF GOD; EVERY PRECIOUS STONE ADORNED YOU: RUBY, TOPAZ, EMERALD, CHRYSOLITE, ONYX, JASPER, SAPPHIRE, TURQUOISE, AND BERYL. GOLD WORK OF TAMBOURINES AND OF PIPES WAS IN YOU. IN THE DAY THAT YOU WERE CREATED THEY WERE PREPARED."**

2. Isaiah 14:12 tells us of a fallen angel and refers to it as having been cut down, a phrase also used of *trees*, **"How you have fallen from heaven, morning star, son of the dawn! How you are <u>cut down</u> to the ground, who laid the nations low"** Ezekiel 31:18 lists and compares the characteristics of the trees. Does it make sense that God would talk to dead wood and tell a piece of dead wood that he would be kicked out of Heaven, Eden, Paradise, and onto lower earth? We know that God kicked Satan and his group out of heaven. Therefore, the trees referred to in Ezekiel 31:18 represent fallen angels. The only tree from the garden that was not kicked out was the *Tree* of life.

3. Judges 9:9-15 is a peculiar group of scriptures it begins referring to people and end up referring to talking *trees*. The *trees* are trying to decide which tree is best suited, and willing to assume the throne. **"But the olive tree said to them, Should I leave my fatness, with which by me they honor God and man, and go to wave back and forth over the trees? The**

trees said to the fig tree, Come you, and reign over us. But the fig tree said to them, Should I leave my sweetness, and my good fruit, and go to wave back and forth over the trees? The trees said to the vine, Come you, and reign over us. The vine said to them, Should I leave my new wine, which cheers God and man, and go to wave back and forth over the trees? Then said all the trees to the bramble, Come you, and reign over us. The bramble said to the trees, If in truth you anoint me king over you, then come and take refuge in my shade; and if not, let fire come out of the bramble, and devour the cedars of Lebanon." I have planted several trees and plants, none of which were suited to lead. In fact, quite often, the most expensive of the lot perished, long before maturity. Obviously, tree is a metaphor and symbol of a person, place, trait, or spirit.

4. "**The Lord <u>called your name</u>, a green olive tree, beautiful with goodly fruit: with the noise of a great tumult He has kindled fire on it, and the branches of it are broken.**" Jeremiah 11:16 refers to the Lord calling a good and faithful servant the name or type of tree. Then God destroys the tree because of unrighteous behavior. Notice God refers to those that took after this servant as *fruit*. The servant is therefore the tree and the servants offspring the *fruit*.

5. Ezekiel 31:3-18 lists eloquent metaphors that go to great lengths to explain not only how beautiful Lucifer was when created but goes on to tell us that the angels compared their beauty against each other. "**Behold, the Assyrian was a cedar in Lebanon with beautiful branches, and with a forest-like shade, and of high stature; and its top was among the thick boughs. The waters nourished it, the deep made it to grow: the rivers of it ran round about its plantation; and it sent out its channels to all the trees of the field. Therefore, its stature was exalted above all the trees of the field; and its boughs were multiplied, and its branches became long by reason of many waters, when it shot them forth. All the birds of the sky made their nests in its boughs; and under its branches did all**

the animals of the field bring forth their young; and under its shadow lived all great nations. Thus, was it beautiful in its greatness, in the length of its branches; for its root was by many waters. The cedars in the garden of God could not hide it; the fir trees were not like its boughs, and the plane trees were not as its branches; nor was any tree in the garden of God like it in its beauty. I MADE IT BEAUTIFUL BY THE MULTITUDE OF ITS BRANCHES, SO THAT ALL THE TREES OF EDEN THAT WERE IN THE GARDEN OF GOD ENVIED IT. Therefore thus said the Lord God: 'BECAUSE YOU ARE EXALTED IN STATURE, AND HE HAS SET HIS TOP AMONG THE THICK BOUGHS, AND HIS HEART IS LIFTED UP IN HIS HEIGHT; I WILL EVEN DELIVER HIM INTO THE HAND OF THE MIGHTY ONE OF THE NATIONS; HE SHALL SURELY DEAL WITH HIM; I HAVE DRIVEN HIM OUT FOR HIS WICKEDNESS. STRANGERS, THE TERRIBLE OF THE NATIONS, HAVE CUT HIM OFF, AND HAVE LEFT HIM: ON THE MOUNTAINS AND IN ALL THE VALLEYS HIS BRANCHES ARE FALLEN, AND HIS BOUGHS ARE BROKEN BY ALL THE WATERCOURSES OF THE LAND; AND ALL THE PEOPLES OF THE EARTH ARE GONE DOWN FROM HIS SHADOW, AND HAVE LEFT HIM. ON HIS RUIN ALL THE BIRDS OF THE SKY SHALL DWELL, AND ALL THE ANIMALS OF THE FIELD SHALL BE ON HIS BRANCHES; TO THE END THAT NONE OF ALL THE TREES BY THE WATERS EXALT THEMSELVES IN THEIR STATURE, NEITHER SET THEIR TOP AMONG THE THICK BOUGHS, NOR THAT THEIR MIGHTY ONES STAND UP ON THEIR HEIGHT, EVEN ALL WHO DRINK WATER: FOR THEY ARE ALL DELIVERED TO DEATH, TO THE LOWER PARTS OF THE EARTH, IN THE MIDST OF THE CHILDREN OF MEN, WITH THOSE WHO GO DOWN TO THE PIT. Thus says the Lord God: IN THE DAY WHEN HE WENT DOWN TO SHEOL I CAUSED A MOURNING: I COVERED THE DEEP FOR HIM, AND I RESTRAINED THE RIVERS OF IT; AND THE GREAT WATERS WERE STAYED; AND I CAUSED LEBANON TO MOURN FOR HIM, AND ALL THE TREES OF THE FIELD FAINTED FOR HIM. I MADE THE NATIONS TO SHAKE AT THE SOUND OF HIS FALL, WHEN I CAST HIM DOWN TO SHEOL WITH THOSE WHO DESCEND INTO THE PIT; AND

ALL THE TREES OF EDEN, THE *CHOICE* AND BEST OF LEBANON, ALL THAT DRINK WATER, WERE COMFORTED IN THE LOWER PARTS OF THE EARTH. THEY ALSO WENT DOWN INTO SHEOL WITH HIM TO THOSE WHO ARE SLAIN BY THE SWORD; YES, THOSE WHO WERE HIS ARM THAT LIVED UNDER HIS SHADOW IN THE MIDST OF THE NATIONS. TO WHOM ARE YOU THUS LIKE IN GLORY AND IN GREATNESS AMONG THE TREES OF EDEN? YET SHALL YOU BE BROUGHT DOWN WITH THE TREES OF EDEN TO THE LOWER PARTS OF THE EARTH: YOU SHALL LIE IN THE MIDST OF THE UNCIRCUMCISED, WITH THOSE WHO ARE SLAIN BY THE SWORD. THIS IS PHARAOH AND ALL HIS MULTITUDE', says the Lord God."

In my humble opinion Ezekiel 28:16 & 17 show just how deep God's sorrow goes. Not only did the Father loose His favorite new toy but also He had to cast His favorite angel out. Before He cast His favorite tree down, He first had to cut it down. The other trees in the garden are mentioned in verse 14 and then again in verse 16. The Bible refers to angels as the trees and as stones of fire.

In verse fourteen, the Lord explains the reason He cast out His prize tree. God explains that this tree was puffed up and proud. Satan exalted himself above all the other trees. The other trees, like Satan, God also cut down and cast into the pit. All the members of Satan's group, God cut and cast down with their leader. Perhaps this is the reason why the word Seraphim actually appears only twice in the Bible. In Judges 9:8-15, the *trees* hold an election. This group was looking for a new leader because they no longer worshipped God. There are distinctions made in verse Ezekiel 28:15 and 31:9 of the *trees* that differentiate these trees from all the other trees. The *trees* in verse 28:15 and 31:9 were God's *trees*, His *choice* stock the *trees* from His soil. The angels in 31:9 were all *fruits* of God's *Tree* they were not men. David reminds us that man is beneath angels/trees. These trees stood in God's inner court drinking from the water; the Living Water. In order to prevent another mutiny, God cast out all of the angels/trees that stood by the Water into Sheol.

This has phenomenal implications. *Cutting down* means God cast all of the angels from the inner court into Sheol and assigned other

Cherubs to prevent the fallen angels' return. This means that Micah'El, Gabri'El, nor Ari'El stood in the inner court, or at the very least the angels, Micah'El, Gabri'El, and Uri'El did not side with Lucifer. This also seems to imply that the normal function of the Cherubs did not involve being part of the inner court.

In Ezekiel 28:16 the Lord calls Lucifer the anointed (Sanctified, consecrated) Cherub. Unlike the regular Cherubs, Lucifer was part of the inner court. In fact, Ezekiel 28:13 tells us that Lucifer sang praises to the Lord. Indeed, God created Satan with special abilities enabling him to sing to the Lord. The Cherubs are apparently a special group of angels that function like deacons in heaven. Cherubs perform certain functions reserved for trusted servants that were loyal and unwavering[154]. Because of their trustworthiness, Cherubs held positions of esteem in the Kingdom but they stayed just outside the inner court. What I found to be intriguing was the two following points;

POINT ONE ABOUT CHERUBS - Revelations 12:4 states that Lucifer took one-third of the stars from heaven when he fell. The stars (bright lights that illuminate the heavens) that left with Lucifer were none other than the angels that drank the Water (Ezekiel 31:16). This implies that the 1/3 that fell were all from the inner court. However, the 1/3 that fell only included one Cherub--Lucifer.

POINT TWO ABOUT CHERUBS - The Cherubs that remained faithful stood against Lucifer for all time. Despite Cherubs high position in the Kingdom, it was the inner circle from whence the trouble in heaven sprang. God therefore found it necessary to cast His inner court into the pit. Then God also had to cast man out of the garden. We know by Judges 9:8 that the trees (angels) were of a particular chorus[155]--type. The inner court cast out in Ezekiel 31 most likely consisted of the Seraphs; this explains why scripture does not mention them again. As part of this Revelation, it now becomes clear why praise and singing is so important to the Almighty. Both creatures created to sing God's praises He cast asunder. David's music was obviously music to His ears and brought joy to God's heart. Perhaps this is why Jesus was able to relate the joy in the

---

[154] 2 Samuel 22:4, Genesis 3:24.
[155] Angel type is called *Chorus* because they sing to the Lord.

story of the prodigal son. Singing had come home and God found it in the heart of King David.

I belabored this point for a reason, and that is to explain that the trees spoken of in the Garden of Eden were spirits[156]. The spirits in the Garden of Eden were God's Holy Spirit and the spirit of Lucifer. Adam chose sides and as Jesus said, **HE THAT IS NOT; WITH ME IS AGAINST ME**; God spewed Adam out of His heart.

In keeping with the theme of this book, there is a lack of trees in the church; a lack of Cherubs. In the history of the church, the trouble in the church has always come from inside the church. It is obvious that the same spirit/tree that Adam partook of still exists. Lucifer is still beguiling God's inner courts, secreting God's inner court from His bosom.

As I write to you the story of Joseph comes to mind. There were twelve brothers but Isra`El loved Joseph above them all. When Joseph was taken from Isra`EL the Bible tells us that his heart was broken. God knows the feeling of losing His beloved; Lucifer, Adam, and Jesus. What we see throughout the Bible is that those who God *chooses* and sets apart He isolates. God set people apart to steward His creation, like Adam in the Garden and Jesus on the earth. Unfortunately, many of the elect *choose* to partake of the forbidden tree.

Too many of us *choose* the knowledge of good and evil trying to become like God. However, when we partake of the spirit of Lucifer we also die in the spirit. When baptized, we are baptized into God's Holy Spirit. When we partake of Lucifer we become part of Lucifer's tree one of his fruit. Undoubtedly, this is why the priests told Jesus in Matthew 12:24 that He was able to cast out demons because He was fruit from the tree of Lucifer. Jesus responded that if that were the case by whom then did the priests cast out demons? The truth is that the priests were the fruit of the tree of Lucifer and could therefore cast out demons. This quid pro quo in the spirit kingdom allows Satan to perform far more wonders than he actually can. Satan appears to have ultimate power, but he cheats. Many of the people masquerading as priests do Satan's bidding. When priests do Satan's bidding it appears that Satan is more powerful than he actually is.

At the time of Jesus, there was a group of spiritualists called *Essenes* also performed miracles. The reason these other groups were able

---

[156] Proverbs 11:30, 13:12, 15:4, 27:18.

to perform wonders was that they also understood spiritual dynamics. *Essenes* understood that demonic influence causes many troubles, ailments, and predicaments. The false prophets therefore cured and healed by convincing their fellow demons to leave. The others conspired with the demons. They all worked for the same under lord. Jesus knew this and indicated His knowledge when He asked by whose power the priest cast out demons.

THE SECRETS OF THE TREES

1. **THE TREE OF LIFE - "HE THAT HATH AN EAR, LET HIM HEAR WHAT THE SPIRIT SAITH UNTO THE CHURCHES; TO HIM THAT OVERCOMETH WILL I GIVE TO EAT OF THE TREE OF LIFE, WHICH IS IN THE MIDST OF THE PARADISE OF GOD** - Revelations 2:7." The Tree of life is the Spirit of God it is this tree from which we draw strength and life. It is from this spirit that Adam was supposed to draw life. Of the wooden trees, God told Adam to eat and sustain his flesh. Of this tree, God told Adam that he could get life, if he chose to eat.

In the garden, the *tree* did not move because the Lord required Adam and Eve to make a *choice*. God required Adam to walk away from the carnal (not yet sinful) nature of life. The proper *choice* for Adam and Eve would have resulted in eternal life and exaltation; these are the rewards for righteousness. However, when the Lord came and dwelt among men He came as a moving, growing, and spreading vine, still giving life and still bearing fruit. Consequently, believers when we live the righteous life and are exalted our status changes. We live an eternal existence as heavenly sons of God i.e. to be as the angels (Revelations 21:6).

2. **THE TREE OF THE KNOWLEDGE OF GOOD AND EVIL** - Genesis 2:17 It is from this *tree* that God told man that he would sustain neither spirit nor his flesh. God promised Adam to eat of this tree results in death, spiritual death. Like the *Tree* of Life, this *tree* is not a real tree but a spiritual *tree*.

3. **CEDARS OF LEBANON** - Ezekiel 31:3-18 God describes Lucifer and his cadre of fallen angels in this passage. The Cedars of Lebanon at the time were the prettiest trees in the region. The Cedars of Lebanon stood tall against the sky beautiful in both strength and stature. The cedar's leaves made shade, the second most valuable commodity in the desert. God likens Lucifer to these trees because of his beauty and stature. God goes on to use the strength of the trees as a metaphor for Lucifer's pride. In most cases comparison to something beautiful is a good thing, the problem with the comparison is that God does not use the traits of Cedars to represent all the traits that caused Satan to fall.

4. **THE TREE FOR THE HEALING OF THE NATIONS** - In Revelations 22:2 we again see that the Tree of Life cannot be a wooden giant. What tree do you know that has leaves on it for the healing of the nations? Obviously, the references to the months of the year and the manner of 12 fruits allude to the 12 tribes of Israel. What tree bears twelve different fruits and bears fruit every month of the year? The same tree that bears the twelve different fruits, stands near the throne of God, the one for the healing of the nations, is none other than the Savior of the world.

5. **THE ACCURSED TREE** - The accursed tree in the Kingdom of Heaven was in the inner court. In the church; that persecuted Jesus, the accursed tree stood in the inner court. It is also a sad fact that Judas was accursed tree stood in Jesus' inner court. Joseph's brothers were the accursed trees that stood in Jacob's inner court. Believers still have problems stemming from the inner court. The problem in the church is the spirit of Lucifer. By his great wisdom and his trafficking Lucifer increased his riches. Lucifer's heart puffed up because of riches.

The world is far less dangerous than the beguiling trees in the forest. When we deal with the world, we wear our armor because we expect to do battle. The truest battle in the Kingdom is always going to be one on one; when you are alone. When you find yourself where God wants you to be in life, you will find isolation. Like Saul, David, Jonah, and Jesus you will cry out; *"Father why hast Thou forsaken me?"*

Lucifer always attacks from the inner circle. Lucifer always comes, through the weakest vessel. The weaker vessel does not mean a woman, although it can. In the garden, the weaker vessel simply meant a point of entry. Always pretending that the woman is the weaker vessel is a flaw in our manhood and our traditions. Despite all her shortcomings, Mary the prostitute was a far stronger vessel than the eleven men[157]. Mary the prostitute was the one sent to tell the eleven weaker vessels that He whom they followed arose. It is of this weaker vessel Jesus says they will tell her story whenever they tell His. Jesus never said that about any of the eleven. Lucifer will always come into your inner circle through your vulnerable points. The more Christian a lifestyle you live, the more vulnerable points you have. Vulnerable points like charity, love, trust, forgiveness, etc.

God laid out the blue print in the beginning of the book of Matthew. In Matthew 4:1[158], Satan tempted Jesus one on one. Temptation did not occur at Jesus' low point in life but at His highest. Jesus received God's Holy Spirit and was presented the world the Son of God. Jesus was where He was supposed to be. In Matthew 16:23 why did Jesus tell Satan to get behind Him? It is because Jesus recognized Satan from the wilderness encounter. Jesus also recognized Satan from the garden where Satan once stood as a tree that drank water from Him. Jesus recognized the demons in Luke 4:33 as well as in the boy in *Mark* 5:9 and the demons knew Jesus well. The demons knew Jesus to be the true Vine--the Vine from whence they sprung; and they worshipped Him as the true Vine. The demons most certainly recognized Jesus not only because they identified Him but also because they knew prophecy. God told the cut-down trees the judgment, so they knew what would happen to them. The demons knew that the time for them to be cast in to the pit was not yet, so they reminded the Master of his own law.

---

[157] Mark 14:9.
[158] **"Then was Jesus led up of the Spirit into the wilderness to be tempted of the devil."**

To understand more fully the uses of the terms *tree* and *vine* refer we pause for a botanical interlude[159];
1. *Plant (p.948a)…lacking the power of motion.*
2. *Shrub (p.1135) a woody plant of relatively low height, distinguished from a tree by having several stems rather than a single trunk.*
3. *Vine (p.1349 <1a>) a plant having a flexible stem supported by climbing, twining, or creeping along. The purpose of this interlude is to elucidate the differences between the types of plant life. This information helps in the synopsis of the information. Bear in mind that the main difference between the tree and the vine is that the vine is mobile.*

A common ascription to the word *exalt* is to glorify, praise or honor. However, another definition holds more meaning to us as believers. As discussed, there is a hierarchy in the Creation of God. This information shows what exaltation means in the spirit world. To exalt also means to rise in rank, character, or status; elevate[160]. When we are exalted or abased, God alters our level on the scale. This is not a difficult concept but the results are devastating.

At one time Lucifer held the second highest and most coveted position in the universe. Although Satan's termination was completely his fault, like most of us he blames someone else. Remember believers the wages of sin are death. When we stand before the Maker, let it be because we have earned a crown of glory not because we *choose* to sin ourselves to death.

6. **THE WOODEN CROSS** - Of all the wooden giants none is of more importance to humanity that the cross. This wooden giant was so heavy Jesus needed the help of another human to carry the weight. From the cross, we learn many spiritual warfare secrets.
    1. The greatest battles to the flesh take place in the spirit.
    2. No flesh can defeat Satan's kingdom alone.
    3. Sometimes it takes a Godly stranger to undergird your strength.

---

[159] American Heritage Dictionary.
[160] American Heritage Dictionary, (page 471 <1>).

4. Those closest to you often are not trustworthy.
5. No flesh can stand up under the weight (effect) of sin.
6. No matter how much fleshly help you have the last step are the most important and these are the steps you MUST take alone.
7. We must waged the battle for God, those you try to help will be the same one nailing you to the cross.
8. The evil ones always have more support than the good.
The weight of sin does not have to destroy you. Sin only destroys those willing to give in to it.
9. The flesh though conceived in sin, does not have to be sinful.
10. We can overcome the flesh by the power of God's Holy Spirit.
11. In the darkest hour, God many not seem present, but the truth is there is no victory without God.

I think there is one more important secret we learn from the tree of crucifixion. Even when impaled on the cross we can still reach out in love. Pain compliance techniques motivate the flesh. Like fasting, fleshly discomfort must not stop the work of the kingdom. It is ok to feel pain, but as the Marine Corps instilled, the enemy will have to kill me before I die. As long as it is just pain, we can overcome. Remember, weeping only endures for the night, and joy comes in the morning. Christ is only gone for the night, the time He says that no man may work. When He returns the Tree of Life will come in the clouds, from then on, your pain will multiply and God will be as far away from you as He has ever been. Draw close to Him now while His mercy abounds. When the *B*east controls, there will be no rest for the weary, no peace for the humble, and no mercy for the merciful.

THE FORBIDDEN TREE

What is the forbidden *tree*, and the *fruit* thereof? The answer is simple but intricate. For hundreds of years scholars eluded that the *fruit* was sex, an apple, or some other allegory. The answer however lies in God's word. Believers, we have trained ourselves to look on the Bible as a book. The Bible is not, it is more of a jigsaw puzzle; nay a song. The verses all tie in but they do not necessarily follow a chronological or topical line. In the same way, God assembled the earth He assembled His word. God's word ebbs and flows at His will. Genesis 3:22 lays down clearly that the eating of the *tree* is an *illegitimate exaltation*.

Illegitimate exaltation is a change not authorized by God it is therefore evil. Evil poisoned the creation against God therefore so God acted. What does this mean in everyday terms? Nothing in everyday terms, but in heaven it meant war. Remember it was not Satan's murder, and wickedness that begun the war. The violence in Satan was a by-product of the true problem. The true problem is that Satan wanted to be greater than God.

There is nothing innately wrong with people wanting to better themselves. Satan however wanted to exceed himself. There is a lifestyle God created humans to live. To try to climb out of that design is evidence of which *tree* you have partaken. Nimrod is the first true example of the heart of Satan. Cain was just a glimpse but Nimrod was more like the tree. Once this became evident God's response was immediate and decisive, "**And the Lord said, 'GO TO, LET US BUILD US A CITY AND A TOWER, WHOSE TOP (MAY REACH) UNTO HEAVEN; AND LET US MAKE US A NAME, LEST WE BE SCATTERED ABROAD UPON THE FACE OF THE WHOLE EARTH'. And they said, 'Go to, let us build us a city and a tower, whose top (may reach) unto heaven; and let us make us a name, lest we be scattered abroad upon the face of the whole earth'. And the Lord said, 'BEHOLD, THE PEOPLE (IS) ONE, AND THEY HAVE ALL ONE LANGUAGE; AND THIS THEY BEGIN TO DO: AND NOW NOTHING WILL BE RESTRAINED FROM THEM, WHICH THEY HAVE IMAGINED TO DO. GO TO, LET US GO DOWN, AND THERE CONFOUND THEIR LANGUAGE, THAT THEY MAY NOT UNDERSTAND ONE ANOTHER'S SPEECH'. So the Lord scattered them abroad from thence upon the face of all the earth: and they left off to build the city** - Genesis 11:4-8." Here you see the same scenario as in Ezekiel wherein God steps in and scatters Satan's handy work before it devastated the earth realm.

If you do not understand the problem, then let us look together to the book of Romans for further clarification. "**Because that, when they knew God, they glorified (Him) not as God, neither were thankful; but became vain in their imaginations, and their foolish heart was**

darkened. Professing themselves to be wise, they became fools, And changed the glory of the incorruptible God into an image made like to corruptible man, and to birds, and four footed beasts, and creeping things. Wherefore God also gave them up to uncleanness through the lusts of their own hearts, to dishonour their own bodies between themselves: Who changed the truth of God into a lie, and worshipped and served the creature more than the Creator, Who is blessed forever, Amen - 1:21-25." Here it is plain to see that the issue is not the knowledge in and of itself. Nor was the problem simply eating a proverbial apple. The problem was the condition of the heart. The issue is that all things in creation, whatsoever they maybe, God designed to worship Him. Worship also entails being happy in your station and worshipping the one that created you instead worshipping the creature you are.

Whenever we desire to be more than God created us to be, we are not in the will of God. This is not to say self-improvement is bad or ungodly. However, there are boundaries in God's will, seek them out, and obey. Believers seek not to be more than God created--but learn therefore to be perfect, just as your Father in heaven is perfect. Do not try to be more than God created for you. What God created you to be you are equipped for, all else results in spiritual death.

Amen

Part VIII

Spiritual Warfare: Satan's Revenge

"I [AM] HE THAT LIVETH, AND WAS DEAD; AND, BEHOLD, I AM ALIVE FOR EVERMORE, AMEN; AND HAVE THE KEYS OF HELL AND OF DEATH. WRITE THE THINGS WHICH THOU HAST SEEN, AND THE THINGS WHICH ARE, AND THE THINGS WHICH SHALL BE HEREAFTER - Revelations 1:18-19."

Chapter Twenty-one
The Origin of Spiritual Warfare

"And there was war in heaven: Michael and his angels fought against the dragon; and the dragon fought and his angels, and they prevailed not, neither was their place found anymore in heaven - Revelations 12:7."

As believers, we seek the truth and try to obey. How can believers obey if we do not know the rules? To this end, I group the following scriptures in order to facilitate closer study without constantly listing the entire chapter. This in no manner is rewriting the scripture; it is simply putting the issues discussed in the immediate area of the discussion.

With this information in hand, we look together at the components of the Creation. The Creation components we look at are;

1. Serpent in the Creation story.

2. Tree in the Creation story.

3. Fruit in the Creation story.

4. Prophecy in the Creation story.

Only through, understanding of the premier story of sin in the Bible, can we will unveil the primordial event in spiritual warfare.

In Spiritual warfare, the primary component is human *choice*. *Spiritual warfare is* not actually warring between spirits; it is *a warlike competition between spirits.* The spirits are not vying for your soul because *choice* determines where your soul ends up. **The spirits war for your choice**. Although the Father must draw you, you do not have to respond. Although Jesus died for your sins, you do not have to accept the gift of salvation. Moreover, although you do not have to sin and go to hell you are free to do so. What freedom results in is a conflict between parties interested in winning over your heart (*choice*), and soul.

The dangers of the lights, in Patmos are numerous and most result is spiritual death. To elucidate the danger of the lights in Patmos more clearly we again refer to the first documented case of the lights in Patmos.

This account comes from the book of Genesis the third chapter. It covers the first appearance of the lights in Patmos on earth. Thusly, we begin construction of our Spiritual Warfare wall in Genesis 3.

BRICK ONE - THE QUESTION

"**Now** {*Serpent*}[161]**, was more subtle than any *beast* of the field which the Lord God had made. He said to the woman, "Has God really said, you shall not eat of any tree of the garden**? - Genesis 3:1" We note in Palms 8:5-8, the hierarchy of life, and shows that the beasts of the fields are the lowest life forms. Also, be cognizant that the curse in Genesis 3 also makes sinful man beast of the fields, as they too are cut off from God and must toil, and fight to survive.

How easily could the vice-president ask a question about a Constitutional Law and the answer cast doubt in our minds? How much doubt would that create in our minds, not about the words of the law but the meaning of the words. The subtlety of Satan's question is not readily apparent, but the undertone of the question is two-fold. Lucifer was an angel Adam and Eve were familiar with-- Lucifer was in the Garden with God.

1. Lucifer, the bearer of light, God's right-hand angel, the only other Celestial being found in the garden asked the question.

2. The second part of the question is a little more sinister. Simply put it is --What did God mean?

BRICK TWO - THE FREUDIAN SLIP

"**The woman said to the** {*Serpent*}**, "Of the fruit of the trees of the garden we may eat, but of the fruit of the tree which is in the middle of the garden, God has said, YOU SHALL NOT EAT OF IT, NEITHER SHALL YOU TOUCH IT, LEST YOU DIE** - Genesis 3:2 & 3"

Adam and Eve did not understand the difference between regular food and spirit food. It is a tricky distinction sometimes to know what regular food is and what is spiritual food. Because Adam and Eve did not understand spiritual matters--they could not conceive of the two deaths[162].

---

[161] Consider Seraphim or fiery dragon because they are also meanings of serpent.
[162] Revelations 2:11.

My personal favorite fruits are Watermelon, Sour-sop, and Mangos. Despite the dozens of fruits, my knowledge has not been increased one iota. Neither did Watermelon, Sour-sop, or Mangos place my life in jeopardy, and cut me off from the Father. Look at the following scripture regarding spiritual food and see that the scripture is not as clear before Christ as it is after Christ. **"HE THAT HATH AN EAR, LET HIM HEAR WHAT THE SPIRIT SAITH UNTO THE CHURCHES; TO HIM THAT OVERCOMETH WILL I GIVE TO EAT OF THE TREE OF LIFE, WHICH IS IN THE MIDST OF THE PARADISE OF GOD**- Revelations 2:7"

God developed a system by which He could help humanity. The Kingdom Mysteries enable God to work through nature to keep Satan at bay. God did not *curse* the earth; He used it to keep satanic influences under control. *Cursing the ground for our sakes* was God's way of nullifying Adams dominion. God could not revoke dominion, so He change the thing man formerly had dominion over. In doing do God saved the purity of creation. This is why the Cherubs were necessary in front of the tree of life. The Tree of Life gives eternal Life. If Adam and Eve had been able to eat of the Tree of Life, sin would have had an eternal hold on the earth. God already gave dominion of the earth to the man-creature. With Adam's sinful nature, sin would have had irrevocable control over the earth realm. Not even Jesus can take back what the Father gives. We must never forget that Adam did not give up dominion over the earth. Adam abdicated the throne, and that abdication made redemption by Jesus possible. Through nature, God communicated His will to mankind.

BRICK THREE- FOOD FOR THOUGHT

"The {*serpent*} said to the woman, "You won't surely die, for God knows that in the day you eat it, your eyes will be opened, and you will be like God, knowing good and evil - Genesis 3:4 & 5"

Here again, Lucifer shows his subtlety by asserting that the words God used actually meant something different. This is correct, God spoke spiritually, because Satan knew that the two humans did not understand the two-fold nature of their existence and fueled the woman's confusion and disbelief of God's statement.

The statement in Genesis 3:4 & 5 is by far the most insidious set of words in the history of spiritual warfare. Remember; God cast Lucifer out because he desired to exalt his kingdom above God's. This statement sets the creation of Lucifer's kingdom on earth. No one worshipped Lucifer;

God forbid it and cast him out. Therefore, Lucifer set about building followers (merchandising) here in the earth realm.

Satanic lies always have a twinge of truth to them. Adam and Eve did not die physically--God instantly cut off their spirits. The statement, "They would be like God," is actually true, as confirmed by Genesis (3:22)[163]. Adam and Eve did not become like God--they became like their god the devil. The Bible says that a tree is known by its *fruit*; therefore, Adam and Eve were fruit of the tree from which they ate. Adam and Eve were fruit of death and of sin. This means that the tree that Adam and Eve were fruit of was not the tree of Life, but of death--the fallen angel Lucifer.

It is not just the knowledge of good and evil that makes men like God, it is living righteously once we have attained this knowledge. This also is confirmed by Genesis 3:22, for the angels still in heaven when God spoke thusly--were there because they were still upright (righteous). Satan was quite happy to share the information with Adam and Eve. Satan's statement is one of the first indications of the narcissistic nature of the fallen angel. Satan increased his flock of followers with the first two humans in history.

BRICK FOUR - WINDOWS TO THE SOUL

"When the woman saw that the tree was good for food[164]**, and that it was a delight to the eyes, and that the tree was to be desired to make one wise, she took of the fruit of it, and ate; and she gave some to her husband with her, and he ate**- Genesis 3:6"

To really understand this portion of the scriptures we undertake reading Proverbs 8:1-3 & 14-21 - **"Doesn't wisdom cry out? Doesn't understanding raise her voice? On the top of high places by the way, where the paths meet, she stands. Beside the gates, at the entry of the city, at the entry doors, she cries aloud: [8:14] Counsel and sound knowledge are mine. I have understanding and power. By me kings reign, and princes decree justice. By me princes rule; nobles, and all the righteous rulers of the earth. I love those who**

---

[163] **"And the Lord God said, 'BEHOLD, THE MAN IS BECOME AS ONE OF US, TO KNOW GOOD AND EVIL: AND NOW, LEST HE PUT FORTH HIS HAND, AND TAKE ALSO OF THE TREE OF LIFE, AND EAT, AND LIVE FOREVER'."**

[164] American Heritage Dictionary (p.520 <4>). *Something that nourishes or sustains in a way suggestive of physical nourishment.*

love me. Those who seek me diligently will find me. With me are riches, honor, enduring wealth, and prosperity. My fruit is better than gold, yes, than fine gold; my yield than *choice* silver. I walk in the way of righteousness, in the midst of the paths of justice; that I may give wealth to those who love me. I fill their treasuries." In this passage, we see several metaphors; the most important for us is verse 19. Herein, we see *Lady wisdom* talking to us and telling us that *she* gives *fruit* that is better than gold, and her yield *choice*r than silver. The use of metaphor and onomatopoeia makes scripture difficult to understand. However, this is the only way that the Lord can begin to explain His magnificence to creatures as small minded as humans. Wisdom is a compilation of knowledge tidbits, wisdom it is not a woman. Wisdom is a non-physical, non-womb possessing entity that therefore cannot literally bear fruit. Nevertheless, this passage sheds light on the beguilement of the humans. Satan sold Adam and Eve on the idea that biting into wisdom would make Adam and Eve like God. How could the woman, not see the fruit that she was offered as, "a delight to the eyes, and desire it to make one wise?" When we read Proverbs 8 and see what wisdom describes as her fruit, can we not understand (though not condone) Eve's decision? Who among us, if offered the *"fruit that is tastier that gold,"* by God's most trusted advisor would not partake?

We all sit back and condemn Eve because we blame her and Adam for sin. Yes, they both sinned, Adam more so than Eve. However, Adam and Eve did not understand the concept of sin. That being the case; what can we, the clergy, laity, ministers, pastors, rabbis, and priests, say about our sin and sin-filled lifestyles? Eve did not know the concept of sin and damnation, and she had no clear understanding of the effects of sin. How then do we the teachers, preachers, evangelists, prophets and apostles reconcile our lives of sin, unforgiveness, theft, and injustice--yet teach about sin. Eve had the promise of wisdom, knowledge, wealth, and long life. What are we promised other then death; yet we still sin.

Believing as she did, Eve did what any companion would do upon receiving a great treasure or gift; she shared it with her mate. Imagine; being one of the only two people in the world and God's right hand man offers you a chance to go from your present life state up to the next level (Exaltation). Eve's sin was the sin that all humans are guilty of at one point in their life; wanting something, to which they do not normally have access. How many pastors, churches, organizations, presidents, fathers, children, wives, and friends have destroyed things for want of something more? Those of us that are truly happy and successful learn to find satisfaction at any level in life.

Jesus speaks of this particular facet of human ignorance in the Matthew 20:22[165]. Wherein not only does the verse deal with the all-important statement that we do not know what we are asking--but it also covers the typical human response; we are able. Jesus again deals with the same human facet in the book of Luke--this time He dealt with this pervasive of all human proclivities--covetousness. In this most gracious of all statements made by our Redeemer, the anointed of the house of David entreats the Almighty for our sakes. **"Then said Jesus, FATHER, FORGIVE THEM; FOR THEY KNOW NOT WHAT THEY DO**...- Luke 23:34"

Those of us that have ears to hear let us hear. In the garden, Adam and Eve sinned and God immediately cast them out. Throughout the Old Testament God dealt with sin harshly--many found harsh mercy in the sight of God. The most important thing Jesus ever said on our behalf was the words in Luke 23:34. The great Advocate interposed Himself on our behalf. In doing so Christ provided that no longer will those of us that fall victim to covetousness, greed, selfishness or stupidity, find ourselves cast out and beyond redemption. This statement preemptively makes atonement for those of us, who like Eve--fall victim to our heart's wicked *choices*.

Although the poem *Slaves* refers to the American slave trade, the concept exists throughout the history of those freed from bondage. Take the children of Israel as our prime examples. How long did it take them to try to return to the ways of their slave lives and slave masters?

SLAVES

"The sun rose in the morning and we prepared to return to the fields, and I hoped at the day's end master'd be pleased with our yield. So I woke the other field hands "Git up! The day is begun. It's time for us to return to our cotton pickin fun."

---

[165] **"But Jesus answered, 'YOU DON'T KNOW WHAT YOU ARE ASKING. ARE YOU ABLE TO DRINK THE CUP THAT I AM ABOUT TO DRINK, AND BE IMMERSED WITH THE IMMERSION THAT I AM IMMERSED WITH?' They said to Him, 'We are able'.**"

> *The heat in the field is unbearable, as the sun beat down our backs, the only thing worse is the master's whip as it cracks. So diligently, we picked cotton, and made it into nice bails, hoping if we pleased him; us he would not impale.*
>
> *As the sun-begun setting and the day was about to end, we droned off to our hovels, for tomorrow it will begin again. Then the news came downwind, the Northman would set us free. No more picking cotton or being whipped down to our knees.*
>
> *But when the Slavery ended, and they removed the fences of chain-link, we's all so happy that we never learned to think. And now in present day, we still remain as slaves, but instead of picking cotton, we're slaves to our own ways."*

There are many sins we are guilty of, but the things we do in our humanity are the most prevalent. Our selfish desires hold us captive far beyond the wiles and the tricks of the devil. Satan does not cause us to sin; that lie we promulgated to abate guilt and responsibility. What Satan specializes in is using our lusts and desires against us. To believe that he creates lusts and desires is a lie from the pit of hell.

I close this point with a short story that involves God, the devil, and the patsy (me). I was sitting in a parking lot waiting on a man to come home. I had been sitting there for several hours (it was my job to do so). There had been no movement in the parking lot. Finally, a young girl of average age and build walked across in front of me. I watched her walk as Satan spoke to me. Satan whispered, "Grab her!" I was startled at first then he whispered again, "Grab her!" As soon as Satan finished talking the Lord spoke over him, *"That is all he does, that is what he specializes in. All he does is try to get you to start, if he could but get you to actually grab her, the rest would have been up to you. He never said rape her, hurt her, beat her, or anything else, he knows that whatever harm you did to her would have come from your inner desire to do it to somebody. The devil does not have to give you those types of desires they are already in your heart."* Of course, I was not a happy camper but the simple fact is that this is not a Revelation it was actually a refresher course. The Master already told us this very same thing over two thousand years ago[166].

---

[166] Matthew 15:11 & Matthew 12:34.

BRICK FIVE - SEEING WITHOUT EYES

"**The eyes of both of them were opened, and they knew that they were naked. They sewed fig leaves together, and made themselves coverings. They heard the voice of the Lord God walking**[167] **in the garden in the cool of the day, and the man and his wife hid themselves from the presence of the Lord God among the trees of the garden. The Lord God called to the man, and said to him, 'WHERE ARE YOU?'** - Genesis 3:7-9" The phrase regarding Adam and Eve's eyes opening refers to removal of the spiritual veil[168]. In John 9:1-12 Jesus opened the eyes of the man born blind so that the man would know, that Light had come into the world. The word says that when God opened Adam and Eve's eyes they saw that they were naked. In Genesis 2:25 the Bible says that Adam and Eve were naked and not ashamed. After God opened Adam and Eve's eyes, they were ashamed. Adam and Eve were ashamed because for the first time they saw the flesh through the eyes of their new spirits, the spirit of the tree from which they were now fruit.

Adam did not become a Living soul until God breathed life into his nostrils. The soul, however alive was still under the dominion of the man[169]. Adam's flesh although alive was not sinful and did not know good and evil. To know good and evil is to know God and His nemesis Lucifer. Adam was only familiar with Lucifer as the right hand man of God, not the fallen angel. Referring to Ezekiel 28, we find therein a wealth of information as to the ordeal the man creature underwent in the Garden of God with Lucifer the bearer of light. It was not until Adam partook of Satan that Adam knew good and evil.

The word *naked* is symbolic of the natural state. Therefore, what Adam was actually saying to God is *I am natural* (i.e. fleshly) and no longer spiritual (supernatural). Adam never knew his natural state. Prior to self-awareness God made Adam a living soul. Adam therefore lived

---

[167] This is a peculiar usage of the verb considering the context. Some translations use *sound* instead of voice. However, when you apply one of the meanings of the verb walk it lends much more reason to the passage. *To roam about in a visible form.* American Heritage Dictionary (p.1360 <6>).

[168] Luke 8:10 "**And He said, 'UNTO YOU IT IS GIVEN TO KNOW THE MYSTERIES OF THE KINGDOM OF GOD: BUT TO OTHERS IN PARABLES; THAT SEEING THEY MIGHT NOT SEE, AND HEARING THEY MIGHT NOT UNDERSTAND'.**"

[169] Genesis 1:26-31.

here on the earth but was supernatural. God knew that the knowledge of the two states was beyond Adam and Eve's ability, therefore someone supernatural, must have told Adam and Eve about the natural and the super-natural. The only other alternative was that they had to have eaten of the tree of the knowledge of good and evil, so God asked the logical question.

In Luke 8:10, if Satan told the humans of their dual nature they would not have understood. Satan therefore did the only thing he could. Satan encouraged Adam and Eve to see through him in the spirit world. This is exactly what diviners do; they look through their father (Satan) into the other world. The cost of this vision is expensive. The only way to see through Satan is to die spiritually.

Just as the opposite of love is not hate, but indifference, the antithesis of holy or righteous is natural. What this means is that when you are in God you are above nature, so Peter was able walk on water, or we can tell mountains to move. However, when you are natural (carnal, fleshly, naked) you live in the death and darkness of this world. Sinful darkness necessitates the sacrifice of animals, circumcision, and the shed Blood of Christ. The death of the flesh is necessary to commune with God. God will not dwell with sin, therefore God waits until the flesh dies, or is crucified so that He may reconcile[170] Himself to His living souls.

Adam and Eve realized that they were going to be in the presence of God. They at least realized that they were no longer worthy to stand upright in God's presence so they hid themselves and were ashamed. Unlike the tree of their sin, Adam and Eve only possessed the baser elements of sin. Satan however, as pointed out in Ezekiel 28:17 was puffed up and God dealt with Satan another way.

God calls to Adam and asked where he was? It was not that God did not know, He was acknowledging the fact that He and the man were separate. Adam was not hidden in the literal sense from God. Adam's sin--filled flesh acted as a veil to Adam's soul. God only communes with Living souls, notice He did not speak with Adam until He had breathed life into Him. What God inquired of Adam was you are not among the Living where do you exist now?

---

[170] Romans 5:10.

When Adam and Eve ate of Satan's *tree*, they died to God[171]. God no longer saw Adam and Eve standing in His holy of holies. Adam and Eve were no longer lived above the beast. Adam and Eve were equal with the beasts of the field...not in the Darwinian sense, but because they no longer had dominion over the earth.

Imagine developing an atomic bomb. Then you give the secrets to the atomic bombs your child. Imagine the possibility for destruction. Every time that child gets angry, upset, confused, or even sleepy you run the risk of destruction. In addition, the child's inability to govern so great a power makes Satan's job easier. The ignorance and naivety of the child create a gamut of inroads for Satan to exploit. The fact the parents ill-equip their kids for the lives and tasks they give them evidences in the failures and suicides. Beloved, when you truly are ready to receive power and greatness from God ask not for money, wealth, or material things, pray God gives you wisdom.

BRICK SIX - A HEDGE TOO SMALL

"The man said, 'I heard Your voice in the garden, and I was afraid, because I was naked; and I hid myself.' God said, 'WHO TOLD YOU THAT YOU WERE NAKED? HAVE YOU EATEN FROM THE TREE THAT I COMMANDED YOU NOT TO EAT FROM?'- Genesis 3:10." Notice the difference between the words in verse 8 and verse 10. Here the words do not say that they 'heard the voice of God walking'; remember God cut them off spiritually. Therefore, they no longer saw God in His glory. Adam and Eve reverted to the method of communication that existed between God and everything else in Creation. Adam no longer lived above the natural, God no longer walked with him God's voice alone was sufficient. The presence of the Lord is always been on Holy ground. This is why it takes so much praise and worship to reach God. God is not hiding; praise and worship does for believers what the living sacrifices did prior to Christ[172]. Praise and worship makes communication possible.

Adam showed a trait seldom shown of today's sinners and apostate believers. Adam was both afraid and ashamed. When Adam spoke to

---

[171] Dead in the same sense, the prodigal son was dead in Luke 15:32, **"IT WAS MEET THAT WE SHOULD MAKE MERRY, AND BE GLAD: FOR THIS THY BROTHER WAS DEAD, AND IS ALIVE AGAIN; AND WAS LOST, AND IS FOUND."**
[172] Jeremiah 33:11, Hebrews 13:15.

God, he used a word that gave away the whole game. God did not ask why Adam hid, nor why he was ashamed. God simply asked Adam who it was that told him that he was naked.

God's response to the man was inquisitive. God knew that the man had no reason to be ashamed. The term *naked* in the sense that Adam used it meant exposed to God. In other words, Adam covered himself to shield his unrighteousness from the eyes of the Lord. It did not mean unclad, naked, or nude, but it referred to the raw nature of his soul unrefined, undignified, and unfortunately unrighteous. God then put to Adam the logical question. God asked Adam did he partake of the forbidden tree. Here again I find difficulty in understanding why for so many years learned theologians have promulgated that the curse was due to partaking of the fruit of the tree of the knowledge of good and evil. The text is clear in that God asked, "**HAVE YOU EATEN FROM THE TREE THAT I COMMANDED YOU NOT TO EAT FROM**?" To assert that it was due to simply eating the fruit is not accurate and it does a disservice to the Lord our God. To explain the difference, I utilize biological terms.

Millions of tiny cells comprise the human body; they come in all shapes, tasks, and varieties. A variety of ailments infect cells. The two most common areas of infection are bacteria and viruses. The treatments for bacteria and viruses differ only in method. In both cases, the objective is to rid the cells of disease. In the case of bacteria treatment is simple, kill the bacteria with antibiotics and the return to normalcy is automatic. In the case of a virus, however, the treatment is not as different as is the nature of the ailment. Anti-viral medicine kills the virus. The problem lies in how to accomplish this task. The bacterium destroys the cells so all you have to do is seek out the bacterium and destroy it. The virus however intermingles with the cell and often itself becomes a part of or inseparable from the cell. This makes destroying the virus very difficult and in extreme cases such as cancers, and HIV impossible to do without killing the host cells as well.

This is the difference between eating of the fruit and eating of the tree. When we eat of the tree of salvation brother Paul informs us in 2 Corinthians 5:17 that we become new creatures. We do not have little pieces of God's Holy Spirit in us; God's Holy Spirit courses through our cells and transforms us into new creatures. The new creature that we become is a negation of the natural state.

The church incorrectly teaches *addition* as the remedy for sin (i.e. add fasting, praying, tithing to become righteous), the converse it true. **Humans cannot add to what they are to become righteous, they must go in the opposite direction. Nothing a human adds will override the sinful nature of the flesh.** Adam was born empty and God filled Him with breath. Adam however opted to fill his heart with the nature of Satan. As a result, humans are born filled with sin and trouble[173]. The act of circumcision singled out the Children of Israel because they chose a life of restraint. Man must put away, crucify, or put to death, the sinful nature of his flesh. God can only fill the empty heart[174].

A man once told a story. In the story, a man walks into a Karate school and speaks to the master of the school. As he speaks, he tells the master what he knows, all the styles he is proficient in and about his special skills. The man talks as the master pours tea into a small cup. The master continues to pour as the man talks. When the tea spills out the man says, "Hey you are spilling the tea." To that the master replies, "Cup that is full has no more room. In the same manner, a heart filled with sin we must first empty so God has room to enter.

In Galatians 5:22 Paul lists the *fruits* of the spirit as love, joy, peace, patience, kindness, goodness, and faith. In no way does Paul imply that we become new creatures because of the fruit of the spirit. Instead, Paul reminds us that our very natures change when we align ourselves to our new lifestyle to the lifestyle of God's Holy Spirit.

Believers, Adam and Eve did not simply partake of the fruit (bacteria) they ate of the tree (virus) itself and their natures changed forever. Adam and Eve became the fruit of Satan's tree. The evidence of the fruitfulness of Satan's tree was sin. Not only were Adam and Eve's souls cut off, their flesh was irrevocably changed. Their flesh became murderous, envious, jealous, and deceitful…as evident through their (fruit) children.

---

[173] Job 14:1 - "**Man [that is] born of a woman [is] of few days, and full of trouble.**"
[174] Kingdom Principle – Sin never goes away, it is a life of dying to, avoiding, and refraining from sin that God calls righteous. The old habits do not die we *choose* to stay away.

BRICK SEVEN - SHARE AND SHARE ALIKE

"The man said, "The woman whom you gave to be with me, she gave me of the tree, and I ate." The Lord God said to the woman, "WHAT IS THIS YOU HAVE DONE?" The woman said, "The serpent beguiled me, and I ate - Genesis 3:12 &13" As to how the woman actually gave Adam of the tree, I have not ascertained. My speculation is not revelation so I will not attempt to instruct as to how she gave Adam of the tree. However, what is evident by the text is that the effect that the tree had on the man was different from the effect it had on the woman. Moreover, what is also evident is that the man said that he partook of the tree not fruit. Whatever the interaction was, it involved the tree, not merely the byproduct of the tree.

Adam's first response to God was to blame the woman. Then Adam admitted his crime by virtue of using the term naked. The woman however, showed no remorse. Although Eve told the truth, the scriptures never allude to fear or her shame. This is important to spiritual warriors because it is imperative to understand that the true nature of sin is to pervert whatever qualities and attributes exist in a person. There is no explanation given by the scripture as to why the man gave into the woman, the man himself answers that question. Adam trusted the woman that God gave him. Because Adam was closer to Eve than to God, he harkened unto Eve's voice. I do not mean Adam was closer in proximity to Eve; Adam was more intimately involved with the woman. God was Adam's spirit but the man lived in the flesh, on a fleshly planet, with a fleshly woman. It was never good for the man to be here on the planet not dwelling close to the Father. Although God made Adam a living soul it was not it was not until God made woman did He say that the man was whole.

The woman, on the other hand, believers judge evil. In Genesis 2:20, God created Eve as a helpmeet for Adam. In her capacity, the woman only had one task, to help the man stay righteous. Satan, like liquor only exacerbates with what we are already. All Satan had to do was capitalize on Eve's nature and Eve did the rest. Satan sold Eve on the idea of a better life, and Eve in turn carried the same offer to her mate. The beguilement was not in taking the offer to Adam it was in accepting Satan's truth in the first place. After Satan beguiles believers, he goes away and leaves the rest of the damage to us. Historically believers have done such a bang up job of helping Satan that he does not get involved.

BRICK EIGHT - AN ANGEL ON HIS BELLY

"**The Lord God said to the serpent, 'BECAUSE YOU HAVE DONE THIS, CURSED ARE YOU ABOVE ALL LIVESTOCK, AND ABOVE EVERY ANIMAL OF THE FIELD. ON YOUR BELLY SHALL YOU GO, AND YOU SHALL EAT DUST ALL THE DAYS OF YOUR LIFE. I WILL PUT ENMITY BETWEEN YOU AND THE WOMAN, AND BETWEEN YOUR OFFSPRING AND HER OFFSPRING. HE WILL BRUISE YOUR HEAD, AND YOU WILL BRUISE HIS HEEL'** - Genesis 3:14 & 15." Many teachings have gone forth that the snake slithers because of the curse of the Almighty. I however, am not sanguine with that postulate for various reasons. Firstly, why would God use the accursed serpent for healing the wilderness? Although many assert that the lifted serpent represents the coming Christ and His bearing of our sins, there is a major difference between Christ and Satan. God cursed Satan; and God never cursed Jesus.

There is no scripture describing Jesus as any type of snake, reptile, or any other type or belly crawler, and there is a poignant reason for this. The belly crawling is not a physical attribute; it is a statement to the person's unrighteousness. The following scriptures expose what belly crawling actually is:

1. Deuteronomy 32:4 - "**The Rock, His work is perfect, for all His ways are justice: Righteous and *upright* is He.**"

2. Job 1:8 - "**The Lord said to Satan, 'HAVE YOU CONSIDERED MY SERVANT, JOB? FOR THERE IS NONE LIKE HIM IN THE EARTH, A BLAMELESS AND AN *UPRIGHT* MAN, ONE WHO FEARS GOD, AND TURNS AWAY FROM EVIL'.**"

3. Ecclesiastes 7:29 - "**Behold, this only have I found: that God made man *upright*, but they search for many schemes.**"

4. Isaiah 59:14 - "**Justice is turned away backward, and righteousness stands afar off; for truth is fallen in the street, and *uprightness* can't enter.**"

5. Micah 7:2 - "**The Godly man has perished out of the earth, and there is no one *upright* among men. They all lie** (Serpent

like qualities but they are not vipers) **in wait for blood; every man hunts his brother with a net.**"

6. Malachi 2:6 - "**The law of truth was in his mouth, and unrighteousness was not found in his lips. He walked with me in peace and *uprightness,* and turned many away from iniquity.**"

Secondly, I offer to Aaron and Moses' snake battle with the Egyptians. The Lord allowed Aaron and Moses' serpents to swallow the other serpents. Although this does have spiritual undertones, there is no scripture to indicate that Satan swallowed other serpents. Even though the great dragon could most certainly swallow the smaller reptiles, why would the smaller reptiles serve Satan?

The following two scriptures seem to indicate the entity we assert was a serpent differs from the snake.

1. "**The burden of the beasts of the south: into the land of trouble and anguish, from whence [come] the young and old lion, the viper** (snake) **and fiery flying serpent** (demon or devil), **they will carry their riches upon the shoulders of young asses, and their treasures upon the bunches of camels, to a people [that] shall not profit [them]** - Isaiah 30:6."

2. "**And when Paul had gathered a bundle of sticks, and laid [them] on the fire, there came a viper** (snake) **out of the heat, and fastened on his hand** - Acts 28:3" What is important to notice here is that the belly crawling, venomous creature we assert was in the garden is not called a serpent here, it is called a viper. More curious is that Isaiah separates the viper from the fiery serpent. We have already looked up the terms that also mean fiery serpent and none of them are vipers.

Consequently, the statement, "**ON YOUR BELLY SHALL YOU GO,**" is not a curse it is a description of the accursed state. In other words, God was not saying I made you unrighteous He was elucidating the results of an unrighteous life. Ezekiel 28:2-3 indicates that when he was righteous Lucifer stood before God's throne. Lucifer controlled and sat in the seas. Lucifer stood amongst the stones of fire. Lucifer walked with God in the Garden in Eden. In short, Lucifer enjoyed the status befitting the Lord of Lord and the King of Kings, and as a result, became full of pride.

The actual curse not only removed Lucifer's ability to stand upright in the sight of God, "**CURSED ARE YOU ABOVE ALL LIVESTOCK, AND ABOVE EVERY ANIMAL OF THE FIELD**." The result of the curse is the belly crawling. God also removed Satan from his position in the heavenly hierarchy. The enmity between man and Satan was not only part of the curse it is the natural offshoot of God placing Satan beneath the man-creature in the hierarchy.

There is a difference between a curse and a pronouncement. The curse is the actual sentence and the pronouncement is what the sentence includes. An example: a man commits the crime of murder and found guilty by a jury. The convicted stands before the judge and receives his sentence. The judgment (curse) is life in prison. Life in prison is the curse. What is included therefore is;

1. The convicted lives in a small cell.
2. The convicted wears an orange jumpsuit.
3. The convicted never comes and goes at will.
4. The convicted will eat when told sleep when told.
5. The convicted will never be free with your family again.
6. The convicted never votes again.

The latter items listed are not curses but a clarification of what affect the curse shall have on your life. The curse although explicit and clear is only inclusive; it does not explain in detail what you are excluded from...the pronouncement does this. After God cut down Lucifer the tree, God in His justice explained the new boundaries. The Lord reminds Lucifer that he ate the Living waters. We know that the Living, flowing waters flow from the Heart of God, which explains how we know that Jesus is the Tree of life. Since expulsion, God tells Satan he will eat dust all the days of his life. The context of the crawling serpent tends to lead us in the direction of dust referring to the results of belly crawling. In fact, when Satan dwelt in the mountain of God he ate of Life. However, if we remember the references to eating earlier, what God is telling Satan is now he will exist on death.

Dust is a reference to the result of dead flesh. However, we must also remember that to die, the death God spoke of in was not a literal death but a spiritual death[175]. Obviously, the reference in Numbers 23:10 refers

---

[175] Numbers 23:10 - "**Who can count the dust of Jacob, or number the fourth part of Israel? Let me die the death of the righteous, let my last end be like his!**"

to the children of Jacob. We refer to the children of Jacob as dust due to the generational birthing and dying of Jacobs's descendants. We cannot count their dust they are so plentiful. Part of the accursed state is that Satan no longer feasts on the Living water that flows from the Mount of God. Now Satan has to eat death. We are not speaking of making meals of humans, but of eating death, the death represented by the dust-destined creatures. Remember, Adam and Eve died the instant they ate of the tree, yet their bodies did not die immediately. Satan eats the sin-affected vessels our spirits dwell in because that is what he wants to rule. Therefore, Satan's life comes from the death of the man-creatures.

Like the writer Milton suggests in <u>Paradise Lost</u>, Satan believes it is better to rule in Hell than to have to serve in Heaven. Satan's *choice* to live a life other than the God ordained life resulted in death, for him and the man-creatures...but at least he gets to play god.

The last stanza of Genesis 3:14 & 15 is of course the prophetic promise of Redemption of the earth by Jesus. He crushes Satan's kingdom (his head) and Satan bruises Jesus' heal--upon the cross. I find it remarkable that schools still teach that the serpent in the garden was a snake. How could this be possible when no snake ever bit Jesus, nor did Jesus never killed any snakes anywhere in scripture or history.

BRICK NINE - BURNING EARS

"BECAUSE YOU HAVE LISTENED TO YOUR WIFE'S VOICE, AND HAVE EATEN OF THE TREE, OF WHICH I COMMANDED YOU, SAYING, 'YOU SHALL NOT EAT OF IT,' CURSED IS THE GROUND FOR YOUR SAKE...{...FOR OUT OF IT YOU WERE TAKEN. FOR YOU ARE DUST, AND TO DUST YOU SHALL RETURN - Genesis 3:17-19." Pay close attention to the structure of God's condemnation. *We see that God first addresses the fact that Adam listened to his wife above the Lord; Disobedience is the primordial sin in the universe.* Disobedience caused havoc in the Heaven and brought about sin-nature in this world. Disobedience goes against the nature of who God is, God has said thusly; **"I AM THE ALPHA AND THE OMEGA, THE BEGINNING AND THE END."** God made it clear what order of preference His words should take in our lives[176]. God is not as concerned with actions as He is with the motivation. Whatsoever we do in the flesh can be undone or simply

---

[176] Exodus 20:3-6.

ignored. This is why forgiveness is attainable; God easily erases the rudimentary problems humans create. God conversely does not overlook disobedience so easily He considers it witchcraft.

The commandments God gave in writing to Moses, first existed in heaven then in the garden. The commandments of God are tenants of righteousness. Since God is the beginning, His laws existed since the beginning. As long as righteousness existed, laws have existed. In Genesis 20:5, the Almighty deals with disobedience not because of its results but because it is contrary to His will. There is nothing we can do that God cannot undo but He tells us that disobedience results in death.

1. It is the nature of children to take after their father. Therefore, if we are disobedient, we are not children of God but sons of Satan. Paul deals with sonship in Ephesians 2:2, "...**In which you once walked according to the course of this world, according to the prince of the powers of the air, the spirit who now works in the children of disobedience**." If we therefore are sons of disobedience and Satan is the father, then the equation becomes simple--Satan is our daddy! There are only three fathers in the annals of Christianity;
   1. God the Holy Father.
   2. Satan the father of evil and the father lies.
   3. Adam the father of the man-creatures and of fleshly sin.

Consequently, if we do not honor our Father in heaven we must follow one of the two other fathers.

When we abandon God's will, we no longer act like sons; we act like bastards. Son-ship implies love and honor[177]. A son by blood is nothing; it simply means you have a sire. When we are accepted as sons by our Father it is due to love and discipline (Proverbs 8:17). The equation is simple, John 14:15 says, "**IF YOU LOVE ME, KEEP MY COMMANDMENTS**," and 1 John 2:22 makes it clear. "**Who is the liar but he who denies that Jesus is the Messiah? This is the Anti-Christ, he who denies the Father and the Son**," we cannot love God and constantly walk in disobedience.

The second part of God's condemnation is the simpler of the matter linguistically. Tradition says that the eating of the fruit caused the fall of man. However, if you read Genesis 3:17-19, God punished Adam

---

[177] Hebrews 10:26, 2 Peter 2:20-22.

for listening to his wife. God's response to the couple's relationship was to punish the women, and to take all responsibility for Godly things away from the man. Like Moses in the wilderness, Adam broke faith with God. Just as in the case of Moses, once man breaks faith with God regains control of the promise. Notice I did not say that God removes the promise; He secures it so it can be passed on, redeemed, or at least not ruined. Adam lost paradise and God did not allow Moses' anger into the promise land. God's intention is always to assuage leaders from passing on their bad habits.

BRICK TEN - EXPULSION FROM THE GARDEN

"So He drove out the man; and He placed at the east of the garden of Eden Cherubims, and a flaming sword which turned every way, to keep the way of the tree of life - Genesis 3:24." There were two pivotal trees in the garden, the Tree of Life and the Tree of the Knowledge of Good and Evil. The tree of Life that is mentioned is none other than the same tree mentioned in Revelations 2:7 and 22:2.

God told Adam that he could eat freely of all of the trees in the garden. This therefore included the Tree of Life, for it too stood in the midst of the garden in Eden. Sadly what this means is that Jesus was rejected, or at least mis-understood in the garden.

With this new information in hand and with the lament that Ezekiel refers to we can only begin to understand the sadness the Creator felt when Adam His newest creature chose death instead of Life. Not only was there unrighteousness in the heavens but it had now spread to the garden in Eden and out into the earth.

A QUICK GUIDE TO THE FALL FROM GRACE
1. **The Question** - Satan asked a simple question of Eve.
2. **The Freudian Slip** - Eve changes the words of God.
3. **Food for Thought** - Satan exposes Eve to kingdom mysteries.
4. **Windows to the Soul** - Satan gets a glimpse into Eve's heart.
5. **Seeing Without Eyes** - God removes the veil of innocence.
6. **A Hedge Too Small** - Adam and Eve attempt to conceal their sin.
7. **Share and Share Alike** - Eve shares her sin with her mate.
8. **An Angel on His Belly** - God curses Satan.
9. **Burning Ears** - Adam learns the penalty for harking to one other than God.
10. **Expulsion** - God expels Adam and Eve from the Garden, and bars man from the earth.

THE INESCAPABLE CONCLUSION

There is an old adage, "He who has the king's ear has the power." Nowhere is this truer than in the realm of spiritual warfare. The power of Satan does not give him control over Christians it is the fact that for too long Satan had the Christian ear. The fall of man was not to Satan's credit, it was an inside job. The first betrayal in human history was not between Can and Abel it occurred in the garden between husband and wife.

Believers, Spiritual warfare did not begin in the conflict between God and Lucifer, nor Satan and Man. Spiritual warfare began with Satan's lack of self-control. Spiritual warfare for humans began with Adam's lack of self-control.

The sad fact of the fall is that the same reason Adam fell exists today among believers. Genesis 21 clearly states that the woman, Eve (the mother of all things), was fashioned from the rib, which God took from the man. This means two phenomenal spiritual things.

1. The deep spiritual mystery of the fall of 'man' is laid out in Genesis 3:17. The revelation is that the woman fashioned from the rib was truly flesh of Adam's flesh and bone of Adam's bone. Therefore, the admonition God laid upon Adam excluded Eve the personality and dealt with Adam: The source. In other words the Lord our God, Creator, and Provider of the worlds did not deal with the fruit[178], He dealt with the tree. Eve is the fruit of Adam. Adam was the first living human and the first living soul. The characteristics of the woman (fruit) had to first exist in the man[179] (Eve's tree). Consequently, the admonition was not simply because Adam failed to maintain dominion over the earth and everything in the garden (1:28) it was also because he had failed to subdue himself. When God gave Adam dominion, that dominion included himself.

2. Because Adam could not rule himself, he lost dominion over the earth. In doing so, Adam also lost dominion over his offspring. All of the fruit of Adam was accursed and like Cain and Able became unruly[180]. However, the accursedness continued beyond Cain and Able, it continued until the unruly flesh that Adam created died. Believers this is why Jesus

---

[178] Matthew 7:16-20.
[179] Ephesians 5:29 & 33.
[180] Ephesians 2:2.

the Christ also had to conquer the flesh[181] to take dominion over every living thing. Jesus, the Son of man, had to retake the dominion Adam gave Satan over God's delegated area. God's Holy Spirit could not claim the earth realm because God gave it forever to the man creature. Therefore, in order that God not lie, He fashioned a special man creature to undo the damage that his predecessor Adam caused.

God placed man in the garden to tend and take care of the garden. In the modern church there are two permanent caretakers of Gods church. The two caretakers of the church are the deacons and the elders. Paul's letter to Timothy deals with the qualifications for the two offices. Incidentally, these are the only two offices with specific qualifications. Paul's letter to Timothy specifically deals with the gender and marital status of deacons and the elders. Later in verses, 4 and 5 Paul deals with the issues at Adam failed: The inability to rule self and the home. The man that proves himself a faithful servant according to Paul secures a great confidence and a high standing in God's kingdom.

Adam was a bad steward over the garden, over self, and over the woman. Jesus was a great steward over all that the Father gave Him, and ruled Himself even better than He ruled the earth, grave, and sin. Matthew 18:4 deals exclusively with ruling self? Jesus explained the greatest of the disciples would be the one that humbles himself the most. As we mentioned before Adam is the father of all humans. Based on human behavior, we conclude that our father is no longer the Creator after whom we are fashioned. The likening of the men to children shows several things;

1. The likening of the men to children shows dependence.
2. The likening of the men to children shows denial.
3. The likening of the men to children shows submission.
4. The likening of the men to children shows absolute trust.
5. The likening of the men to children shows vulnerability.
6. The likening of the men to children shows gentleness.

Therefore, if we are fruit of a tree and Jesus tells us that we are the devil's fruit, it makes sense that we have the devils characteristics. Characteristics such as vanity, lust, greed, selfishness, lying, stealing,

---

[181] John 17:1.

murder, theft, covetousness and a host of other sins are in us because we pass them on through inheritance. Vanity, lust, greed, are not genetic they can be changed. The human heart makes the flesh sinful. Our *daddy* Satan had these diseases and he passed them on to us his fruit.

The reason all the fatherly relationships in the Bible had problems and were plagued with bloodshed is that those men took after their father, the devil. The purpose of a father is to guide his family, protect them, and rear them in a righteous direction. The troubles that we have in our children are because these problems existed first in our flesh. Since we cannot control our own flesh, we cannot control our children without conflict. The conflicts we have with our children reflect are the same problems the Creator has with us. To conquer ourselves, is to conquer our children and vice versa. Bad fatherhood is a symptom of the blood that flows in our veins[182], the only way to conquer self, and our families is to replace the blood in our veins with the shed Blood of Christ. Only when we are born of the shed blood of Christ will we take on and therefore be able to pass on the Godly traits of our Father which art in Heaven.

It must be the free *choice* of men to subjugate their will to God's will and let Him deliver us from evil. There is no victory in spiritual warfare without spiritual power. Humans have no power; God gave the power to Christ, in heaven and in earth. No matter what relationship you have, Christ is still the power in the earth realm, only His power counteracts the power of the evil one. Many people believe that signs and wonders are evidence of their own power. Anyone that tells you this is making you a spiritual warfare casualty. ALL spiritual gifts are *gifts*, which mean they come from somewhere else; we do not make, create, or earn them. We neither create nor destroy the gifts from God. God's Holy Spirit maintains the gifts via our relationship. The better the relationship with God the more readily available is God's power. The more strained our relationship is with God the less likely we are to be able to operate in God's Holy Spirit.

---

[182] "**The Lord saw that the wickedness of man was great in the earth, and that every imagination of the thoughts of his heart was only evil continually. The Lord was sorry that He had made man on the earth, and it grieved him in His heart. The Lord said, 'I WILL DESTROY MAN WHOM I HAVE CREATED FROM THE SURFACE OF THE GROUND; MAN, ALONG WITH ANIMALS, CREEPING THINGS, AND BIRDS OF THE SKY; FOR I AM SORRY THAT I HAVE MADE THEM'** – Genesis 6:5-7."

The ultimate gift in the universe is salvation. Salvation coupled with choice creates eternal bliss or damnation. Salvation is a gift that cannot be earned or forfeit. No one, not even the Christ earned salvation. Jesus like us *chose* salvation, and then He fought to maintain righteousness. Salvations is not what church, Bible, study, prayer and fasting maintain they maintain righteousness. Salvation does not maintain a relationship with God righteousness does that. Without salvation, no one is eligible for a relationship with God (outer court). Only righteousness gets you into the inner court, and a lifestyle of righteousness gets you into the Holy of holies.

Many times like Moses, we pout the dirty shoes back on which precludes us from the Holy of Holies. When we take them off, we can again sup with the Father. Our constant removal of our shoes makes believers lives tumultuous. If you have not learned anything from Moses? Learn and observe this lesson; DO NOT COME BACK DOWN THE MOUNTAIN. This was the major difference between Moses and Jesus, and Paul. Once Jesus and Paul went up they NEVER came back down. This does not mean they stayed in the wilderness like the Baptist, what is means is once you consecrate your heart enough to enter the Holy of holies, allow no one and nothing to drag you back into filth.

This principle is the single most important reason God requires monogamy in marriage. Once consecrated, a thing can easily get dirty again. That thing can be cleaned again but it will never be the same as it was when pure. Many marriages survive adultery but none are ever the same. Some people claim the affair saved their marriage. What a sad concept, this is to say that had they not sinned they would have never craved salvation. No one realizes what they had when the loose it, people are just greedy. How could you not realize the gifts of your spouse until they leave, are you blind; not just stupid, greedy and immature. This is why there so much idolatry, because we are greedy and immature, we do not want to wait for God, we do not appreciate His grace until the bottom falls out of our lives. God can and will save you but the relationship you have with Him from that moment will always be rescuer.

The inescapable conclusion is that Spiritual Warfare is more like babysitting than actual combat. If the stakes were not so sigh, the issue would be a laughing matter, two gods vying for the hearts of stupid mortals. Zeus fought for Persus, and his son Hercules. Hera fought for her son Calabos. Isis and Osiris constantly fought over mortals.

Mythology is replete with the concept of gods waging war over mortals. Despite which god wins, the reward is not very high.

The scripture that explains why the Father in heaven even cares about the inconsiderate, selfish, evil humans is in Judges 9. There are numerous scripture including John 3:16 that tell us that God redeemed us because He loves us. By why does He love humans? In judges 9 the *True Vine* says that men *cheer God up*. I cannot begin to explain the great gaps in Bible history and theory pertaining to creation and why humans appear to be the creatures of choice. Actually, I could begin, but it would be reckless to speculate. I will give you food for thought regarding this issue. The True Vine called humans *new wine*, Isaiah and Jeremiah allude to life before Adam, cities etc., and God telling the sun not shine and God turning the world upside down. If there was life before Adam, in whatever form it did not please God. According to Judges 9, something about the human creature cheered God up. There was something in the man creature that gave God hope. There was something special about the man creature that made God tire Himself out creating him. I put it to you that the thing that made God give humans such favor is *choice*. God looked and saw that despite our wickedness and the cost to save human, many of them would *choose* to love Him back.

In Genesis 18, God told Abraham that He would spare Sodom and Gomorrah if there were 10 righteous men in the two cities. The two cities represented humans; our sin waxes great in the sight of God. Abraham interceded on behalf of Lot, and God favored him because Abraham *chose* to serve God. God knew there would be few men like Enoch, Abraham, Daniel, etc. so He did it with one deft move.

From this deluge of information that we can conclude that God and His Son are not our enemy. We can also deduce humans of any religion are not our enemy. We can also understand that Satan is just a parasite, a spiritual tick that lives on the blood of wicked hearts. GOD MAKES IT CLEAR; IF YOU WANT TO SEE ME, PURIFY YOU HEART. If your heart was not wicked, your life would not be wicked. The issues of your life come from your heart, if your life is stressed, fearful and desperate; it is because the things that defile us ARE INSIDE US. Satan does not defile you, WE DEFILE OURSELVES. THE DARKNESS IN THE WORLD IS NOT BECAUSE OD SATAN WE ARE THE DARKNESS. The world is a horrible place because of the things in the hearts of men. Like a stray dog, Satan hangs around where the free food is stockpiled and abundant. If you want freedom from Satan, get the things that attract him out of your heart. Stop using your imagination to satisfy your lusts, learn to serve the Lord with humility, purity, and joy, then God promises that Satan will flee.

    Believers God is not just a savior, He is a lover, and friend, why not seek his heart like David, or His face like Moses? Why only look to Him for His gifts or grace. Why have a one nightstand with a lover that offers their heart and soul? Or should I say--Why have a one nightstand with a lover their offers you their heart and your soul.

Amen

Chapter Twenty-two
Dousing Satan's Fire

"When the devil had completed every temptation, he departed from Him for a season - Luke 4:13."

Fire is a peculiar entity; it has almost all of the characteristics of a living thing. Fire's similarity to living things is what makes discernment difficult. If a person cannot discern the true flame of God from amongst the lights in Patmos--how can we ever resist or hope to douse the flame.

An old parable warns, "Those who wish to be served by magic often end up its slave." In terms of demons, the following is always true. *Those who wish to have demons serve them by demons eventually end up their slave.* This concept also is true for those that wish to fire serve them.

How wonderful a thing is this *choice*. *Choice* cost God creation yet made Him send His only begotten Son. *Choice* made a king kill a husband to sleep with his wife, yet die trying to please God and build His temple. *Choice* was the wondrous entity that made Moses relinquish his princeship. *Choice* then caused Moses to break faith with the Lord our God. The light that burns in Patmos is the same fire that burns in each believer's heart. The *lights in Patmos* are none other than the burning desires of *choice*.

When Eve looked upon the tree, the Bible says that in her heart she saw that it was good to eat and a desirable thing. The simple fact is that *choice* is a desirable thing. This is because *choice* is synonymous with freedom. Only slaves cannot readily make *choices*.

It was precisely because Adam and Eve were free that they had the ability to make a *choice*; even the wrong *choice*. God loves His children; He therefore gave them the freedom to *choose*. Even God's children, called angels, have *choice*. At least one-third of God's *children* chose to rebel against God and suffer His wrath. Many skeptics of the Lord's methods contend that it is sheer folly of the Lord to give humans *choice*. What skeptics do not understand is that for a parent or a king, *choice* is the ultimate expression of love. Some of the most wonderful, loving, kind, parents in history sired rotten kids. What makes these parents wonderful,

THE 39 STEPS TO DOUSING SATAN'S FIRE

I make use of myself as an example of what not to do and what mistakes not to make in determining a relationship with God. Let us look together at the poem *The Lights in Patmos* systematically identifying find ways to dim the false lights. As we explore the origin of human-spiritual warfare, allow me to express the main components by use of a poem. This poem is not to trivialize this adventure in God's word but to express it more fluently. Unlike many of my other poems, I specifically wrote this poem/parable[183] for this work. As such, it covers the greatest weaknesses in our spiritual battles. Let us examine each of these weaknesses together.

Alone in my exile feeling grace and mercies pain, I looked over and I saw a lavish Flame. I looked over the ocean to see if this was a game, wondering if this guiding light possibly had a name?

I walked up to the fire and spoke into its heat, but Flame said nothing the silence was complete. At least I was not alone on my island full of light, no longer scared of darkness, and there was no more night.

I wondered of Flame; and where Flame had been, although I really did not care because now I had a friend.

As I lay down to bed at night my Flame tucked me in, all the while saying, "I have overlooked your sin." Flame never said much, he was simply always near, but because of his lavish warmth, I no longer lived in fear.

One day I asked him, "Flame are you my God?" Flame answered finally his answer very odd. "Yes friend I am your God, I serve your very heart, Yes friend," said Flame, "I've been here from your start."

Then I really rejoiced for now I knew His name, now I had a title to call my brilliant Flame. It was only when I asked that I realized what was done, after years of following Flame, I asked about the Son.

Flame explained he was there to keep the temp nice, but I quickly corrected him and said, "I meant the Christ." Flame then flickered and backed away a bit, then the Flame began again but never finished it.

---

[183] Ecclesiastes 12: 9-11.

I asked again of the Christ, this time Flame cooled off, every time he spoke of Christ Flame began to cough. "I do not understand. Is it something I have done, why will not you tell me about your begotten Son?"

"Well we look alike," said Flame 'Identical twins', sometimes He fills in for me sometimes I fill in for Him. He's very kind and gentle, and never puts up a fuss; it is simply more convenient to let him represent us." Is He here among us now since you Two are One? Perhaps I can talk to Him and give thanks for what was done."

"I alone am sovereign you first must go through me, only by bowing down to me will your soul ever be free." "If it takes that," I said, "For my soul to be safe, I will bow before you." Then I knelt down in haste.

I looked up at Flame and bellowed from my chest, "I believe you died for me and with my mouth I confess." "Ah! Roared Flame; now live in my shade." I exclaimed falling backwards, "In what darkness must I bathe?"

"Now you belong to me for you have called me God." I replied, "But you deceived me with your words and with your rod." "I used no rod on you 'twas you said all the words, if you truly knew your God then you would have heard."

He reached down to grab me and take me to his abode when all of a sudden from the sea a sparkling tidal wave arose. The sparkling wave roared towards us but Flame held me fast. When the wave reached the shore, Flame released his grasp. Flame tried to run away but the wave soon overtook. The wave rolled passed me, as a hand did not allow my look.

The hand held me fast as the wave pounced on Flame, with a scalding hiss came the end of Flame's game. Then the water receded and went back to sea, the hand moved from my eyes and for the first time I could see. "Thank you," I shouted to the now lapping waves; overhead the gulls shouted, "All who call upon Him shall be saved."

That is when I realized what I had learned to see, was not the Glory of God but the glow of the enemy. I learned that day to see my God's glory shine, and that Satan glow comes from the evil in my mind.

1. **Alone in my exile feeling grace and mercies pain,** - The first line indicates self-pity and ingratitude. God's ways are His own. This type

of flawed thinking breeds resentment and anger and weakens faith. Self-pity and ingratitude are the typical response to life's hardships, failings, and challenges.

2. *I looked over and I saw a lavish flame* - One will rarely recognize God at the first encounter. Our imagination is simply not versed enough to receive His visage. We must not hasten to worship that which we know not. Had God not explained to Moses that He was God, not a burning bush Moses would have worshipped the hedge instead of the King of kings.

3. *I looked over the ocean to see if this was a game,* - Faith must start somewhere; however, faith must NEVER start without the word and the guidance of God. The faith walks in the Bible all started with an encounter with God. Blind guessing and impetuous emotionality are not a basis for faith. When God gives impossible tasks, your *choice* to movie is faith. Creating ridiculous situations for God to bail us out of is not faith it is bond. The Bible says we should not test the Lord our God. The second scenario is nothing but testing the Lord.

4. *Wondering if this guiding light possibly had a name?* - If you do not know the name of a god then why would you dedicate your life to them? Our God has many names the one that you should concern yourself with for now is Love. If there is no love in what your god asks or requires, it is not the God of Abraham, Isaac, and Jacob. The measure of our God is found in 1 Corinthians 13--try your God against this list.
1. God is patient.
2. God is kind.
3. God does not envy.
4. God does not brag.
5. God is not proud.
6. God does not behave itself inappropriately.
7. God does not seek its own way.
8. God is not provoked.
9. God takes no account of evil.
10. God does not rejoice in unrighteousness.
11. God bears all things.

12. God believes all things.
13. God hopes all things.
14. God endures all things.
15. God never fails.
16. God is the beginning and the ending.

5. ***I walked up to flame and spoke into its heat,*** - The fire in the heart of our God does not burn or scorch His children. Our God is kind and gentle, though He is King. What manner of king burns you then requires your love? What kind of king rewards faithful service with death? Satan is that kind of king his wages are still death. It is precisely because Satan does not love you that he kills, steals, and destroys.

6. ***But flame said nothing the silence was complete.*** - This is one of the most difficult characteristics of the relationship to deal with. Everybody hates the silent treatment and no one does the silent treatment quite like God. It seems as though God is silent at all the wrong times and will not shut up at all the wrong times. Silence creates anguish because it seems as though when we really need His input to make a decision He sits silently by and watches. This is why it is imperative to be in a relationship with God's Holy Spirit because at times when Heaven is silent we must continue in the will of God.

The silent treatment tests your relationship with God. It is during God's silence that the intimate times pay off. You need to know how to scuba dive before you dive into the ocean. You also need to know the will of God before you enter the Wilderness. We always pretend not to know the will of God when we want things. Nevertheless, there are not that many decisions that the Bible does not cover.

7. ***At least I was not alone on my island full of light***; - This is a common mistake amongst the lonely. There is more loneliness in the Christian lifestyle than you would believe. One of the chief causes of grief, bad decisions, and bad relationships is loneliness. The same loneliness that made David plead with God is the same tool used to allow believers time to see the truth. Jonah is the best example of the effect of silent treatment. Jonah cries out from what he describes as the depths of hell. Additionally, the 40 days the children of Israel

waited for Moses shows how the lack of revelation often leads to falling away. Proverbs 29:18 explains that the lack of revelation causes the people to cast off their restraints. This is not saying that people perish because they cannot further God's plans. What Solomon tells us is that without revelation there is no growth. Without revelation, the people stagnate and eventually become complacent.

8. *No longer scared of darkness, and there was no more night.* - In this instance, we find the single most common cause of sin--fear. Fear causes more sin than greed does. Fear manifests itself in many ways that all too often do not appear as fear. Fear also leads to a host of other emotions and actions such as anger, resentment, despair, hatred, greed, insecurity, and selfishness. Darkness, as we know is one of the greatest fear causing entities. Darkness does not cause fear we fear the unknown. Darkness is the greatest expression of the unknown. Darkness causes fear because it deprives us of the sense we rely on the most. Reliance on this most evident of senses is also the greatest enemy to faith, because we rely so heavily on sight.

9. *I wondered of flame and where the flame had been,* - Many hours of the free day people spend sitting and wondering where God is, and what is He doing. This is not always a lack of faith; it is a lack of evidence. Wondering is ok it is the wandering that leads us into beds, windows, and other people's arms that we need to avoid.

10. *Although I really did not care because now I had a friend.*- Accommodation is the easiest way to fall into temptation. Most believers are inpatient. Impatience causes believers to fall prey to the wiles of the devil. Hunger causes us to ask God for food instead of temperance. Loneliness causes believers to fornicate instead of asking for grace. Sadness causes us to give up or lash out instead of asking for comfort. Believers must never settle for the ungodly just so we can have someone or something.

11. *As I lay down to bed at night my flame tucked me in,* - Comfort zones create false security in our lives. One of the surest signs of God's Holy Spirit is that unlike the enemy He constantly urges us towards righteousness. God uses no force, no coercion, just a subtle,

loving, chastisement into God's way of Living. Remember, there are two deaths; therefore there must be two lives[184]. Jesus assures that His flock shall not taste of the second death. Verily I say unto you that you SHALL IN NO WAY TASTE OF THE SECOND LIFE WITHOUT JESUS.

12. *All the while saying, "I have overlooked your sin."* - This statement as all of Satan's statements have a portion of truth but overall is a lie. There is no, NO overlooking of sin. Sin is never overlooked by God it is forgiven. Remember all sin is against God; God determines how to handle it. God's *choice* is to forgive those who ask, and to let those who desire death--die.

13. *Flame never said much, he was simply always near;* - This is why intimacy with God is imperative. With a quiet, unobtrusive, companion it is almost impossible to discern whether they are benevolent or evil. Only familiarity with Gods loving Spirit will enable this level of discernment. Both spirits speak to us quietly, and constantly. The only way to differentiate the voice is as a child does at school. Every one of us remembers the clarity with which we could distinguish mom's voice at the playground. What enabled us to distinguish was the number of times we heard the voice, her sounds, and what she said. Praying unceasingly as Paul suggest keeps constant communication open to God. During this communication we hear his voice

14. *But because of his lavish warmth, I no longer lived in fear.* - God never promised you warmth to conquer fear. He promised that the spirit that He gives casts out fear. The beauty within this scripture is that the type of love God refers to is the John 3:16 type of love. Our fearful, selfish, nature does not understand God's type of love therefore, we are fearful. Rest assured that when we walk in His Spirit love conquers fear.

15. *One day I asked him, "Flame are you my god?" The flame answered finally his answer very odd;* - You should not have to ask

---

[184] Revelations 2:11.

this question. God and Satan have nothing in common. Satan NEVER pretends to be God. However, what Satan does is pretend to be the phantom that you create to be God. If you believe that God looks like Santa Clause, Satan can pretend to be Santa. If you believe God gives you everything you ask for then Satan will do that. What God does not allow Satan to do is appear to or commune with the lost and tell them he is God.

Time is the true test of the spirit with which you commune. Because our God is loving, He gave an entire book of ways to determine whether the spirit you encountered is Him or not. God designed your spirit to respond to the One, True, and Living God. After all God's sheep know His voice. Only those that God called ever hear His voice or recognize His Spirit.

16. *"Yes friend I am your god, I serve your very heart, yes friend," said flame, "I've been here from your start."* - Again we see the false light in Patmos rear its head. The statement in phrase 16 PROVES the light we accustom ourselves to in the wilderness is not the Light of God. In stanza 16 the fire in Patmos states, 'I serve your very heart." Flame's statement in no way resembles God's promise to give you the desires of your heart, but is not the same. **"IF YE ABIDE IN ME, AND MY WORDS ABIDE IN YOU, ASK WHATSOEVER YE WILL, AND IT SHALL BE DONE UNTO YOU** - John 15:7." God in no way serves our will. Not only is there a condition placed on this promise, it is a loving gesture to His faithful, beloved kids…not cessation to our sinful greed.

17. *Then I really rejoiced for now I knew his name,* - How pathetic believers are as a group. We prefer to seek the name of the Lord rather than His face. In the Bible, those that truly loved the Lord sought God's heart or God's face. Only benchwarmers seek God's name. Much like brand name products, what good is a name with no product? A bottle of Tide is useless without the actual chemicals that do the cleaning. Like a bottle of Tide without chemicals, God's name is useless to those He does not serve.

As any other King, God also wields His power the way He desires. Only God's people get to use His name. High science teaches through witchcraft, that to obtain God's name is to have all the power in the universe. This is only because high science does not understand God. Before God had a name, He was God. To have God's name means you have access to a powerful tool. However, because your power-saw says Craftsman on the side does not mean you control the company.

18. ***Now I had a title to call my brilliant flame.*** - Why do we continue to try to name our God? This attempt serves no purpose in our religion other then idolatry. '**I AM**' is only the name God ever gives in the Bible. '**I AM**' is not God's name. God wants you to identify with His love, not his name. The Bible clearly says that God is Love. Therefore, as far as Christians are concerned God's name is Love. The Lord our God serves as a king serves His kingdom He is a servant king. As a servant king God may serve but He is still king. Therefore, when you seek to name your King, any of His 78 names found in the Bible will do. Nevertheless, try Our Father which art in heaven; Jesus seemed to think it was a good *choice* of title.

19. ***It was only when I asked that I realized what was done, after years of following flame, I asked about the sun.*** - The poet points out that it took him years to realize that he really knew nothing about the god he worshipped. Like many believers, we know little about our precious Savior. Ignorance causes weak faith and backsliding. Not knowing God or His will means that you are operating in a foreign spiritual plane.

No wonder God does not answer many of our prayers, are we sure, when we pray, we pray to the right god? Jesus goes on to say **THY WILL BE DONE** remember. If we do not know who to pray to, how can we pray His will? What a horrible course of action to ask questions of a god after years of worship and servitude. What a sad life to serve a god and then realize that the god you served is not the true God of creation.

Contrary to popular teaching, asking questions of God is not a sin. Moses, Abraham, and many other men of God questioned the Father, and they received answers not punishment. Even the Christ questioned His Father both in the Garden and then on the cross; and He still sits at God's right hand. I urge you to talk to your Father and ask questions before you spend years following a foreign god.

20. *Flame explained he was there to keep the temp nice*, - This answer should have startled the poet because it flew in the face of the order God set about. God told us that He placed the sun in the sky for light. The Bible does not address the climate control issue in Genesis. It is not that God does not answer simplistically when He does. However, God never changes the truth to make it easier to understand.

21. *But I quickly corrected him and said, "I meant the Christ."* - Should you really have to explain yourself to the God that told you He knew what you wanted even before you ever asked[185]?

22. *The light then flickered and backed away a bit*, - Another great indicator of the true nature of our God is that His truth burns the tongue of the adversary. The Life in God cannot dwell in the dead, and they cannot dwell with Him. Any Spirit that does not worship God as God is not of God. Therefore, the scripture admonishes us to try the spirit by the Spirit.

23. *Then the flame began again but never finished it.* - The dead never rejoice in Life. Therefore, they do not spend much time discussing life. During simple, short interactions, demons can maintain their false light. That is why intimacy with God is a lifestyle not a happenstance. When Satan transforms into a being of light, he does not actually glow. Paul's reference is to Lucifer. What Lucifer does is not glow, but pretended that he is still a stone of fire. As a stone of fire Satan appears to be a creature of light, a righteous entity.

24. *I asked again of Christ this time flame cooled off*, - The way, the truth, and the Life always cool, down the fiery serpent. Much like your wife cools down when you speak of something making you happy other than her Satan wanes when you worship any other. God is not the only jealous ruler in the universe. The words in Judges 9 tell us that there is punitive action from Satan for those who claim to worship him and fail.

---

[185] Matthew 6:8.

25. ***Every time he spoke of Christ, flame began to cough. I do not understand. Is it something I have done, why will not you tell me about your begotten Son?"*** - The evil spirit has little to say about the begotten Son of Heaven. This will always be the case because there are few things that the fallen angels can say to the Son. One thing they say is that He is the Son. In every interaction, the demons had with Christ they either worshipped Him while He was a far off, or they acknowledged Him as the Son.

Despite dissenting from God's kingdom, demons must still acknowledge Jesus as King. The reason Satan did not acknowledge Him as king in the wilderness was that Satan was still not sure. Satan had seen and tempted so many prophets they he undoubtedly thought Jesus was just another one. This is why Satan told Jesus that if He was the Son of God He should do certain things as proof.

The difference between prophets and Christ is that prophets used signs and wonders to show the power of God. Christ's very existence showed the power of God. Jesus never performed any miracles as proof[186]. Why would the King show ID to prove who He was? The Truth is the truth whether you believe it or not.

On the cross, there were two thieves. The two thieves represented the two categories of humans:
1. Those that believe and
2. Those that do not believe.

Even until the last moments of his reign Satan still was not sure if this was the Christ for the scripture says, **"But we speak the wisdom of God in a mystery, even the hidden wisdom, which God ordained before the world unto our glory; which none of the princes of this world knew: for had they known [it], they would not have crucified the Lord of glory** - 1 Corinthians 2:7-8."

26. ***"Well we look alike," said flame "Identical twins, sometimes he fills in for me sometimes I fill in for him. He's very kind, and gentle, and never puts up a fuss; it is simply more convenient to let him represent us."*** - This is one of the more intricate lies of Satan. Here we see Satan starting his lie saying that he and the Lord look alike. The reason I say that this is intricate is because there are some

---
[186] Matthew 12:39.

references in the Bible that lend credibility to this line. The reason this seems credible is that believers settle for Hollywood's version of what God looks like.

According to scripture, Satan transforms himself into a being of light. The reason this is confusing is that Hollywood sold the idea that glow in the dark people are what celestial beings look like. Hollywood convinced the world that celestial beings glow in the dark and fly wonderful, feathered wings.

The scripture is clear that no man can look upon God and live. Even when Moses hid in the cleft of the rock, all he was able to see was the hind parts of God. Despite what you think you see in your visions, God does not appear in the forms we envision.

THE MIDST OF THE SEAS

The same type of confusion arises when Satan says that He and God exchanged places. Ezekiel 28:2 clearly states that Satan sat in the seat of God. Here is Revelation on this statement. Satan is jeering at God with this scenario. To sit in the seat of God, Satan shows the control he has over the *sea*. This *sea* is not the ocean, remember Satan in the prince of the power of the air. The *sea* referred to in this statement is the same sea referred to in Revelations 4:6, and 15:2. The *sea* that Satan lords over is the *sea* of souls, the people of earth that do not know God.

It is a fact that Lucifer was second in command. As such, Satan occupied the seat on the right hand of the Father. This statement has a far more sinister meaning to those in this world. The fact of the matter is that Satan did sit in the seat of God, spiritually speaking. God did not give Satan His throne, we the people requested another king. The reason Satan sits in the seat of God is that God's people still worship Satan as lord and king instead of the Father. Satan therefore does not hesitate to exercise the power humans give him. Again, we see the brilliance that illuminates from the fallen angel.

Flame's reference to personality traits of the Son give the believer the sense of familiarity needed to create a comfort zone. As you can see, Flame lacks depth as well as credibility. Satan is telling you what he is not. Satan certainly does not know much about God.

Even the prince of this age, former aide de camp of the Lord did not recognize God's Spirit here on earth.

27. "*Is he here among us now since you two are one? Perhaps I can talk to him and thank you for what he has done.*" - Truly, it is sad that a believer would feel it necessary to ask our enemy to identify our God. Why would anyone delivered by the blood of a King feel the need to go through an intermediary again? God forever tore the veil in two so that we could see for ourselves the glory and truth of God. What possible reason could we find to seek the truth in the tongue of a liar? Permit me to give you some soul saving advice. IF YOU ARE NOT SURE WHICH GOD YOU ARE SPEAKING TO, DO NOT SPEAK. The same applies to listening. God is patient and will make Himself known to you. In order that you hear, you must know His words. If faith comes by *hearing* and *hearing* by the word of God, YOU MUST HAVE THE WORDS OF GOD TO *HEAR*. God is not offended by questions and playing it safe. Reread the scriptures and you will find all of God's faithful and beloved asked questions.

28. "*I alone am sovereign you first must go through me, only by bowing down to me will your soul ever be free.*" - Yet another glossy lie from the enemy of the truth. Those unfamiliar with scripture will believe Satan's lie. It is because we spend insufficient time in communion with the Lord that we do not hear God's words. When Phillip and Andrew inquired of the Lord whether they should reveal who He was Jesus replied, "**MY SHEEP KNOW MY VOICE**." I add this corollary; His sheep also know His words. If you knew God's word, you would know that stanza 28 is not scripture. The scripture is, "**I AM THE WAY, THE TRUTH, AND THE LIFE, NO MAN COMES TO THE FATHER BUT THROUGH ME**." The two verses are close but a world apart. Adherence to the scripture is LIFE and to Satan's lie in stanza 28 is death.

I alone am sovereign you first must go through me, only by bowing down to me will your soul ever be free."	"**I AM THE WAY, THE TRUTH AND THE LIFE, NO MAN COMES TO THE FATHER BUT THROUGH ME.**"

In reference to the bowing down, we read the following two verses. In both verses, you see that we are not required to bow to God for salvation. If God does not require our bowing at His feet then there is no cause in the universe to bow before anyone. There is also no other way to God in the universe than Jesus. Anything other route or method than the following two listed roads to salvation is a device of men, or a lie of the devil.

1. **"For God so loved the world that He gave His only begotten Son, that whosoever believeth in Him shall not perish but have everlasting life** - John 3:16."

2. **"For whosoever shall call upon the name of the Lord shall be saved** - Romans 10:13."

The most insidious portion of this stanza from the poem is the promise of freedom. There is no freedom in bowing, serving, or loving Satan, following Satan, or listening to Satan. Many fall prey Satan's lie and bow before men and idols to find salvation. Damnation is the only thing you find on your knees before other gods.

29. *"If it takes that," I said, "for my soul to be safe I will bow before you." Then I knelt down in haste.* - If you do not know what it takes to save your soul, can you ever truly be saved? Darkness frightens most people. Yet believers race into eternal darkness with little information and even less understanding about our souls. If we worship anything, we should research it and learn about what it is we commit ourselves. How sad to make a covenant and still not be assured about your eternal soul. You may not understand God, but He promises you safety and honesty. God plainly explains what He requires of you, and all what you are entitled to you before He invites or draws you to commit.

30. *I looked up at flame and bellowed from my chest, "I believe you died for me and with my mouth I confess." "Ah! Roared flame; now live in my shade."* - Pride brings a man low is a Proverb from Solomon. Pride made the man in the poem bellow. Pride is the opposite mannerism from the way we should come to God. No man walks into the emergency room of a hospital shouting about his ailments. As it should be when we heed the call home of the Master.

It is not because of great deeds God calls us; it is an act of love. There is no reason to be prideful. On the contrary, we should hide our faces in shame. We should be ashamed that the world crucified an innocent man for our wretched deeds. We should not gloat in sin; remember what it cost a man that knew no sin. To seek solace in the fact that Christ was born for this task is horrible. That the world took a man to slaughter; like a lamb, so we could sleep with the wife of another, smoke crack, or indulge in other lusts of the flesh should humiliate all believers.

The shade spoken of in this stanza is the same shade referred to in Judges 9. Satan neither emits nor reflects light, the shade is nothing other than the darkness of death. Satan is a creature of darkness. It is into this darkness Satan invites you.

Flame's prideful roar of the devil is because Satan rejoices when he beguiles souls from the hand of the Redeemer. Even in this flawed concept Satan's ignorance shows. Those that the Father claims Satan cannot steal[187]. Like a waiting vulture, Satan is destined to feast on those that *choose* to walk away from the Hand of the God that saved them. Just as the blind should not lead the blind the living should not feed the dead. Satan cannot feast on you while you live. He has to wait for you to die spiritually for you to become palatable to him.

31. *I exclaimed falling backwards, "in what darkness must I bathe?"* - There is only one type of darkness--that is the darkness of death. When Paul says we were once darkness what he is saying is that once we were death[188]. Allow me to explain this to you in terms of humans. There is a rather stupid movie called Night of the Living Dead. The concept in this film is that the dead have risen, walk, and do things normally reserved for the living. Spiritually this is what Paul says Christians do. Those that are not of Christ, in other words not ALIVE are wasting their time worshipping Christ. Jesus says, **"DEPART FROM ME YOU DOERS OF INIQUITY FOR I KNOW YOU NOT**[189]**."** The living dead, look like God's people, they talk like

---

[187] John 6:37.
[188] Or at least in death.
[189] Matthew 7:23.

God's people and they perform miracles like God's people, but their names are not in the Lamb's Book of Life.

Flame is therefore saying that the poet must now bathe in the shade of death. Remember in order for it to be death it has to contain dead things. When Jesus walked under the earth for three days, He spoke to the dead and the dead in Christ. Remember there are two deaths but the second death is where you reside when you serve Satan.

32. "*Now you belong to me for you have called me god.*" - In Exodus 20:3-5, God issued a commandment about worshipping others Gods. Although God tells us that He is a jealous God there is an additional reason not to worship other gods. There is no way to worship a god, and not serve it. We may not see addiction as serving and bowing down. We must understand however, that when your actions exist to service an addiction, craving, or desire which occupies most of your thoughts, as far as God is concerned that thing, addiction, craving, or desire is your god (Idolatry).

When Flame says that we belong to him, he is speaking the truth. We do not belong in the ownership sense, but in the same way, you belong to a pilot when you fly on his plane. You are a free person, but you have given up that freedom and autonomy to ride in his plane.

Paul admonishes us not to surrender to strong drink. The term *given* means to surrender your free will to power (effect) of the drink. In this sense, there is little difference between an alcoholic and a person a social drinker. They both are dependent on the liquor to create a desired effect.

33. "*But you deceived me with your words and with your rod.*" - Although Satan is the deceiver, reread the poet's words and you will see that the deception was not Satan's but the poets own. Much like Eve in the garden, the poet had ulterior motives for interacting with God. The poet wanted to worship something so badly that he decided to fill the hole in his life with his own understanding. Professing himself to be wise, the poet chose to worship a god of his own understanding. How many nights do believers stay awake praying and crying to gods they create and submit to? It is not by chance that many of the cults and false religions have compromising gods. It is easy to compromise if that is all it takes to get followers.

Christians on the other hand have an uncompromising yet forgiving God. There is a difference, the compromising god allows you to live and die in your sin. Our God forgives our sin and requires that we change. In this way, we do not have to live and you certainly do not have to die in sin.

34. "*I used no rod on you 'twas you said all the words, if you truly knew your god then you would have heard.*" - This is another evidence of a lack of love from Flame. A father that does not chastise his children does not love them. Any parent that allows his children to fail, and live a life less than the best available because they do not discipline is a terrible parent and does not love their children. Should Flame have to say to you that you do not know your god? Is it not sad that even the enemy of our souls can recognize the fact that you do not worship in spirit and truth.

35. *He reached down to grab me and take me to his abode when all of a sudden from the sea a sparkling tidal wave arose.* - Notice Jesus says, **"WHOMEVER THE FATHER GIVES TO I SHALL IN NO WISE CAST OUT."** Jesus' ability to lay claim to a people stems from a covenant with God in Heaven. The covenant, the binding contract, and the people's obedience to God's law is what makes believers His children.

However, this relationship works in the same manner with Satan. A covenant, the binding contract and the people's obedience to Satan's is what makes people outside of Christ Satan's children. Anton S. Lavey, even compiled a Bible for the children of Satan[190]. It is an interesting book, it does not teach as much as it modifies. An example is that the satanic Bible reverse prayers and rituals found in the Bible. The true followers of the satanic lie simply see the lie for what it is-- the negation of the truth. This is the nature of belonging, doing as your master bids. Once God pays for souls, they become His property. However, if after attaining freedom from Satan you chose to go back, you again become the property of your former owner Satan[191].

---

[190] The Satanic Bible. Lavey, Antony.
[191] 2 Peter 2:2-22.

36. ***The sparkling wave roared towards us but flame held me fast. When the wave reached the shore flame released his grasp.*** - The power of God's Holy Spirit is inexplicable. When God shows up to rescue lost sheep, He shows up in two forms simultaneously. The first thing you see when God shows up to help is what you need. The second thing you see when you see God is what He is really. No matter what your circumstances are God never changes. He always moves in accordance with His law.

The poet also found that Satan never releases his grasp until necessary. In most instances however, Satan simply has to play possum to defeat believers. Satan however cannot defeat our Redeemer. This is why God admonishes us to submit to Him first, then resist Satan and he shall flee.

37. ***Flame tried to run away but the wave soon overtook. The wave rolled passed me as a hand prevented my look.*** - This portion of the poem is prophetic in that it delineates the time line spoken of in the Bible. There is a finite period for Satan's freedom. This stanza refers to Satan's timely demise. Satan runs across time to escape the person he took time to plot and kill. Since Jesus crushed Satan's kingdom he runs around on earth looking for dead, rotting scraps of meat like a vulture[192].

The reference to God's protection is part of the mystery of His will. Although God tore the veil in two the Lord still does His bidding out of the sight and understanding of humans. The raw purity of God's truth would destroy our wretched sinful bodies. Therefore, God protects humans from His raw power.

38. ***The hand held me fast as the wave pounced on flame, with a scalding hiss came the end of flame's game.*** - The ability to be more than one thing or place at a time is what makes God great. He is at least 78 things at a time in the Bible. Who knows how many other things God is. In this stanza, we find that the only thing in the universe that can actually douse the flame. In this stanza we verify the only power in the universe greater than both evil and good. There are three great powers in the universe;

---

[192] Job 2:2.

1. *Self* - The soul of the human creature that has *choice*.
2. *Selfish* - The fallen angel that wants all for himself.
3. *Selfless* - The image of a God that gave His only begotten Son.

We the people have to make decisions every minute of everyday as to which category we fall. When making decisions we should bear in mind that only one of these three powers has the ability and the desire to provide for us and keep us safe. If you wish to live, the logical *choice* is Life.

39. Then the water receded and went back to sea, the hand moved from my eyes and for the first time I could see. - The poet makes the statement that for the first time he could see. This is because for the first time he looked through someone else's eyes. Seeing in spiritual terms is a gift from God. God opens the eyes of those that *choose* Life so they can see His will. Most people do not see the truth because their eyes are not open. This is not to say that God blinds people. It is to say that we are born blind. It takes the hands and heart of God to open our eyes that we may see and our ears that we may hear and our hearts that we may feel.

Our unassuming Father does not gloat, nor does He spike the ball in the end zone when He rescues the lost. After God rescues, He simply returns to His abode waiting and hoping to rescue another lost sheep.

40. "Thank you," I shouted to the now lapping waves; overhead the gulls shouted, "All that call upon Him shall be saved." - Notice in the poem God did not stay around for the thank you either. It is not that God does not love gratitude. God is a good father. As a good father, God does what is necessary for His children--whether they say thank you or not. At the same time, the gulls remind us that everyone that calls upon Him He saves.

Although both concepts are important, salvation is more important than gratitude. It is good to give thanks to the Lord for His mercy endures forever. Hell also lasts forever, be sure that before you spend your life being grateful you allow God to save your soul.

41. *That is when I realized what I had learned to see, was not the Glory of God but the glow of the enemy*. - This is where discernment becomes dispensable. Being able to stand in front of an audience and tell them about a financial breakthrough is easy. To stand in front of that same crowd and say that they are poor because of their sin is more difficult. The reason most people never attain sight or wisdom is because they cannot handle sight or wisdom.

With much wisdom, there is much sorrow. Therefore, vision, the ability to see, also causes much sorrow. When you learn to see as God does, you learn to see what God sees. When you learn to love as He does, you learn to hurt as God does. The cup that we beg to drink from God spares us in most cases. We simply cannot handle the pain of life if we saw it all. As did God when He looked upon the marred visage of Christ we too would look away from the sordid, carnal creatures, we call brothers and sisters.

42. *I learned that day to see my God's glory shine, and that Satan glow comes from the evil in my mind*. - God's glory is difficult to see because we are looking with the wrong eyes. I often hear people say that they are going to look for a soul mate when they go dancing. I find it ironic that they look in the flesh for their soul mates. Inability to understand that God is always with His children is what causes backsliding. The relationship between God and His people is mirrored in wedding vows; for richer or for poorer, in sickness and in health, in the good times and the bad; until death does us part. Perhaps this is why so many marriages fail, they do not believe in God so they cannot fathom the depth of covenant?

Remember, God is the beginning, middle, and ending of faith. This is probably the single most important of the keys to dousing Satan's fire. When the pilot of a plane encounters turbulence, and other difficulties he does not panic because he knows what the plane's design allows it to do and what kind of abuse it can take. Faith in his plane comes from hours of training, and hours spent in close quarters with this plane. This is how faith in God develops, hours of training, prayer, crying and spent in close quarters. Those that lack faith also lack knowledge. The lack of knowledge the Bible says is the reason God's people perish.

The information we desperately need is not prayer or scripture it is time spent in close quarters with God's Holy Spirit.

I pray that you notice that this chapter is *Dousing Satan's fire* not extinguishing Satan's fire. The two concepts are hues of each other but they differ immensely.
1. Dousing Satan's fire means that we diminish it or even put it out briefly.
2. Extinguishing Satan's fire means that we terminated every spark, the light cooled beyond incineration, and the lights no longer has the ability to revive.

Even if you cannot extinguish the effect of Satan's fire in our lives we can douse it effectively if you do nothing but spend time sitting in silence crying out to the Lord. I am not saying shed tears but I do suggest audibly calling upon the Lord. It takes time and you will hurt until God shows up but God promises you He will show up. If you cannot believe God's words, then stop wasting your time right now. If you do not believe that God saves, then should you believe anything that He says?

The following words come from the movie Shaka Zulu. The words are part of a conversation between the Emperor Shaka the king of the Zulus and the man that deceived him. Beware believers that we do not have a similar conversation with God because of our inability to renew in the Will of God.

Chaka - "Tell me Fabana, how do you catch a monkey?"

Fabana - "Well, a gourd is used with a narrow neck. Bait is used; a piece of fruit or something shinny. The monkey puts his hand down in to the gourd and grabs the bait. Then he is trapped, because he cannot get his hand out."

Chaka - "Once he realizes he is trapped why does the monkey not let go of the bait?"

Fabana - "Because his greed makes him blind."

Chaka - "And what is he greedy for?"

Fabana - "I supposed for what he thinks he cannot have."

Chaka - "Bait your gourd again, my heart longs for something-- shinny."

In the garden, Adam and Eve would not release the shinny bait Satan promised. Eve's heart longed for something shinny and she had a *choice* between the two lights she saw in the garden. It took the shed blood of Jesus Christ to free us from the shinny contents of Satan's gourd. I pray that believers do not meddle with the bait in the gourd again. Sadly, the prosperity doctrine is shinny, the promise of favor for tithe is shinny, the promise of opening the windows of heaven is shinny but none are what the Father wants for us. The light He wishes to shine in our lives is His fire, His glory. Imagine the lights in heaven around the throne of the King of Kings.

Amen

Chapter Twenty-three
Smoking or Non-smoking

"**While he [was] yet speaking, there came also another, and said, 'The fire of God is fallen from heaven, and hath burned up the sheep, and the servants, and consumed them; and I only am escaped alone to tell thee**' - Job1:16"

This work ends with scripture about the eternal flame of hell. I have never been nor do I intend to become a herald of hellfire and damnation. There is urgency in evangelism but this urgency stems not from fear but out of love. There is no way to have the love of God in your heart and not urgently render aid and mercy to the captives and the blind. Although fear of the Lord is the beginning of wisdom, admitting our humanity is the beginning of freedom.

Before any man becomes free, he must first admit that he is a slave. IF YOU ARE NOT A CAPTIVE, GOD HAS NO REASON TO FREE YOU. Free men are not in bondage to their sin they are rebellious, therefore beyond the assistance of God. This does not mean that the rebellious cannot return, but the scriptures tell us that the rebellious *choose* not to return. With this in mind I, point out that *choice* is predicated in honesty. When we *choose* based on our preference then we are often honest. For example, I always prefer cheesecake as my *choice* of desert. I will eat Apple pie, but my *choice* is and always will be Cheesecake.

Believers, God reads the contents of the human heart. Although we may not engage in fornication, He knows we lust. Although we may not kill, we have hate in our hearts. He also knows that although we call ourselves Christian we follow our own desires. It is our *choice* to follow our own heart, which permanently prevents humanity from achieving greatness in Christ. One of the things that differentiated Christ from the rest of Christendom is that He dedicated every waking moment to serving the will of God. By conscience design, Christ subjugated and subdued His will in difference to His flesh.

No matter what else you read about Christ's divine nature, Immaculate Conception, prayer life, fasting, miracles, kindness, love, teaching, compassion, or color it is one thing that made Christ special. The thing that made Christ special was that He *chose* to live and die for the will of the Father. This evidence we see throughout the gospels. Nowhere is it more important than in the Garden of Gethsemane. Mark 14:36 "**And He said, 'ABBA FATHER ALL THINGS ARE POSSIBLE UNTO THEE: TAKE AWAY THIS CUP FROM ME: NEVER THE LESS NOT WHAT I WILL BUT WHAT THOU WILL'.**" I find the statement "**NOT WHAT I WILL, BUT WHAT THOU WILL**," re*mark*able. There are two re*mark*able components to this statement. The first component was *choice*; we have already discussed this component.

The second component is that Jesus clearly states that it was NOT His will. Most of my life I heard preachers indicate that Jesus wanted to die for us. I have never found this validated in the scriptures. The scriptures seem to contradict this concept. It was not Christ's preference to die for our sins it was His *choice*. Like my *choice* to eat apple pie, I have eaten apple pie, but I desired Cheesecake the entire time. Why did Jesus lay down His life? Because to do the His Father's will was His food (choice).

What we learn from Jesus' suffering is a valuable lesson in obedience. What we see is that God's will must be our highest mandate. Jesus never wanted to die, to live a life devoid of human pleasures He *chose* to do because He understood that the Father's will was a better way than the efforts He had to offer. The human though fleshly by design DOES NOT HAVE TO SIN. Sin does not separate humans from God; the unrepentant heart repels God.

Amen

Appendices

Appendix A
Commentary

Where Does Your Treasure ?

"**Trust not in oppression, and become not vain in robbery: if riches increase, set not your heart [upon them** - Psalms 62:10'"

Commentary
Fool's Gold

The prosperity doctrine is of the greatest examples of following false lights, self worship, and materialism. The get rich mentality, which indeed pervades the church even today, caused thousands to rush to California for a piece of the proverbial pie. "Gold, gold, gold; there's gold in them thar hills," echoed through the mountains during the famous California gold rush. This gold rush occurred when unearthed gold in the California Mountains, sold and created instant wealth. People created towns to accommodate gold rushers. When the rush ended, the towns soon faded back into the prairies from which they came.

During the famous California gold rush, many men and women uprooted their everyday, safe, lives and went west in search of easy money. Actually, this was an ironic concept, for even though gold expedited wealth mining it was not easy. Although laborious, the difficulty Gold-miners faced was only part of the danger. There were many other dangers. Some of these dangers included claim jumpers, mine cave-ins, banditos, starvation, dehydration, and dishonest bankers.

Another difficulty in mining was that a gold like substance commonly unearthed and then taken to mineralogists as gold. This substance soon developed its own name. That name was 'Fool's Gold'. There was a simple test for fool's gold, pour either nitric or sulphuric acid on the metal substance. If the substance was true gold, there was an effervescent bubbling and then the purer metal remained. In the case of fool's gold, the bubbling did not cease. The substance dissolved into the acid releasing a pungent, unpleasant odor. The substance earned the name fool's gold because it took just as much labor to mine and ship this ore, but it yielded nothing in return.

The label *Fool's Gold* did not arise because it was stupid to fall prey to it. The label arose because you ended up feeling and looking foolish after putting so much time into a vain effort. The gold ore lay beneath the surface and needed mining. Miners dug until they saw a yellowish, metallic substance, and then they would unearth it, clean it, and have it tested. The gold then attained its value based on the purity of the sample.

Many people wasted life savings and only recovered fool's gold. Many people lost their lives staking out and laying claim to land full of fool's gold. The reason many people fell victim to fool's gold is that the substance had many of the same characteristics as gold. It was the same color; it weighed the same, and existed in the same places as the real gold.

Brokers price gold by purity, weight, mining, and refining cost. Again, we see that placing outrageous value on gold, diamonds, gemstones etc., shows that we have no understanding of what is valuable. How valuable can a substance really be if the price of it is contingent on whether or not people want it? Salvation has value whether you want it or not. Salvation's value is innate--meaning built in. The baubles we kill and die for have no innate value, yet we give up; and or, sacrifice the most valuable asset we have for them. We sacrifice our lives for pieces of dirt that do not even know we exist.

There is often swelling in a new thing much like in modern churches. But as a friend points out, "Swelling does not mean growth." When we create churches and ministries because of 'gold rushing', they do not last. Not only do they not last but they also produce weak, glossy eyed believers. These glossy-eyed believers are tepid and unprepared to handle the nuances of their Christian life. This is not because God's Holy Spirit is not present. It is because these believers like the gold rushers are only there because they are seeking gold. Anytime your quest takes you on a hunt for the dirt and rocks of this world, and switches your focus from God you WILL NEVER FIND LIFE. There is no Life in money, gold, or any other mineral from the dirt.

The promissory note is where paper money and checks evolved. The purpose of the promissory note was to make transporting money safer and easier. Despite the ease of carrying paper notes, they had no value unless honored, or vouched for. This meant two things;

1. Someone must accept the note.
2. Someone must provide the value of the promise.

This is the difference between money and treasure. Both money and treasure items have value. Treasure, however, is valuable regardless of who wants it or who understands it. For example, 99% of Christians would agree that wealth is a blessing. However, how many Christians realize that sanity is a far greater treasure. How many Christians realize that non-nightmare filled nights and the sweet sleep of God is far greater than money?

The reason we call paper money 'bills' is that they have no value unless someone vouches or pays for them. Think of all the bills you have on your counter at home, they are valueless unless you *choose* to pay them. Although the service has been rendered the bill is still unpaid. In other words, a bill is only valuable if someone *chooses* to make good the value. The Bank in heaven accepts checks or vouchers from one person and one person only, Jesus the Christ. Jesus the Christ is the only person authorized to pay any bills required to give Life and give it more abundantly.

Salvation cost God His only begotten Son. It does not matter whether or not we want this most precious gift; salvation is valuable. The fact of the matter is that the most valuable stone in the history of humanity was a tried stone, a precious Cornerstone. We do not measure salvation in karats, but by the effect it has on life; past, present, and future. If any of the stones you know of can alter time, go into hell, redeem the lost, and atone for your sins tell me where to find them. I will bring the excavating equipment and mine with you! What fool heartiness to sacrifice our most valuable treasures (freedom and life) for rocks[193].

Let me tell you a story. A certain doctor had two patients; both came to see him one day. As they waited patiently, one of them sang. He sang the same song repeatedly. The singing patient wore dirty clothes and knew the doctor from shining his shoes. The other patient was dressed well and sat quietly. He had nice clothes, nice jewelry, and kept looking at his watch. He was going to be late for work. After approximately 45 minutes, the richer of the two asked the other why he kept singing the same verse, "I ain't by no means tired." The poorer of the two said, "These ain't just words to me, they told me I was going to die five years ago, I ain't gonna never stop singing about Jesus." The man continued to sing in his tattered clothes, while the richer of the two went back to silently watching his watch. I ask you, which one of them was the wealthiest?

The first documented case of fool's gold in the Bible occurs in Genesis, wherein Eve and then Adam fall prey to fool's gold. Believers, Satan (the angel formerly known as Lucifer) appeared to Eve and Adam in

---

[193] "**Professing themselves to be wise they became foolish** - Romans 1:34."

his created form. Satan's original form was bright, shinning, and beautiful, the way he was the day God created him.

Just as we find real gold near fool's gold, we found Lucifer in the same as real Gold. Satan stood in the Garden of God he was there with God[194]. Eve and Adam saw a shinning object and thought it was the real McCoy. Satan knew about fool's gold long before Eve and Adam; he is the epitome of fool's gold. We know Satan existed amidst real gold. Lucifer had many of the same characteristics as gold, but we never put him to the test. Much to our downfall, Adam and Eve did not have the means to test Lucifer to see just how badly he stank.

According to Ezekiel 28, Lucifer *mark*eted himself to the angels and because of this; the Almighty cast him out of heaven. God Almighty cast out Lucifer and all the angels Lucifer recruited from amongst the stones of fire. In the garden God walked with Adam and spoke to Adam; and Satan was there. Satan knew the words of God and said them with Godly eloquence.

The problem with fool's gold was that the uneducated miners did not know how to differentiate between real gold and the fool's gold. Many miners actually developed their own methods of differentiating. The method always cost more time than it was worth and was always trial and error.

This is also the case with many believers. The lack of knowledge of the test kits blocks believer's ability to discern the difference between the fool's gold and real gold. What this actually means is that we cannot tell the difference between salvation and damnation, life and death. Many believers still cannot distinguish between real gold and fool's gold for two reasons.
1. They do not know or study the word and therefore cannot use the word as a test against Satan.
2. They do not know God nor do they know His voice, they therefore cannot tell the difference between Satan and the Lord.

In the case of the shinny, valueless, metal fool's gold, the acid reacted with the trace elements. This reaction released ammonia or sulfur and caused a pungent, burning gas. The Almighty gave us the two test kits, witness, or more commonly known as *Testaments*. By these two testaments, the stench of Satan can be uncovered continually.

---

[194] Ezekiel 31:15.

Brothers and sisters we too are miners; seekers of True Gold. Believers use their own mining methods, stake out claims called churches and ministries and then prospect, hoping to find God. Believers dig and blast away their lives, and pieces of other people's lives in an effort to hit the mother lode. The mother lode (Meaning the richest vein with the largest yield) in the kingdom of God is God's Holy Spirit. When we hit the mother lode it is, there we should stay. Many prospectors forsook the true treasure, looking for the bright shiny material we have heard so much about. However, what we hear most about is not True Gold it is the fool's gold of this world, the foolish pleasantries of the flesh. When we find what we believe to be gold, we race off to have it tested. Only to find that it is fool's gold, or even worse it was the real gold but we left the bulk of it unguarded in order to bring in our find. When we return to the gold left behind, we often find someone else has squatting on our claim.

Claim jumpers lay hold to our gifts and live in our blessings and prosperity. The claim jumpers now possess these things not because they stole them, but because we gave them up, abandoned, or simply failed to grow in them. The other type of claim jumpers, cowboys called 'Bushwhackers'. Cowboys call them bushwhackers because they lay in wait behind bushes, and when the chance arises they jump out and *wack* you. Spiritual bushwhackers also hide in the bushes. The bush of *choice* for a bushwhacker is the Bramble elected in Judges 9. Spiritual bushwhackers hide in the shade of the Bramble and strike out from their place of death. When bushwhackers hear of a new strike (patch of gold), they move in and *'wack'* (kill) the true owners. Bushwhackers move in not because they have a desire to live in God's Holy Spirit, but because they do not want you to live in God's Holy Spirit. Bushwhackers also have a plan. Bushwhacker's plan is to stop as many of God's prospectors from striking gold as possible. Bushwhackers do not wish to see God they simply desire to live in their flesh to the utmost pleasure of the flesh[195].

I took the time to draw this point out because the real gold is not in the ground but in your heart. For a believer, the human heart is the Holy of Holies. The true treasure we should guard is the portable Holy of Holies: the human heart[196]. From this place set aside for God that God's Holy Spirit ebbs and flows. What fellowship has light with darkness Paul

---

[195] Romans 1:25.
[196] Matthew 5:8, 15:18, 6:21, and John 7:38.

asks and Jesus confirms. If Light dwells in your heart, Light will flow from your mouth. If however, darkness flows from your mouth then darkness is also in your heart. Believers...blessed are the pure in heart for they shall SEE GOD. The light in Patmos is any object that looks like real gold but is fool's gold. When Satan presented himself in the garden, he implied that God actually had not spoken the truth[197]. What Satan told Eve was that she could live anyway she wanted to, defy God, and still reap all the rewards. This is how all-successful deception begins, with a portion of distorted truth. What Satan implied is accurate. Any believer may live any life they desire and they shall surely reap the rewards of that life style[198]. The greed in our hearts convinces us that the rewards of a sinful life style are the same blessings reserved for those in Christ.

WHEN THE TITHE IS FOOL'S GOLD

The tithe does not assure you anything. Blessed assurance stems from a relationship with God. The best example of this comes from Acts chapter 5. If the tithe was so important why would Peter say the following in verses 3 & 4 "**But Peter said, 'Ananias, why hath Satan filled thine heart to lie to the Holy Ghost, and to keep back (part) of the price of the land? Whiles it remained, was it not thine own? And after it was sold, was it not in thine own power? Why hast thou conceived this thing in thine heart? Thou hast not lied unto men, but unto God'.**" Peter tells the couple that the money from the sale of the land was theirs to do with what they desired. Notice Peter makes the point of telling them that the money was theirs, thus not nullifying the law of the tithe but keeping it in its proper place. Man is not above the law Paul tells us but a righteous man obeys the law. Accordingly, Peter tells the couple it would have been better not to give the money than to break covenant with the Lord, the amount of the money that was not the issue. Neither time did Peter say they had robbed God, he said they lied to God's Holy Spirit.

How can a man rob God? What exactly is a heavenly stick-up? What does God posses that man can steal? What does God consider precious? For the answer to this we look to Judges 9:12-13 which says

---

[197] I explained this in the chapter, the bearer of light.
[198] "**For the wages of sin [is] death; but the gift of God [is] eternal life through Jesus Christ our Lord** - Romans 6:23."

"The trees said to the vine, 'Come and reign over us. The vine said to them, 'Should I leave my new wine, which cheers God and man, and go to wave back and forth over the trees?" The human creature, the creature God gave *choice* is God's prize possession, so much so He gave His only begotten Son. "**BUT WOE TO YOU; SCRIBES AND PHARISEES, HYPOCRITES! BECAUSE YOU SHUT UP THE KINGDOM OF HEAVEN AGAINST MEN; FOR YOU DON'T ENTER IN YOURSELVES, NEITHER DO YOU ALLOW THOSE WHO ARE ENTERING IN TO ENTER. WOE TO YOU, SCRIBES AND PHARISEES, HYPOCRITES! FOR YOU TRAVEL AROUND BY SEA AND LAND TO MAKE ONE PROSELYTE; AND WHEN HE BECOMES ONE, YOU MAKE HIM TWICE AS MUCH OF A SON OF HELL AS YOURSELVES** - Matthew 23:13-15."

How can a man rob God? A man robs God by standing in the way of those He died to redeem. The moneychangers in the temple were not thieves simply because they changed money, but because they turned the truth into a lie. People that looked to God for truth and justice saw in His temple theft, lies, and deceit. When people encountered the representatives of the God of Abraham, Isaac, and Jacob, they found their God to be a conniving liar.

The Shed Blood of Christ is the only assurance of salvation. While you live outside the Blood and Body of Christ, you make yourself food for Satan. That is why Christians are sick, weak, poor, unhappy, and powerless. This is not because Christians do not tithe but because you have no relationship with God. Moreover, this state of Lifelessness leads to famine-like hunger. When we reach this level of hunger, anything will do. When we reach this level of death: there is nothing left for us to do but to eat death; then we are never satisfied. This process leads to destruction.

The prosperity doctrine reeks of death, and our greed and lust for it proves it is unholy. 1 Timothy 6:10 reminds us of some very important truths. "**For the love of money is the root of all-evil: which while some coveted after, they have erred from the faith, and pierced themselves through with many sorrows**." The prosperity doctrine has diverted the mission of the church for almost 50 years. So much so that we have allowed evil to run rampant in the church and then out into the world. Much like the church at Corinth, we no longer lead the world in morality--they look to themselves for that. The world resorted to the law for righteousness because they no longer saw any righteousness in the church. We crave most in life the thing that is least important money. The love of money is the root of all sorts of evil, not the love of god. When you learn to love Life not this life but God's Life, you will be joyful and rich. Not with dollars and cents but with the only thing life is for-- Love.

ACCEPTABLE CHRISTIANITY IS FOOL'S GOLD

Believers we, should never dwell amongst non-believers unless we are there to lead them from of bondage. The only time Jesus went amongst the sinners was to pull them from the clutches of Satan. Jesus never dwelt among sinners; never accepted sinners praise, and most certainly never accepted sinners rewards.

For too long the church has flirted with the world of entertainment. I ask you, can it be ministry when the world praises music and cannot tell that you are singing about God? To the world it is just good music. Believers, the joyful noise we make is unto God. I assure you that the things that please God joy do not delight the world. For proof of this, ask God's Son.

I enjoy good entertainment as much as the next person does. However, we must maintain a distinct line between believers and non-believers. The scriptures specifically tell us not to conform to the things of this world but to come away from the things of this world. Non-believers do a better job of removing themselves from Christians than Christian's do of not trying to be with and act like non-believers. Non-believers do not try to gain acceptance from Christians. Non-believers never seek Christian approval. Christians on the other hand do everything we can to ride along side non-believers. Christians even take their titles and try to make them our own titles like, 'first lady'. I have never seen a president's wife claim to the title of bishop or pastor's wife. Why then do believers try to ascribe empty titles to God's people? It is as if to imply that there is royalty here on earth. Tradition lends to the fact that monarchs are divine by nature. This is a lie only celestial beings are divine. No king in history, other than Jesus came down from, or ascended to heaven.

However, these same practitioners of this farce will then bellow from the pulpit that we are of a Royal priesthood. This phrase 'Royal priesthood' therefore means two things;
1. We serve a king or kingdom.
2. We serve this king/kingdom in a spiritual capacity.

There is no king or emperor higher than our High Priest. If we are truly God's priests, we should rejoice in the titles given to us by our King, our Prince of peace. Titles such as *servant*, *bondservant*, *disciple*, *worshipper*, and *people of God* should be looked on as gold. Then again this chapter is about the fool's gold many of God's people still desire.

Jesus told of the world's disdain for the true word of God[199]. Not only does the world not hate crossover Christian music; the world's does not recognize crossover Christian music as the word of God. If the sinners that we are admonished to minister to do not know that we are talking about God how can they hear and accept Christ?

We turn on shows and award ceremonies wherein half of the performers are either naked or vulgar. Then near the end of the show, one or two people come out and wail a few words on a vocal cord then retire calling it gospel. There is seldom mention of God, sometimes the vulgar, worldly performers give a rendition of a popular Christian song. Even worse, some lifelong advocate of sin and immorality from a dark life style filled with drugs, or homosexuality sings an all time gospel great and we applaud Satan's people for singing to our God. Brothers and sisters, God rejects these people's songs (just like the offerings of Cain) and the singers are not accepting God. The singers are simply disarming you; they are bushwhackers. The bushwhackers of this world hide behind the bramble that speaks in Judges 9. Satan in Job speaks of the believer's hedge. The hedge is to shield believers from the evil one not to shield us in our sin. Worldly acceptance is fool's gold[200]. Examine worldly acceptance and you will see that it stinks. Not everyone is guilty, many of the worst CDs in production gladly call the name of God…to them we owe honor.

In instances where we *mark*et fool's gold as ministry, it does not uplift, praise God's Holy Spirit, or edify; therefore, it is not ministry. The

---

[199] John 15:18 "**IF THE WORLD HATE YOU, YE KNOW THAT IT HATED ME BEFORE [IT HATED] YOU.**"

[200] James 4:4 "**Ye adulterers and adulteresses, know ye not that the friendship of the world is enmity with God? Whosoever therefore will be a friend of the world is the enemy of God.**"

book of Ephesians clearly states that the purpose of ministry is to perfect the saints. A runner cannot improve his running by practicing archery. In this same manner, only Christ can perfect a Christian. A song performed by a Christian does not mean that it is ministry; it just means that it was a song sung by a Christian. Conversely, a gospel song sung by a heathen is just that, another performance.

What '*crossover*' ministry offers to believers and non-believers is a weak, watered down version of God's way. I understand the crossover concept, but the flaw in it is that there is no reason to change. There is no way to make Jesus inoffensive and disarming. It is like trying to convince a lamb that the salivating lion only wants to be intimate. The prey ALWAYS knows the enemy. **Christ and sin are enemies forever, they cannot reconcile**[201].

If a person can maintain their lifestyle, change very little if at all and then claim to be a Christian - who would not? Believers, the problem with fool's gold is it has no value at all. *Ministry that does not bring about change in the sinner or help perfect the saints is not ministry and has no value at all.*

Let us pause a moment and define the term Ministry using the scriptures as our guide. "**He gave some...for the perfecting of the holy ones, to the work of serving, to the building up of the body of {the} Messiah; until we all attain to the unity of the faith, and of the knowledge of the Son of God**[202]." Ministry therefore only has one purpose; to perfect saints into **the unity of the faith, and of the knowledge of the Son of God** not to entertain. In other words, the purpose of ministry it is to take sinners and move them towards the perfected state in Christ. Hence, the term Christian therefore means that we are becoming Christ-like. A Martian is from Mars, a Haitian from Haiti so we as Christians must be from Christ. If we therefore are from Christ, why do we have more characteristics of God's enemy? Jesus gives us the simple answer in John 8:44. This simply means we are more like Satan than Jesus is a state the Bible calls darkness. The Bible says we are not in darkness but darkness itself.

Believers; crossover, politically correct ministry/music is fool's gold. There can be no conviction or change without God's Holy Spirit.

---

[201] Genesis 3:13.
[202] The World English Bible -Ephesians 4:11-13.

For lack of a simpler explanation, a song is an invitation, if we never sing about God's Holy Spirit how can He be invited? If God is not invited, why should He come in and sup with us? Only the works of God's Holy Spirit bring about change and salvation. Since non-believers do not know God's Holy Spirit, we must teach them of grace and mercy. It is the message of God's unfailing love that brings lost souls home; not the beat of the music.

In the book of Acts, the sons of Sceva tried to cast out demons[203]. The demons said to them, **"Paul and Silas we know, but who are you?"** In the case of fool's gold lost souls hear the music and say, "Jesus and God's Holy Spirit we know, but who are you singing about?" This is because too often we never mention or even allude to God's Holy Spirit. Songs that do not sing about change, or explain the new life, and the new Light are not ministry. According to Paul, the purpose of the four-fold ministry is for the perfecting of the saints and the building up of the body of Christ[204]. How then can a lost sheep become a perfected saint if there is no change? This implies that the sinner's heart is perfect. We know this is not the case. Therefore, can we do the sinner a service when all we do is make them feel good, and hope falsely that there is a tomorrow?

The entertainment industry is not interested in education or ministry. Even in the Gospel (entertainment), industry the emphasis is on making money and entertainment. They do not promote artists because of their ministry; they promote based on the marketability of the music and the artist. Some the worst music in history we produced and market successfully simply because we like the artist. However, the Gospel industry is not doing this as a favor this is how they make a living, by the multitude of their merchandising and their trafficking[205].

Much as it was with Adam and Eve, the people of God have such weak fellowship with God they cannot discern the truth. Much like the man in the poem, Adam and Eve yearned to serve God with their flesh not with their hearts. This is why Satan appeals to the flesh not the heart and why God never appeals to the flesh. Those who seek God seek Him in the

---

[203] Acts 19:14 - Notice it was all seven of the man's sons. Seven being the number of completion this means that their attempt was a complete failure.
[204] Building the body has two meanings just as it does in the weight room. In the weight room, we build the body by first strengthening the body we have. Secondly, we then add to the body things like new muscles and a new diet.
[205] Ezekiel 28:16.

spirit. Those who cherish gold seek gold in the flesh and will always find fool's gold. Fool's gold is the *nightclub paradox* at work. We go a place filled with drunks, scantily clad women, and suggestive lewd dancing to find our soul mate? If the person you found in the club you found with your 'soul' perhaps you should reevaluate the condition of your soul.

Conversely, when you seek the Lord, do so with your heart. God can fill an empty spirit; but He must break a sinful spirit. It is better to be lonely and searching than lost and satisfied. It is better to dig longer and find real gold than to rush off to market to sell nothing. The new convert most often characterizes the sale of nothing. In the new converts case this is because they have no relationship with God.

If a man is taken hostage, he is in the custody and the care of the hostage taker, but they have no relationship. What we discovered in the Stockholm Syndrome is that prolonged exposure to the hostage taker often results in the hostage developing a bond. Many times the hostage sways completely to the hostage takers side, giving little thought to their predicament. This is how a relationship with God develops; with quite intimate time, listening to what He has to say. In Stockholm, the hostage taker DID NOT have the victim's best interest at heart; this is why it is fool's gold. God on the other hand has your best interest at heart; all He wants is the time, the quite time to tell you what He wants for you. Allow God to take you hostage; this is the only time that He is guarantees your freedom and safety. The word addict comes from Latin. The slaves Romans took after conquests they called addicts. We have been addicts in the literal sense of the word are entire life, let God take you hostage, become His bondservant and let freedom reign.

There is a parable that instructs us that a fool and his money are soon parted. Until I got older, I did not realize the wisdom of this parable. This is not a reference to theft, squandering, or losing the money; it is a reference to the fact that this life is but a whisper. This life is fool's gold, because it has no real value. The only value this life has is in Christ. Without Christ this life is not a treasure, it is simply an adventure. Salvation is a gift freely given, is does not diminish, tarnish nor does it depreciate; it is the only gold standard that lasts for eternity.

Look with me to the wisdom of Solomon in Ecclesiastes chapter two. I present the scripture in the form of a letter. As you read the words of this fallen king, read them as a letter written to you from his broken heart to your heart that too will break. Imagine spending your entire life striving for something and at the end, this is what you discover about your efforts. Look at what the result is for those who chase wealth, despite Solomon's warning that it will grow wings.

Brothers and Sisters,

"I said in my heart, 'Come now, I will test you with mirth;' therefore enjoy pleasure;' and behold, this also was vanity. I said of laughter, 'It is foolishness; and of mirth, What does it accomplish?'

I searched in my heart how to cheer my flesh with wine, my heart yet guiding me with wisdom, and how to lay hold of folly, until I might see what it was good for the sons of men that they should do under heaven all the days of their lives. I made myself great works. I built myself houses. I planted myself vineyards. I made myself gardens and parks, and I planted trees in them of all kinds of fruit. I made myself pools of water, to water from it the forest where trees were reared. I bought male servants and female servants, and had servants born in my house. I also had great possessions of herds and flocks, above all who were before me in Jerusalem; I also gathered silver and gold for myself, and the treasure of kings and of the Provinces. I got myself male and female singers, and the delights of the sons of men—musical instruments, and that of all sorts.

So I was great, and increased more than all who were before me in Jerusalem. My wisdom also remained with me. Whatever my eyes desired, I did not keep from them. I didn't withhold my heart from any joy, for my heart rejoiced because of all my labor, and this was my portion from all my labor. Then I looked at all the works that my hands had worked, and at the labor that I had labored to do; and behold, all was vanity and a chasing after wind, and there was no profit under the sun.

I turned myself to consider wisdom, madness, and folly: for what can the king's successor do? Just that which has been done long ago. Then I saw that wisdom excels folly, as far as light excels darkness. The wise man's eyes are in his head, and the fool walks in darkness—and yet I perceived that one event happens to them all. Then I said in my heart, 'As it happens to the fool, so will it happen even to me; and why was I then more wise?'

Then I said in my heart that this also is vanity. For of the wise man, even as of the fool, there is no memory for ever, since in the days to come all will have been long forgotten. Indeed, the wise man must die *just like the fool! So I hated life, because the work that is worked under the sun was grievous to me; for all is vanity and a chasing after wind. I hated all my labor in which I labored under the sun, because I must leave it to the man who comes after me. Who knows whether he will be a wise man or a fool? Yet he will have rule over all of my labor in which I have labored, and in which I have shown myself wise under the sun. This also is vanity.*

Therefore, I began to cause my heart to despair concerning all the labor in which I had labored under the sun. For there is a man whose labor is with wisdom, with knowledge, and with skillfulness; yet he shall leave it for his portion to a man who has not labored for it. This also is vanity and a great evil. For what has a man of all his labor, and of the striving of his heart, in which he labors under the sun? For all his days are sorrows and his travail is grief; yes, even in the night his heart takes no rest. This also is vanity. There is nothing better for a man than that he should eat and drink, and make his soul enjoy good in his labor. This also I saw, that it is from the hand of God.

For who can eat, or who can have enjoyment, more than I? For to the man who pleases him, God gives wisdom, knowledge, and joy; but to the sinner he gives travail, to gather and to heap up, that he may give to him who pleases God. This also is vanity and a chasing after wind[206]*."*

Solomon
The ~~wise~~ broken hearted

---

[206] The World English Bible: Messianic Edition, http://www.eBible.org/Bible/hnv/ july/07

THE TRUE PROSPERITY DOCTRINE

"Bless the Lord, my soul! All that is within me praise His holy name! Bless the Lord, my soul, and don't forget all His benefits; Who forgives all your sins; who heals all your diseases; Who redeems your life from destruction; who crowns you with loving kindness and tender mercies; Who satisfies your desire with good things, so that your youth is renewed like the eagle's. The Lord executes righteous acts, and justice for all who are oppressed. He made known His ways to Moses, His deeds to the children of Israel. The Lord is merciful and gracious, slow to anger, and abundant in loving kindness. He will not always accuse; neither will He stay angry forever. He has not dealt with us according to our sins, nor repaid us for our iniquities. For as the heavens are high above the earth, so great is His loving kindness toward those who fear Him. As far as the east is from the west, so far has He removed our transgressions from us. Like a father has compassion on His children, so the Lord has compassion on those who fear Him. For He knows how we are made. He remembers that we are dust. As for man, his days are like grass. As a flower of the field, so he flourishes. For the wind passes over it, and it is gone. Its place remembers it no more. But the Lord's loving kindness is from everlasting to everlasting with those who fear Him, His righteousness to children's children; to those who keep His covenant, to those who remember to obey His precepts. The Lord has established His throne in the heavens. His kingdom rules over all. Praise the Lord, you angels of His, who are mighty in strength, who fulfill His word, obeying the voice of His word. Praise the Lord, all you armies of His, you servants of His, who do His pleasure. Praise the Lord, all you works of

His, in all places of His dominion. Bless the Lord, my soul! - Psalms 103."

Solomon reminds us in Proverbs 13:22 the wealth of the sinner is laid up for the just. I can honestly say that I have never heard this scripture used accurately. Proverbs 13:22 is always used as a false promise that the money the world possesses God takes and gives to us. This is a false promise. Nowhere in the Bible does God make for His people permanent plans for this earth. All that God has ever done He has done in preparation for that great day God calls His people to live with Him. Why would God turn Christians unto the rich young rulers knowing what He teaches about the effect of wealth? God knows that we will not sell all we have and give it to the poor not even to inherit the kingdom.

The proponents of staying here on earth in the hereafter have some scriptural basis for their concept in Revelations. However, Revelations clearly states what the Revelations saw, "**And I saw a new heaven and a new earth: for the first heaven and the first earth were passed away; and there was no more sea. And I John saw the holy city, new Jerusalem, coming down from God out of heaven, prepared as a bride adorned for her husband**, - Revelations 21:1-2." This scripture nullifies the concept of taking the world's stuff or it being left here for us in the next life. Fields you did not plant and houses you did not build is not telling us that the world built them. Instead, this scripture is God reminding us of the care and the love He has for His children. God builds the houses and the fields[207]. Whether or not God uses people like Nebuchadnezzar to accomplish His will God is still the builder. God owns the cattle on a thousand hills. These He reserves for His children to use to serve His kingdom. Every kingdom needs servants.

Let us look together at Psalms 103 the true prosperity doctrine. It should at least be true for Christians that our greatest treasure is in Christ Himself.

1. "**Bless the Lord, O my soul! All that is within me bless His holy name**!" David reminds us that it more blessed to give than to receive. Imagine the day when you can say bless the Lord instead of Help me Lord. When you can say all I have; I give to you, instead of in need. More concisely stated it is more blessed to be able to give than to be in

---

[207] John 14:2.

need. Understanding the concept as such makes the principle much more useful, and more of blessing than most understand.

2. **"Bless the Lord, my soul, and don't forget all His benefits."** In the job market, the older you get the more important benefits become so it is in this relationship with God. The more apart from the world, you become, the more you need God's love and His mercy. These benefits make all the other Godly benefits work.

3. **"Who forgives all your sins; Who heals all your diseases; Who redeems your life from destruction; Who crowns you with loving kindness and tender mercies; Who satisfies your desire with good things, so that your youth is renewed like the eagle's."** Here, we see that David lists some of the more, important benefits the relationship with his new Shepard avails. Notably no mention of money appears in this list. People do not realize that forgiveness is a continual process. Jesus told us to forgive our brother 7x70, so we understood that forgiveness is not only continual but also complete. Therefore, God's forgiveness is also not only continual but complete.

4. **"The Lord executes righteous acts, and justice for all who are oppressed."** David reminds us again of the wealth of God's mercy. Remember Jesus commented on paying the tithe in Matthew 23:23[208], it should not be difficult to see that the Father and the Son are one. They both remind us that the tithe although important fades in comparison to mercy and faith. What is also important is the reminder from David that God serves the oppressed. Perhaps the Christians that constantly seek wealth should remember that God called us to <u>SERVE</u> the poor.

5. **"He made known His ways to Moses, His deeds to the children of Israel."** David reminds us that our God deserves praise, worship, and to be blessed for all His goodness. David reminds us that to those that stay intimate with the Lord He tells His mysteries and His plans for our future.

---

[208] **"WOE UNTO YOU, SCRIBES AND PHARISEES, HYPOCRITES! FOR YE PAY TITHE OF MINT, ANISE, AND CUMMIN, AND HAVE OMITTED THE WEIGHTIER [MATTERS] OF THE LAW, JUDGMENT, MERCY, AND FAITH: THESE OUGHT YE TO HAVE DONE, AND NOT TO LEAVE THE OTHER UNDONE."**

6. "**The Lord is merciful and gracious, slow to anger, and abundant in loving kindness.**" Yet another listed benefit of intimacy with God. Regarding this scripture, some assert that God's abundant, loving-kindness is material in nature. Nevertheless, the next verse clears this fallacy up for us. It is clear from the following five verses in this scripture that David is referring to the mercy and gentleness of our Father.

7. "**He will not always chide[209]; neither will He stay angry forever. He has not dealt with us according to our sins, nor repaid us for our iniquities. For as the heavens are high above the earth, so great is His loving kindness toward those who fear Him. As far as the east is from the west, so far has He removed our transgressions from us. Like a father has compassion on his children, so the Lord has compassion on those who fear Him.**" I personally find the first line in this verse one of the most revealing stanzas in the Bible. Fear of the Lord is definitely the beginning of wisdom, but it can also be the end of an intimate relationship. For those people who grew up in abusive homes, volatile relationships, and homes that lacked warmth fear is a common thing. Abusive relationships are dreadful examples of love, and give rise to the wrong type of fear of the Lord. An abusive, untrustworthy, insensitive father image lends the victim to see God in this way. Victims see God as judgmental and wrathful. This stanza however clears that up. God is not an angry, vengeful deity, He is a Father. The difference is that God does not lash out at those that lovingly fear His will. To say that God does not punish would be lying, but even when God punishes, it is out of love not anger. The Psalm gets more beautiful when the writer states that God did not deal with us according to our sins. How majestic a God that deals with children based on what is best not what they deserve.

8 "**For He knows how we are made. He remembers that we are dust. As for man, his days are like grass. As a flower of the field, so He flourishes. For the wind passes over it, and it is gone. Its place remembers it no more.**" Brother David (whose name means beloved) writes a peculiar phrase stating that we are dust. This phrase is not peculiar because David reminds us that we are mortal. It is peculiar because even before God's Holy Spirit dwelt among humans David

---

[209] Accuse.

understood that we live outside God. This Revelation is phenomenal because David informs us that at every juncture that God remembers that we are flawed, frail, creatures **unlike** Him. Despite our pathetic, sinful nature God is still God; merciful and kind.

This statement by David also brings us again to the ultimate wealth there is in the universe. **"Jesus answered, 'VERILY, VERILY, I SAY UNTO THEE, EXCEPT A MAN BE BORN OF WATER AND [OF] THE SPIRIT, HE CANNOT ENTER INTO THE KINGDOM OF GOD. THAT WHICH IS BORN OF THE FLESH IS FLESH; AND THAT WHICH IS BORN OF THE SPIRIT IS SPIRIT'."** David knew the importance of salvation long before Christ came. Believers still have not grasped the actual key to the kingdom. There is no mystery or hidden wisdom in this statement. This is fact! **THE KEY TO THE KINGDOM IS AND ALWAYS HAS BEEN CHRIST.**

9. **"But the Lord's loving kindness is from everlasting to everlasting**
   1. **With those who fear Him, His righteousness to children's children;**
   2. **To those who keep his covenant,**
   3. **To those who remember to obey His precepts.**

The Lord has established His throne in the heavens. His kingdom rules over all. Bless the Lord, you angels of His, who are mighty in strength, who fulfill His word, obeying the voice of His word. Bless the Lord, all you armies of His, you servants of His, who do His pleasure. Praise the Lord, all you works of His, in all places of His dominion. Praise the Lord, my soul!" Again, we see in David a wisdom Solomon did not possess, and a type of intimacy with the Lord our God that results in understanding and revelation. We do not consider David a prophet but his revealed wisdom exceeds most if not all of the prophets.

In these last verses, David outlines the kingdom of God and praises Him for all the good things God has done. Here we see David breaking down the triune nature of the kingdom of God. Here we see David breaking down the righteous into three wonderful groups. David also illustrates to us the ways in which believers mimic the three-fold nature of God's design. David is holding true to blessing God from all that is within him, for you see David was all three; Spirit, flesh and dust.

1. *SPIRIT* - The spirit kingdom to which we belong if in Christ.

2. **FLESH** - The human kingdom to which we are born and from which most will never be free.

3. **DUST** - The lower creatures that are outside the body of Christ - a sin filled status called dust.

ALL THAT GLITTERS

"**Now when the apostles which were at Jerusalem heard that Samaria had received the word of God, they sent unto them Peter and John -- Who, when they were come down, prayed for them, that they might receive the Holy Ghost: For as yet he was fallen upon none of them: only they were baptized in the name of the Lord Jesus. Then laid they {their} hands on them, and they received the Holy Ghost. And when Simon saw that through laying on of the apostles' hands the Holy Ghost was given, he offered them money, Saying, Give me also this power, that on whomsoever I lay hands, he may receive the Holy Ghost. But Peter said unto him, Thy money perish with thee, because thou hast thought that the gift of God may be purchased with money. Thou hast neither part nor lot in this matter: for thy heart is not right in the sight of God. Repent therefore of this thy wickedness, and pray God, if perhaps the thought of thine heart may be forgiven thee. For I perceive that thou art in the gall of bitterness, and {in} the bond of iniquity** - Acts 8:14-23." Having gone this far into the fiery lie of fool's gold, I will no longer hold my peace about the prosperity doctrine. Since we are dealing with falsehoods and false glory let us tackle the most pervasive in the church. Someone once said, "Cured of my disease, last night I died of my physician." I bring this thought to your because it spells out in everyday terms the effect the prosperity doctrine has on the church.

This is not to say that prosperity is a lie. We know the Lord our God promised prosperity. However, God made no promises of prosperity without Him. How could the prosperity doctrine actually work when believers have less now than when they started participating? The only people prospering under this prosperity doctrine are the ones peddling the accursed doctrine. Christian edifices are getting larger, but the glory of the Lord fades constantly from the face of the earth.

In all biblical teaching about wealth, has God ever exempted Himself from His peoples' wealth or ordained for them to be wealthy and He not live among them? To be wealthy does not mean that you have money it means a great deal more. Money is a mere trinket. In the grand scheme of things, money means very little by itself[210].

It will take two steps to open your hearts to God's prosperity. Firstly, a Revelation from God is in order. One day while listening to a televangelist beg for money and promise a return on what you give unto the televangelist's bosom the Lord chimed in. {Thus saith the Lord} *"THAT IS WHERE YOU ALL MISSED IT. YES, I PROMISED YOU MILK AND HONEY BUT I NEVER SAID IT WAS THINGS. THE THINGS I PROMISE YOU ARE NEVER DEAD; I COME TO GIVE LIFE AND IT MORE ABUNDANTLY. I NEVER TOLD YOU THE MILK AND HONEY WAS MONEY. THE MILK IS HOW I FEED MY CHILDREN IT IS WHAT THEY NEED TO LIVE. THE HONEY IS THE SWEETNESS OF MY PRESENCE, MY SWEET FRAGRANCE; THE LAND OF MILK AND HONEY IS ANYWHERE I AM AND YOU ARE TOO. THE LAND OF MILK AND HONEY IS MY BOSOM."*

To help you to see this more clearly I cite the following and underline the important terms. The underlined phrases are important to us because they verify that we only access the *land of milk and honey* through God the Father.

1. Exodus13:5 - **"And it shall be when the Lord shall bring thee into the land of the Canaanites, and the Hittites, and the Amorites, and the Hivites, and the Jebusites, which He sware unto thy fathers to give thee, a land flowing with milk and honey, that thou shalt keep this service in this month**."

2. Leviticus 20:20-24 - **"YE SHALL THEREFORE KEEP ALL MY STATUTES, AND ALL MY JUDGMENTS, AND DO THEM: THAT THE LAND, YE SHALL THEREFORE KEEP ALL MY STATUTES, AND ALL MY JUDGMENTS, AND DO THEM: THAT THE LAND, WHITHER I BRING YOU TO DWELL THEREIN, SPUE YOU NOT OUT. BUT I HAVE SAID UNTO YOU, YE SHALL INHERIT THEIR LAND, AND I WILL GIVE IT UNTO YOU TO POSSESS IT, A LAND THAT FLOWETH**

---

[210] James 5.

WITH MILK AND HONEY: I (AM) THE LORD YOUR GOD, WHICH HAVE SEPARATED YOU FROM (OTHER) PEOPLE."

3. Numbers 14:8 - "**If the Lord delight in us, then <u>He will bring</u> us into this land, and give it us; a land which floweth with milk and honey.**"

4. Ezekiel 20:6 - "**IN THE DAY (THAT) I LIFTED UP MINE HAND UNTO THEM, <u>TO BRING THEM</u> FORTH OF THE LAND OF EGYPT INTO A LAND THAT I HAD SPIED FOR THEM, FLOWING WITH MILK AND HONEY, WHICH (IS) THE GLORY OF ALL LANDS.**"

As stated before, the places referred to as paradise in the Bible are places where God is present. It is written that man shall not live by bread alone, but by every word that proceeds out of the mouth of God. It therefore makes sense that there is no Life outside God's; God's wealth must also involve Him. Do we still think so little of God that we believe (As did the children of Israel) that God owes us something? I put it to you that salvation was a gift freely given[211]. What sense does it then make that God would require man to pay for that which He gave freely?

The second phase of understanding comes from a popular but misunderstood passage: The 23rd Psalms. Let us explore the life changing relationship God's wealth has in store. Herein lays the true prosperity of God. Let us explore it point-by-point, not verse by verse. As all of Gods words line up, we must understand that He perfects us in our wealth as well.

Let me remind you of a scripture, "**AND YE SHALL KNOW THE TRUTH AND THE TRUTH SHALL MAKE YOU FREE.**" I remind you of this scripture because invariably personal dogma and/or affinity for men (pastor, bishops, etc.) will cause you to shy away from the obvious. Whether or not you want to accept the Truth, it is and always will be the Truth. The sooner you learn to release yourself from the philosophies[212] of men and cling to the Way, the Truth, and the Life the sooner you will be free. It took several years, and a lengthy walk with the Spirit to understand the stanzas in the 23rd Psalms. These phases do not comprise a

---

[211] Romans 5:15 & 18.
[212] Colossians 2:8.

package deal; they are individual life changes in the relationship with the Heavenly Father.

1. **"The Lord is my shepherd"** - I believe that this is the most important life change in this Psalm. This change sets about all the other changes in the relationship. This change is important because prior to this covenant the Psalmist had another shepherd. If the Psalmists is anything like most Christians, his former shepherd was his fleshly human desire.

2. **"I shall not want"** - We are all familiar with the emptiness of life. In this phase, the Psalmist discovers the true treasure in Life. In David's words, we see that the relationship with God is the only source of all things important in life. The Psalmist then goes on to state absolutely which things are required to have a fulfilled life.

3. **"He makes me lie down in green pastures"** - The lonely, failure-filled, life of lost sheep passes away under the care of the Owner of the cattle on a thousand hills. Green pastures do not represent wealth they represent *balance*. We misinterpret what the pastures represent because they are green, but farmers understand. Green pastures indicate correct proportionality of all things needed to grow crops: sun, rain, wind, soil, and temperature.

4. **"He leads me beside still waters"** - For whatever reason, sheep do not drink from moving water. Although it is grand to have a pond to drink from, the problem of stagnation occurs. Another greatness of the Father is that He provides sweet, still, calm, fresh water for us to drink. I believe the Bible calls it Living Water. How majestic God is, that God even changes our diet from the death sin produces and leads us to drink from His heart.

5. **"He restores my soul"** - What I find wondrous about the Father is how much care He takes to rebuild the damage we do to ourselves. Look, see: God set the stage for peace in our lives. In His peace, God can now restore our soul and there should be less difficulty in righteousness. The restoration of the soul is meticulous work. The restoration of the soul is a work of love. When the Father restores our

souls He removes sin from our lives enabling us back in to His presence.

6. **"He guides me in the paths of righteousness for His name's sake"** - This life change is part of the stewarding of the Father. Pay close attention to the latter part of the stanza. We boldly proclaim the first part from the pulpit neglecting the latter. However, the latter makes the entire relationship important. What God does is not because we are due, or to make us wealthy; it is for His namesake. God is not selfish He is King. Does not the Potter have a right to order the life of His clay pots?[213] The same clay pots that He delivered, restored, provided for, and repainted.

7. **"Yea, though I walk through the valley of the Shadow of death"** - Another beautiful aspect of the new life is that we now get to walk through; I say again THROUGH, the valley of the shadow of death. Before our new Shepherd guided our lives, we would not get to walk through the valley we stayed in the valley. Lost sheep do not pass through the shade of death cast be Satan. The valley of Satan's shadow causes darkness in the earth. It is from this darkness, that God delivers us from. God's bosom overrides the sting of death. Now, as we approach the valley of the dry bones we need not fear permanent residence. All we need to do is remind the 'Gates of Hell' whom our Shepherd is and continue through, without problem, and without fear.

8. **"I will fear no evil"** - Jehovah Jireh is the Shepherd that delivers us from all evil. Part of that which He must deliver us from is our own wretched hearts. We should not fear of evil because it has no control over His sheep. In the 56th Psalm, David reminds us to trust in the Lord and not to fear what the flesh can do to us. I say; Here, Here!

9. **"For Thou art with me"** - Again, we must remember that these life changing layers although not always occurring together always existing tandem. Once we know the truth, HE shall set us free. This new type of intimacy with God affords new confidence. It is this same THOU that

---

[213] Isaiah 45.

reminds us that when we walk in His will--He will be with us until the end of the world.

10. **"Thy rod and Thy staff they comfort me"** - David is probably God's favorite because of this very fact. How many children would say to their parents that their guidance and correction give them comfort? We must remember that whom God loves He chastises. To understand this is to be able to find comfort during the wilderness period. There is a distinct difference between a rod and a staff. Both are instruments of loving guidance used by a caring father. The staff guides the sheep, and keeps them on the straight and narrow. The shepherd's staff also known as a crook often had a hook on the end of it. The hook was to pull the sheep by the neck and guide them back to where they were supposed to be.

The rod, on the other hand, is for punitive measures. Although hell is God's punitive tool, His rod chastises those He loves. Father informs us it is through this course of correction that we will save the child. Bear in mind however, that sparing the rod and spoiling the child does not refer to literal beatings. Chastisement is correction, not punishment. God says who the father does not chastise He does not love. Because God loves us He changes our direction rather than send us to hell.

11. **"Thou preparest a table before me in the presence of mine enemies."** - Although confusing, this phase develops the faith walk. What greater God is there than one that controls so much that He can do this? Who but the God of Abraham, Isaac, and Jacob, would set you up before your enemy only to deliver you. What other purpose than to show you His love, sovereignty, and interest in your life.

12. **"Thou anoints my head with oil"** - The anointing of oil has always indicated acceptance. Let us express this in words from Matthew chapter four, **"THIS IS MY SON IN WHOM I AM WELL PLEASED."** Some contend that this means that we are kings, but that is not accurate. **We are heirs to the kingdom, not heirs to the throne. God has but only one Prince and Heir Apparent - Jesus.** This gesture is also a marker of righteousness and uprightness. Notice that 11 stages including correction, trial, and tribulation occur before acceptance.

13. **"My cup runneth over"** - This cup is not the same cup from which Jesus drank. This cup is a cup of mercy and grace. The blessings that God pours out onto His beloved have no bounds or limits. God's blessings surpass our meager understanding. This is a statement to the lavish blessings of God. We know how expensive wine is, only the wealthy can afford allow it to run over. It also explains that His Spirit and His blessings are far more than we can contain.

14. **"Surely goodness and mercy shall follow me all the days of my life"** - The Psalmist realizes that as a beloved sheep the true wealth of his Father would follow him all the days of his life. Maturity also comes in this new relationship. David learned that goodness and mercy are far more valuable than wealth and popularity.

15. **"And I will dwell in the House of the Lord forever"** - The House of the Lord is the highest place in the universe. Do not confuse the House of the Lord with a temple, church, or synagogue. The House of the Lord is God's actual dwelling place[214]. What does it profit a man to gain the whole world and yet lose his soul? To gain money is pleasing, but to qualify to dwell in the House of the Lord pleases God. Those in Christ will be with Christ forever, in His Father's house; the house with many mansions. Those outside Christ need to pray that their money can buy them a spot in the coolest corner of Hell.

As we move the true prosperity doctrine, allow me to share a story with you. One Sunday, I assisted in the gathering of the tithes and offerings. That Sunday an elder and I discussed the peer pressure churches use when they march the people up to the front to drop the collection in the bucket. The elder said that it was not peer pressure, it made the process simpler. I said that it did not. It is far easier to move the ushers than the entire congregation, not mention it is a security issue. The motivation for moving the crowd is that people are too embarrassed to sit in their seats and let everybody else see that they have no money or are not interested in putting any in the plate.

No sooner than we had finished collecting did I remove an empty envelope from the bucket. On that envelope the following words appeared, "I did not have the money this week, I know you will

---

[214] John 14:2-3.

understand." If tithes and offerings are supposed to have the freeing affect the proponents of the doctrine proclaims, why is this woman in bondage? The book of James informs us that the righteous do not resist. James 5 also reminds us that the riches amassed in this life at the expense of God's sheep will cry out against the wealthy in judgment.

The 23rd Psalm is not a bedtime fable; it is the Christian walk on paper. Those of us that take the Christian walk are not trying to accomplish anything more than a relationship with God. If what we want in this life is God is a relationship with God, then we must learn to make the things He says are important to Him important in our lives.

Paul said that when we were children we thought and did childish things. However Paul says, when we grow up we are to put away childish things. Let us employ this same reasoning to the concept of *prosperous*. For too many centuries, we have over looked the truest and greatest blessings of our Father for the trinkets of this life. A prime example is that many Christians do not consider salvation prosperity. How small a mind that thinks sustenance in this brief life is comparable to eternity with the Creator?

What does it say of a people that spend their entire life preparing for something they cannot control? Yet spend little to no time preparing for the eternity they can control. It is to this mentality the Lord spoke in Matthew 19:24 when He said, **"AND AGAIN I SAY UNTO YOU, IT IS EASIER FOR A CAMEL TO GO THROUGH THE EYE OF A NEEDLE, THAN FOR A RICH MAN TO ENTER INTO THE KINGDOM OF GOD."** Sadly enough the disciples understood immediately that the problem was great for they asked, "Who then can be saved?"

The need for instant gratification is the single reason that the poor will be with us always. It is not due to the lack of material wealth it is due to a lack of understanding of material wealth. Money answers all things the Bible says. This, however, is an admonition of our level of understanding and greed more than a fact. Money does not fix all problems it allows the greedy human creatures a tangible release from problems. If I had terminal cancer, would $10,000 guarantee my health? No, it would not. Many millionaires have died of terminal illnesses that their millions could not fix. The way money answers all things is because for the most part all of the things we crave are buyable. Therefore, we appease our lustful ways by simply throwing dollars to the greedy pining children.

Before we look to the ultimate prosperity doctrine, let us look at a simple test, and answer the following questions. The book of Matthew 27:3-8 records the following; **"Then Judas, which had betrayed Him, when he saw that he was condemned, repented himself, and brought again the thirty pieces of silver to the chief priests and elders. Saying, I have sinned in that I have betrayed the innocent blood. And they said, What (is that) to us? See thou (to that). And he cast down the pieces of silver in the temple, and departed, and went and hanged himself. And the chief priests took the silver pieces, and said, It is not lawful for to put them into the treasury, because it is the price of blood. And the chief priests took the silver pieces, and said, It is not lawful for to put them into the treasury, because it is the price of blood. Wherefore that field was called, the field of blood, unto this day."**

If money answers all things, why did it not ease Judas' burden?
1. Why did Judas throw the money away?
2. With all the money, Judas made why was he unhappy.
3. What did it profit Judas to make the money yet lose his soul?
4. Why did the very men that hired the betrayal take the money out and bury it?

There is a new doctrine spreading through the church called the Gospel of Judas. Some Christians have even argued that Jesus orchestrated the betrayal. Not only is this ridiculous it flies in the face of scripture and reason[215]. There is no way to reconcile destroying your eternity for the here and now; it is of the devil. It is not the money that destroys but the love of money.

No matter how much money we acquire, we can never escape the guilty of innocent blood. Bloodshed for money; the prosperity gained at the cost of innocent blood. How I ask you in closing, does this differ in any way from James 5:1-6? Seek out James 5:1-6 read and then answer in our hearts. If in our hearts it does not bother us to have condemned and killed the righteous for prosperity's sake, then rest ye I pray with your wealth. However, be reminded, that the cries of the defrauded will reach the Lord of the Sabbath who unlike you is Just.

---

[215] **"THE SON OF MAN INDEED GOETH, AS IT IS WRITTEN OF HIM: BUT WOE TO THAT MAN BY WHOM THE SON OF MAN IS BETRAYED! GOOD WERE IT FOR THAT MAN IF HE HAD NEVER BEEN BORN** - Mark 14:21."

Amen
Appendix B
Questions You Should be Able to Answer After Reading this Book

1. Why do people worship the sun or the moon?
2. Why were the sun and moon created so early in the creation story?
3. What do the sun and moon have in common with fire?
4. What are those that worship the sun and the moon actually seeking?
5. Why do people worship the creations instead of the Creator?
6. What is a bearer of light?
7. Which type of light do you bear?
8. List the ways light bearers manifest the light they carry?
9. List all the ways in which believers bear light.
10. Why do demons transform into beings of light?
11. What does the word Pharoah mean?
12. Why would a king call himself pharaoh?
13. Humans after the flood descended from Noah's children, where did the evil spirit come from?
14. Why was Nimrod not called Pharoah?
15. Why did Exodus say there arose a Pharoah that did not know Joseph's God?
16. How did descendants of Adam and Noah not know the God of creation?

17. What are beasts of the field?
18. Is it possible to be proud of Egypt and be in a good relationship with God?
19. Why do humans keep falling for Satan's wiles?
20. Why are the religions and concepts Satan introduces so appealing?
21. How does a person worship self?
22. What is the differance between demon possession and demonic influence.
23. Do demons have the power to power humans?
24. How many ways can demons posses people.
25. What is the difference between demon possession before and after Christ.
26. Where do demons get their power?
27. Explain the difference between the name, number, and mark of the beast?
28. Where does the beast get his power?
29. Why does the beast have a relationship witht the anti-Christ?
30. Does the term 'beast' in Genesis 3 and the term 'beast' in Revelations 13:11&12 the same meaning?
31. Why do demons play possum?
32. Why is this scenario so effective?
33. How do you stop demons playing possum?
34. Why are demons so easily able to play posssum?
35. Do demons only play possum with addictions?
36. What tools are available to douse Satan's fire?

37. Do not quench the Holy Spirit is a scripture, how does one quench the Holy Spirit?
38. Why is it necessary to douse the fire?
39. What is the difference between extinguishing and dousing the fire?
40. How do you tell the difference between God's fire and the fire in Patmos?
41. What is the main spiritual function of the heart?
42. Define singleness of heart and its benefits.
43. How are Christian marriages different from worldly marriages?
44. What is the difference between love and lust?
45. How do you tell the difference between a Godly marriage and an unGodly marriage?
46. What exactly is spiritual warfare?
47. When does spiritual warfare begin for believers?
48. Why does God allow spiritual warfare?
49. What weapons do we have to fight with?
50. What weapons does Satan have to use against us?
51. When does spiritual warfare end for believers?
52. What is the Holy Spirit's role in spiritual warfare?
53. How are weapons formed against you?
54. Can believers and other believers be enemies in spiritual warfare?
55. Can the church be an enemy in spiritual warfare?
56. What is the difference between extinguishing and dousing the fire?
57. How do you tell the difference between God's fire and the fire in Patmos?
58. Why is God's glory likened unto fire?

59. Why did God appear to Moses in the form of a burning buish?
60. What is the baptism of fire and what is its purpose?
61. Why do so many churches teach fire dousing instead of extinguishing?
62. Can you extinguish the fire in Patmos without scripture and the Holy Spirit?
63. What are stones of fire?
64. Why are diamonds intriguing?
65. What makes jewels precious?
66. Why is Jesus called the Corner stone and not diamond or some other gem stone?
67. How are humans supposed to reflect the fire of God?
68. How do you identify the enemy in you?
69. How do you deal with other people spirits?
70. Why is the flesh so attune to the world?
71. Why can't fasting alone save the flesh?
72. Who is the ruler of this age.
73. What is it about Egypt that we miss.

Appendix C
Glossary of Spiritual Warfare Terms

Ashes - Charred remains.
Beast - A deity with debase, lower characteristics.
Bright - A thing that gives off unusual amounts of light.
Bronze - A shining attribute.
Commands- To lead, or be in charge, to order or demand.
Death - To be cut off from God, to be without salvation.
Devil - An ungodly deity, a fallen angel.
Devilution - Evolving satanic traits
Dragon - A mythical creature, a name for Satan, a description of bad behavior.
Dust - Offspring
Eat – To ingest side with, partake of, enjoin, mimic, or become like.
Fire - The glory of God, a reflection of God's glory.
Flesh - The living shell encasing humans, the sin-riddle corpse.
Fruit - Offspring, disciples, followers, people of similar traits.
Glory - A luminescent manifestation of majesty.
Riches - disciples, followers,
Seraphim - *seraph* -The highest order of angel.
Serpent - unrighteous behavior, a loathsome personage.
Shinning - To reflect light.
Tithes - One tenth of increase, part of a Godly relationship.
Tree - Source, leader,
Unrighteous - Out of the will of God.
Upright - Righteous.

Appendix D
Symbolic Language used in the Old and New Testaments[216]

N.B. All of the words on this list are interchangeable with their counter parts. Therefore, every time you see term they may be applicable or vice versa.

Adultery.... Idolatry
Angel.... Messenger or minister
Arm.... Power
Arrows.... Judgments
Babylon.... Rome
Beast.... A tyrannical heathen monarch
Black.... Affliction--anguish
Blindness.... Ignorance
Blood.... Slaughter--depth
Brimstone.... Desolation--torments
Bride.... The Church of God
Bridegroom.... Christ wedded to his Church
Bulls.... Violent enemies
Candlestick....Church
Chariots.... Heavenly hosts
Crown.... Victory--reward
Cup....Divine Blessings/ Divine Judgments
Darkness.... Misery—adversity--ignorance
Day....An indefinite time--a prophetic year
Dogs.... Gentiles--impure persons--persecutors
Door.... An opening
Drunkenness.... Effects of divine judgments
Earthquakes.... Revolutions

---

[216] Nevin, Alfred, Ed., et al. "Symbolic Language Used by the Poets and Prophets of the Old and New Testaments," *The Parallel Bible*. Blue Letter Bible. 1 Aug 2002. 8 Dec 2004. <http://blueletterBible.org/study/parallel/paral17.html>.

Eyes.... Knowledge
Face.... The divine favor
Fat.... Abundance
Fire.... Judgments
Forehead.... A public profession
Furnace.... Affliction
Garments.... Outward appearance
Gates.... Power--security
Girdles...Strength
Goats.... Wicked persons
Grass.... The lower orders, opposed to trees
Hail....Divine vengeance
Hand.... Protection--support
Hand of the Lord.... Divine influence
Harvest.... A time of destruction/reaping
Head.... Rule or ruler
Heavens.... Political or ecclesiastical governments
Horse.... War and conquest
Hunger and thirst.... Spiritual desires
Incense.... Prayer
Jerusalem.... Church of God/ The heavenly state
Keys.... Power and authority
Lamp... A successor or offspring
Light.... Joy—prosperity/ Knowledge—bitterness
Mountains.... A state—Christ's Church
Mystery.... Not unintelligible, but not made plain
Mystery.... Not unintelligible, but not made plain
Naked.... In the sinful state of nature
Night.... Adversity—affliction—ignorance
Oaks.... Men of rank and power
Oil.... Abundance—fertility—joy
Psalms.... Victory
Paradise.... Heaven
Rock.... A secure refuge
Salt.... Purity—barrenness
Sea in commotion.... An army
Seal.... Security—secrecy
Sheep.... Christ's disciples

Shepherds.... Rules, civil or ecclesiastical
Shield.... Defense—protection
Sleep.... Death
Sores.... Spiritual maladies
Star.... A prince or ruler
Sun/moon/stars.... The various governors in a state
Sword.... War and slaughter
Tail.... Subjection—degradation
Teeth... Cruelty
Throne.... Kingdom or government
Travail.... Anguish—anxiety
Trees.... the higher orders/ The great and noble
Vine/vineyard.... The Church of God
Watchtower.... The Prophets
Waters.... Afflictions—multitudes—ordinances
Wilderness.... Afflicted state
Wind.... Judgments—destructive war
Wine.... Spiritual blessings—divine judgments
Winepress.... Slaughter
Wings.... Protection
Wolves.... Furious, ungodly persons
Woman.... City, or body polity / Church of Christ
Yoke.... Labor-restraint

About the Author

The author Michael Donaldson was born in Nassau, Bahamas. On that island, he grew up in a Methodist school and a Pentecostal church; and accepted Christ when he was 14yrs old. He moved to Tennessee in 1988 where for the next seven years he contributed precious little to the Kingdom of Heaven. After returning to Kingdom service in 1995, he spent the next 13 years teaching Spiritual warfare, and making disciples. He is founder and CEO of Ashara Outreach Ministries. The motto of Ashara is, "Building people not churches." Under that mission, Ashara has developed numerous programs[217] to reach the lost sheep. The great joy in Kingdom work manifested itself in his life through prison outreach and working with the Police and Sheriff's departments in Nashville.

"There is beauty in all of God's children which manifests itself in their expression of His love. The only true church of Christ is found in the hearts of people. The edifices we build fail in comparison to give glory and honor to the Lord God Almighty. The love of God shows itself in the hearts of people, and only this dwelling place lasts forever. This is not because man lasts forever, but it is because God lasts forever. Remember, only what you do for Christ will last."

After leaving home at age sixteen and experiencing college at that tender age, Donaldson came to the following conclusion: Kids do not have a clue. "The biggest mistake in my life was ignoring my parents and leaving home at 16, I had no idea what real life was like."

Donaldson's education consists of tenure at Tennessee State University, which resulted in a B.S. in Political Science. Donaldson was a member of Pres. Dorm Council, Student Union Board of Governors, Food Services Committee, Student Court, and spending numerous semesters on the Nat'l Dean's List. From there Donaldson attained a Master's of Science in Public Administration; - policy, and planning, from Cumberland University, where he was inducted into Pi Gamma Mu Int'l Honor Society in Social Science. Donaldson also has studied and attained a Certificate of Theology from Falwell University.

Donaldson is the CEO and founder of Ashara (Rise and be healed) Ministries a non-profit organization created to use creative *mark*eting

---

[217] For more information log onto www.asharaministries.org.

approaches to assist the less fortunate. He is also the founder of Jesuka Martial Arts Discipline - The art of physical-spirituality. He spent the last 12 years teaching various topics ranging from Rape Prevention to preventing kids from becoming sexually active. His listed of published works consists of From a Fishing Trip in Patmos, From a Fishing Trip in Patmos: Disciple Maker's Edition, Black Coffee, and The Butterfly Veil. In addition, the following works The Lights in Patmos, Famine in Patmos, and Jesuka: The Book of Physical Spirituality, are currently underway.

Donaldson worked fifteen years as a Police officer, during which he was decorated 12 times and taught numerous topics. Eight of the thirteen years as policeman were I spent in the Vice Division buying, and selling drugs, dealing with prostitutes and sex crimes. In those eight years, the untold stories of human suffering and misery troubled and frightened him. More than being frightened, exposure to this suffrage moved Donaldson to try to do something to increase awareness and alleviate some of the sorrow.

The results of Donaldson's experience prompted him to write the Wilderness series of Patmos books. The series is not complete, but Donaldson admits that the lessons he learns and the experiences he undergoes never end either. What he knew when he wrote From a fishing Trip in Patmos, has only grown. The reason for the revelation is a better ever increasing relationship with God.

To order other books by this author, send an email to
Shepardsink@yahoo.com or shop the web.
Write to Shepard's Ink
P.O. Box 78211
Nashville, Tn 37207.
or log on to
www.shepardsinkpublishing.com

These books are also made available to believers and new converts in jail through prison outreach ministry please feel free to logon to www.Asharaministries.org and if you know someone in jail send them a copy of these stories. The copies you send to jail MUST however be the paperback cover.

323 | The Lights in Patmos

In the war, weary Middle East an old terror raises its ugly heads. An old war burns again, a war against peace; a war against life. Someone always remembers, someone always sees and someone always knows. The war against terror cannot end until there is peace, and there can be no peace until all that is evil is dead. The innocent suffer, the greedy thrive, and the guilty go free. In this war the last great frontier has still to be liberated, the human heart.

This resource traipses across the weary, torn frontier of the church. This resource offers disciples and disciple makers a portable, useful means to spread the word of God. After completing this resource when you are asked the question; "Where is your church?" The answer will now be, "Wherever I stand or wherever there is a need, that very spot is my church."

Although often dreary and melancholy, these writings are a means, which allow for the abatement of frustration and despair as well as the often ill-advised expressions of love, happiness joy, glee and youth. There will be hard times, and often times we wish we did not have to live through, but it is through these trials that our relationship with God is perfected. No matter how dark life is the Light is never far from us, only the darkness in our hearts can keep Him away.

"The most fun I have had praising the Lord in years."
Donaldson

Available at www.myspace.com/tdogg7

We would love to help you write your dreams down. Each story is precious, let us make yours known.
Allow us to serve your needs with your family or Christian work: Poetry, stories, textbooks, children's books.

And so no one feels left out we also do music production…tell a friends we live to serve you.

The Lights in Patmos

The Lights in Patmos

www.ingramcontent.com/pod-product-compliance
Lightning Source LLC
Chambersburg PA
CBHW051418290426
44109CB00016B/1346